AGILE
MARKETING

Michelle Accardi-Petersen

Agile Marketing

ISBN-13 (pbk): 978-1-4302-3315-2
ISBN-13 (electronic): 978-1-4302-3316-9

Lead Editor: Jeffrey Pepper
Technical Reviewer: Bernard Klopfer
Editorial Board: Steve Anglin, Mark Beckner, Ewan Buckingham, Gary Cornell, Morgan Ertel, Jonathan Gennick, Jonathan Hassell, Robert Hutchinson, Michelle Lowman, James Markham, Matthew Moodie, Jeff Olson, Jeffrey Pepper, Douglas Pundick, Ben Renow-Clarke, Dominic Shakeshaft, Gwenan Spearing, Matt Wade, Tom Welsh
Coordinating Editor: Jennifer L. Blackwell
Copy Editor: Mary Ann Fugate
Compositor: Mary Sudul
Indexer: SPi Global
Cover Designer: Anna Ishschenko

Distributed to the book trade worldwide by Springer Science+Business Media, LLC., 233 Spring Street, 6th Floor, New York, NY 10013. Phone 1-800-SPRINGER, fax (201) 348-4505, e-mail orders-ny@springer-sbm.com, or visit www.springeronline.com.

For information on translations, please e-mail rights@apress.com, or visit www.apress.com.

Apress and friends of ED books may be purchased in bulk for academic, corporate, or promotional use. eBook versions and licenses are also available for most titles. For more information, reference our Special Bulk Sales–eBook Licensing web page at www.apress.com/bulk-sales.

This book is dedicated to my mentor, George Fischer, who has taught me that the power to be successful is not dependent on the constraints put on you by others but on your ability to focus on what's possible.

Contents

About the Author ix

About the Technical Reviewer x

Acknowledgments xi

Introduction xii

Chapter 1: Agile: Marketing's New Method 1

Chapter 2: A Practical Case for Using Agile Methods 45

Chapter 3: Collaborative Leadership 77

Chapter 4: Plan, Fail, Iterate, Succeed 113

Chapter 5: How to Get Moving in Agile 171

Chapter 6: Crowdsourcing or Once Again Formalizing My Practice 189

References 217

Index 219

About the Author

Michelle Accardi-Petersen is currently vice president of Internet marketing at CA Technologies.

Michelle started her career in direct sales and marketing as a licensed real estate agent, where she was an early adopter of the Internet to attract new buyers. After university Michelle started at Infresco Corporation, an independent software subsidiary of CA Technologies focused on revitalizing legacy applications, where she held a variety of positions in product marketing and support. Michelle's innovative approaches to challenges and exceptional service mentality garnered her much praise from both her internal and external customers. It was because of her superior internal and external customer relationships that she was then offered the opportunity to take a leadership position at CA Technologies headquarters in New York, running CA's Global Sales Support program, and later moved into a leadership role in field marketing, helping to create account-based marketing programs for CA's strategic accounts. Michelle has been recognized as an expert in her field by *Gulf Coast Business Review*, which included her in the "40 under 40" in 2009, and *South Florida Business Journal*, which included her in "Women Who Mean Business."

Michelle was raised in Venice, Florida, where she currently lives with her husband. She received her undergraduate degree from the University of South Florida and her MBA from American InterContinental University.

When she isn't on the road traveling and strategizing worldwide sales and marketing tactics at CA Technologies, she is a member of the American Marketing Association and the Data Application Management Association.

About the Technical Reviewer

Bernard S. Klopfer was responsible for reviewing *Agile Marketing* for technical accuracy. With a diversified technical, marketing, consulting, and management background, Bernard S. Klopfer has held executive roles in the software and technology fields for more than 20 years. During this time he has worked with global responsibilities in management consulting, sales and sales enablement, services and engagement management, application development, field marketing, corporate marketing, program development, marketing transformation and, in his current role as VP, Internet Marketing for CA Technologies.

In these capacities, he has driven and managed successful development and implementations of technology for customers and clients worldwide as well as creative marketing initiatives and programs for web, video, print, trade shows and events.

Known for his unique ability to effectively communicate and motivate a broad spectrum of people, Bernard has been recognized for his innovative and pragmatic approach to achieving business goals, consistently and successfully overseeing large, multifaceted international work teams to get the job done.

Acknowledgments

I'd like to give special thanks to my team, especially Bernard Klopfer and Betsy Corey, for making the seemingly impossible always possible—you are amazing; Karen Sleeth and the CA Press team for encouraging my writing and helping along the way; my boss and friend, Ellyn Raftery, for showing me it is possible to have it all and supporting me through this book-writing process. Special thanks to Joanne and Bernie for your friendships and your openness to work with me early on to implement and iterate the agile marketing processes I discuss in the book.

I'd also like to thank my publisher and editors at Apress, especially Jeffrey Pepper and Jennifer Blackwell; also those authors and contributors to this book who paved the way before me on agile who have granted me permissions (there are way too many to mention here).

And last but certainly not least, I thank my husband, Wally, for teaching me that life balance matters, and my parents, for always being there and giving me the gift of open, honest communication

Introduction

This book is for all those in marketing who have ever struggled to get something done because they have been waiting for "everything" to come into place. My hope is that this book helps you by giving you a methodology to iterate from and a faster start.

So why listen to me? Over the early part of my career, I read all the marketing books out there to help me get ahead, like *The 22 Immutable Laws of Marketing, Branding, Blink, Ogilvy on Advertising,* even *Marketing for Dummies,* but none prepared me for what many years of hard knocks in the various marketing departments of a Fortune 500 software company would teach me. I started out as a marketing rookie in a business-to-business marketing department, as a temporary worker for $7/hour, helping the sales and marketing department. I was sure all that I had learned in business school would prepare me and help me succeed, but I was wrong. I quickly learned from some very wise and helpful business mentors along the way that in school what was taught is only theory and was not going to help me sell software or win friends in making a career.

In school you're taught to get the 4 Ps of marketing right (product, price, promotion, and place), and bam—you have success, but it's not always that simple, because what is success? After all, in marketing it is not always black and white how to quantify success especially if you are using more than one promotion and one channel to get to the market. Who is responsible for that success? Does marketing open the door and sales close it? Do the Internet and viral consumption spell success for your program, and who can claim victory or point a finger in your eye with defeat?

Success gets defined by a number of people, not just your boss and his or her boss, but also the other departments, like sales, who depends on leads and finance, and let's not forget the customer, as they have expectations as well. Social media is also changing what success means for today's marketing departments. No longer is it enough to just sell your product: having the most friends, tweets, and crowdsourced ideas are also being judged as part of determining whether your programs are successful. At the center of all of this are the people marketing serves. Marketing needs a method to help bring all of it together, as the 4 Ps of marketing that they teach in school leave out the most important ingredient: the *people* who are your ultimate consumers, the people you service in your company who have expectations of your programs.

In this book, I will talk a lot about people and how you interact with them in order to define the other 4 Ps and success of your programs, your companies, and your own career. People are the center of every idea and metric used to define success, and yet it is rare that marketing departments take a step back and think about the people they serve. Yes, I said the people marketing serves…marketing is a service business. Marketing departments often think of themselves as the hotbed of innovation and forget that their real purpose is to provide a service to sales and their customers, helping to open doors and promote products others are busy creating or using.

Marketing as a service department may not be a new concept, but it does call for a new way to approach the work. When you view your work in marketing as a service, providing the best service and iterating on that over time becomes more important than a one-time flash in the pan marketing campaign. Marketing as a service is defined on the Web as a model of marketing deployment whereby a provider licenses their marketing resources to customers for use as a service on demand. Think of your marketing department and yourself as being on loan to sales or the other stakeholders in your company, whose job it is to make their job easier.

Sometimes being service-oriented may mean checking your ego and pride at the door; no one said it is easy. But this is the core to the new methodology that marketing needs to implement—one that is service-oriented and more agile. I often tell my employees not to fall in love with their projects or programs because things change, and if you are overly invested in one program or project or identify it too much with yourself and your own self-worth, then when the tides of corporate or customer tastes change, you can be left behind. The ability to change is the key ingredient for anything's survival, including a marketing career. This is where agility comes in, and we will be talking throughout this book about practical ways to become more agile in your thinking as well as your marketing. Let's first talk about what being agile means. Okay, I know you're thinking, "I know what being agile means."

Agility in sports means moving with ease, quickly and nimbly in response to a stimulus. Now apply this to marketing, and you find being agile requires the capability of rapidly and efficiently adapting to changes—often balancing your own views of what works with what others want yesterday and delivering at least some level of results today. It is for this reason marketing would be very well served to take a closer look at the development movement called "agile" that is a set of software development methodologies, where requirements and solutions evolve through collaboration of cross-functional teams, and where iteration is key, as what doesn't get done is as important as what does.

Success in marketing today requires collaboration with all the important parties, from those creating the product, those creating the messaging, those creating the program, and those ultimately having to close the deal. I am a big fan of Darwin, as I think he put it best when he said, "It is not the strongest of the species that survive, nor the most intelligent, but the one most responsive to change." As I said earlier, agility and adaptability are paramount to survival in life as well as marketing. If you hold too tightly to your ideas and are not open to seeing things differently and changing, I assure you that you will not survive regardless of how smart you are. The single best skill a marketer in today's world can have is agility. Let's say tomorrow your company decided it wanted to be in a new market with a new product. How long would it take you to get together all the right messaging, and buy the right ad words, create print advertising, update your web site, etc. with the new information. If you are like most companies, a six-month cycle would not be unrealistic. But this is just not fast enough if you are going to beat your competitors. If you wait six months, you risk being me-too-ish. For this reason, the old integrated marketing methods don't work...that is, unless you have an agile process that allows you to move much faster and to adapt to these marketing pressures on the fly where necessary. The biggest issue marketing has today is that it often is disconnected from the business in terms of what it can deliver and when. The fact is that every person I know has an opinion of what works for marketing something. A fundamental issue is that marketing should not be a department's job but a whole company's job. Everyone needs to know how to tell the company story, succinctly and credibly, and when you relegate that authority to a department and don't get all the other departments bought in, you lose. You cannot build a brand on one department; brands are built on people doing things consistently and in a positive matter. Colors, words, advertisements, events, etc.—they are only tools for doing this and alone cannot build a positive image; you need people who believe and live a message to make a good brand. By creating cross-functional teams in every part of your business and extending it out to customers and prospects via crowdsourcing and other devices, you can create a more agile marketing organization. Marketing does more than deliver the message. To be good at marketing today, the services you offer go beyond message delivery. Understanding the nature of the organization and being able to adapt to market, customer, financial, and political changes in the organization are important.

As an example, given today's technology, marketing also provides important services as a channel to communicate back to product development what new trends are in the market and what customers are responding positively and negatively to, so add product development to the list of marketing's customers.

In *Agile Marketing*, you will gain lots of tips from my years of experience in marketing and from those of many whom I reference throughout the book. You will see how agile marketing can benefit your organization, and how social networking can open doors to break down the departmental silos so that marketing is truly a lean, flexible, service organization driving the success of the business.

Helping others definitely will help you, and I hope this book helps give you the framework for even more success. Happy reading!

Agile: Marketing's New Method

Pigs, Chickens, and Other Dr. Seuss Rascals

Today's marketing environment can look intimidating, and even scary to a marketing professional. One of the reasons you may be holding this book in your hand or perhaps your choice of e-book reader is the hope that this book will assist you in navigating, overcoming, and meeting the often daunting challenges that you as a contemporary marketing professional are facing minute by minute. Well, the simple answer is that I truly believe you've come to the right place. If you are still reading, then it is my hope that at a minimum you are intrigued by what is coming next, cynically thinking what *is* coming next, or hopefully wondering what silver bullet this book is going to reveal. Whatever your thoughts at this point, thank you for continuing to read, and while it may not be so much magic, I do think this book will establish a foundation for the adoption and integration of this innovative approach into your thought processes as you approach the challenges you face.

Before going much further, there are two fundamental concepts that are key to driving success in any pursuit, but certainly important in the context of marketing and what this book is all about—agile marketing. These two ideas are simple and straightforward:

1. Being a master of the obvious has a bad reputation, when in actual fact it probably is always the best answer.

2. Be practical in everything you do, and apply it because either you have to or it is often the best approach to accomplishing your goals and being successful.

I will cover both of these ideas in the context of my experience and my nature. I have had the privilege of leading and being part of organizations that have utilized many of these principles, which have been in some part formally introduced by industry experts and gurus. But much like Robert Fulguhm's book emphasized, perhaps the most important thing I ever needed to know about marketing I learned in kindergarten; at least, that is where I first came across Dr. Seuss and *Green Eggs and Ham*. What in the world, you ask, does Dr. Seuss have to do with agile marketing? I can only paraphrase him though and hope it all becomes clear by the end of the book, if not the end of this chapter.

I cannot tell you how many times I have asked a simple and seemingly obvious question of my colleagues: "Can we just try it and see what happens?" It seems that Sam's persistence in getting his prospect to try green eggs and ham might have some relevance for the boardroom, or at least that marketing campaign that your team wants to try....what's the worst that can happen? It could fail, I suppose, but something that is never tried certainly fails from the start. How can it be that simple, you may ask; marketing takes more work than that; you can't just execute everything that comes across your desk. I promise you that if you work in an agile world, you won't execute everything, as your pigs and chickens won't let you...pigs and chickens? Oh, wow, this is getting weird from the start. Just hang in, and I'll explain how being the master of the farm or boardroom will help you gain success in your marketing efforts.

Marketing need not be complicated regardless of what anyone says; marketing is all about simplicity and getting to the heart of why someone needs your product. Lots of people will tell you it is a science or an art, and I'll tell you it is both. But what marketing really requires more than anything else is action, iterative action. It requires people to try something, anything to get to a solution or see the problem at least in a new way. I find people like to make the simple complex; marketing is really about making things simple.

Sometimes you want to scream, "Am I missing something here, or shouldn't we just do a, b, then c," when you are met with blank stares from your colleagues. This is when you likely need agile marketing the most—you are suffering from inflexible marketing, which can drive a company to failure.

Cutting through this inflexibility and executing in the face of the naysayers is a capability that should not be unique to anyone in a successful organization, regardless of whether you are leading the group or an individual contributor. What usually happens when I ask this type of simple question is that I am met with resistance and told things are a lot more complex than a simple solution. I am met with words, generally, but not action. Most of the time, the complexity is self-created, self-sustained, and self-fulfilling. For many problems, there are obvious and common-sense answers, where the more complexity we bring to the table to resolve issues, inputting more data to analyze or gathering metrics for components, does nothing more than complicate things to an extent that may be detrimental to any organization. Again, the point here is not to over-simplify, as things are complex, but when it comes to resolving issues, I believe in the obvious as a good place to start, and action is better than inaction. If you try nothing, you definitely get nothing…if you try a reasonable solution, there is a result and results can generally be changed or improved.

How we arrive at the solution to the issue and what can be done to resolve the complexity are the keys to thought processes that I trust will demonstrate value to the readers of this book. I also believe that in order for you to put the concepts I will discuss here to work, it is important that you truly understand the fundamentals of marketing. So I will start you in the discussion of marketing at a fundamental level. For those of you who think you already know it all, you can put down the book now and continue doing what you've always done to get the same tired results, but for those of you willing to humor me, I am hopeful this refresher may bring you to see what is possible by simply going back to the laws of marketing. You see, in pursuit of my obvious ideology, I came across a book written by Jack Trout, one of the co-authors of *The 22 Immutable Laws of Marketing*, called *In Search of the Obvious: The Antidote for Today's Marketing Mess.*[1] In his book, he talks about the pursuit of the obvious and how it is more than likely the basis of resolution (resolution to what he calls the "mess" marketing is currently in). He interestingly gives credit for what I am going to call the *obvious principle* to a book published in 1916: *Obvious Adams: The Story of a Successful Businessman*, written by Robert R. Updegraff.

---

[1] Jack Trout, *In Search of the Obvious: The Antidote for Today's Marketing Mess* (Hoboken, NJ: Wiley, 2008). Used with permission.

Here are the five guidelines from Updegraff's book:

- This problem when solved will be simple.
- Does it check with human nature?
- Put it on paper.
- Does it explode in people's minds?
- Is the time ripe?

Simply stated, Trout asserts that the pursuit of a marketing strategy is the search for the obvious. If we look at the dictionary definition of the word obvious, we find the following:

"Easy to see or understand, plain, or evident"

This is why obvious is so important. It is the simplicity of that message and specifically a marketing message that drives consumerism. When a marketing message is simple, easy to understand, and evident, it works really well. Trout cites that the first response to this message is people's hesitation with this concept, because of the misconception that the obvious is too simple and does not appeal to the imagination. Likewise, we often think a marketing message has to be very clever and intellectually stimulating to be successful.

If we accept the validity of the obvious as a fundamental premise—which I do, and my experience has taught me—let's examine five ideas from Trout's book:

First, Trout's book warns us of roadblocks that get in the way of the obvious.

- *Wrong focus*: CEOs are not focused on the right stuff. Legions of competitors, constantly changing technologies, faster change of pace, and a flood of information challenge the CEO's attention. The trick to surviving is to know where you are going.
- *Wall Street*: Wall Street brokers pursue growth to ensure their reputations and to increase their take-home pay.
- *No time to think*. Taking away your ability to come up with new innovations because you are too busy.
- *Flawed research*: A flood of data should never be allowed to wash away your common sense and your own feeling for the market. You'll never see the obvious solution.
- *Communication*: The Internet (plus e-mail) brings more clutter. Word-of-mouth marketing is not the next big thing.
- *Advertising people*: Theater, emotion, sloganeering, and creativity are their trap. How to fix this?
- *Marketing people*: They just can't stop tinkering. They sit around and try to figure out how to improve things. What top management fails

to understand is that the road to chaos is paved with improvements. Convergence and brand schizophrenia are often the result.

Secondly, Trout indicates that we must zero in on the proper marketing process.

- *Make sense in the context of the marketplace*: What has the marketplace heard and registered from your competition?
- *Find the differentiating idea*: Look for something that separates you from your competitors. This does not have to be product-related.
- *Have the credentials*: The demonstration of your differentiating idea is your credentials.
- *Communicate your difference*: Better products don't win; better perceptions do.

Thirdly, Trout emphasizes that we must know the essence of marketing.

- It's marketing's responsibility to see that everyone is playing the same tune in unison.
- It's marketing's assignment to turn that tune or differentiating idea into what we call a coherent marketing direction. A differentiating idea is a competitive mental angle.

Fourth, beware of obvious blunders.

- A me-too mindset won't cut it.
- Don't get cute or complex. Describe your product in a simple, understandable way.
- Don't forget that marketing is a battle of perceptions.
- Don't try to copy a competitor's word or position in the prospect's mind.
- Guard against arrogance when becoming successful. You tend to become less objective; arrogance leads to failure.
- Don't try to be all things to all people.
- Don't live exclusively by numbers. When you go down this path, it often leads to bad decisions.
- Don't be unwilling to attack your own business plan, i.e., Xerox with laser printing; Kodak with the digital camera.

Finally, beware of obvious ground rules.[2]

- *Law of the Ear*: Your obvious strategy has to sound right.

---

[2] Jack Trout, "The Law of Perception," in *Branding Strategy* (2007). Used with permission.

- *Law of Division*: Over time, a category will divide and become two or more categories.
- *Law of Perception*: Marketing is not a battle of products; it's a battle of perceptions. The perception is the reality; hence, "obvious ideas exploding in the mind" (Robert Updegraff).
- *Law of Singularity*: In search for the obvious, only one move will produce substantial results. History teaches that the only thing that works in marketing is the single, bold stroke. To find that singular idea or concept, marketing managers have to know what's happening in the marketplace. They have to be down at the front lines. They have to know what's working and what isn't. They have to be involved.
- *Law of Duality*: Every market becomes a two-horse race.
- *Law of Resources*: Without adequate funding, an obvious idea won't get off the ground.

So far we have examined the obvious principle and, for me, a validation by an industry leader, something I have felt all along is an important guideline to success. You don't need to reinvent something if it already works, but adding practical innovations to make something better works as well. Faster to market and to sell more should be what we seek to do in marketing, not to be the smartest or most complicated. And obvious should always be part of the DNA of how you proceed with any marketing endeavor. So that is part one of my fundamental principles, and now on to part two.

I mentioned before about the importance of innovation. It is important to recognize that we are not talking about innovation for the sake of innovation, but a pragmatic approach to innovation or what has been recently defined as pragmatic innovation. Now while this has been defined formally, it has always been my approach to accomplishing the things I need to accomplish. Let's take a look at information from the Wharton School on pragmatic innovation.[3] The story parallels my own experience in a lot of ways, so I show it here as an illustration of what and how this concept of agile marketing and pragmatic innovation evolved.

> *At the age of 18, Dee Kapur left India and arrived in New York City on the first leg of his journey to California to attend Stanford University. His flight was late, and he missed his connecting flight; Kapur found himself*

---

[3] Craig M. Vogel, Jonathan Cagan, and Peter Boatwright, *The Design of Things to Come* (Upper Saddle River, NJ: Prentice Hall, 2005). Used with permission.

stranded in the Big Apple with $200, his suitcase, his tennis racquet, and little sense of what to do. He eventually got to Stanford, and although economically poorer, he gained a new sense of confidence. With no money to his name, he found that he had to be innovative in small ways every day just to make ends meet. His current drive for innovation in business has its roots in such experiences, when he had to seek new and efficient solutions in daunting circumstances.

After earning a degree in mechanical engineering from Stanford and his MBA at Carnegie Mellon, Kapur eventually landed at Ford Motor Company. At Ford, he continued to seek innovative ways to turn supposed barriers into opportunities. At one point, he ran the most profitable line of vehicles in the United States and was part of the group at Ford that helped transform the SUV and a pickup truck from a service vehicle into a lifestyle vehicle. In 2003, after a successful career at Ford, Kapur was named president of the Truck Division of International Truck and Engine.

Kapur believes in what he refers to as pragmatic innovation, a term that perfectly captures the balance between creativity and profit. He recognizes that, even as he leads an organization, he cannot mandate innovation. However, he can institute a management process that fosters it. Kapur models his approach to his employees with one dose inspiration and one dose instruction. The level of interpersonal relationships is reinforced by the practical, by budget allocations, and by reward and recognition. In his work with others and in his business procedures, Kapur holds up innovation as a clear signpost that shows the direction of his leadership. How you allocate your time and money and how you groom your employees show your priorities and establish incentives within a company.

At the end of the day, Kapur keeps an eye on results. Although his upbringing and engineering training continuously ensure attention to facts, logic, and results, often the road to the outcome is newly laid. He likes to set targets for his company that he has "no freakin' idea how to get to." These targets are not just goals; they shape corporate culture. The targets create a demand for unconventional input, and, more often than not, they coalesce into a game plan that would not happen with a "safe" goal. In setting such goals, he has developed an instinct for finding the sweet spot between the acceptable and the impossible. Setting the bar where he does helps motivate those under him and creates an environment of creativity. He also sets a positive example by walking the walk; he strives to be the ideal he wants others to be. He has a directness and honesty that you instantly respect. He wastes neither words nor time. He does not look to blame others; instead, he looks to accomplish goals. He never seeks to embarrass people, and he knows the power of win-win.

Throughout his career, Kapur has looked to identify the people who, like him, are looking at the broader picture. He realizes that you can never bring everyone along with total conviction, but if you build a core team right away, you can change the way a group or project team works. In any organization, he says, approximately 30% of the people are passionate about wanting to win or at least make a difference. The leader's challenge is to identify those people, groom them, harness their energy, and let them be a beacon for others. If one can garner the allegiance of that 30%, that is success. Spend time with the people who want to be motivated. Challenge and "jazz" them, and they will introduce a velocity and energy that will propel the rest along with them.

For Kapur, pragmatic innovation requires a balance of the left and right brain working in unison. Such a balance enables him to see situations in a broader way than many others. He can manage the duality inherent in complex corporate decision-making. He intuitively understands the concept of moving from one level of viewing the problem to another. He attributes this in part to the fact that he not only has an analytical ability to understand engineering and business systems, but also has a feel for the lifestyle side of products, he appreciates the human reaction, and he recognizes the compulsion that drives prospective buyers. He was raised in the Himalayas in India, but he also spent time in Europe when his father was transferred there in the course of his career. He has a global perspective born of his personal life: high school in the Himalayas, several years in Europe as a child, and an exposure to life's possibilities without the luxuries of coddling.

His ability to see the value of the different major players in the process enables him to manage and motivate others and to unify them toward common goals. It is not who is right or wrong, but what needs to be done to get to the next level. In our work with the auto industry, we saw many examples of managers who were loyal to their area of expertise and defensive about the requests for change or perspectives offered by other areas in the company.

Many complain that employees in other areas of the company are myopic. If only they could learn to see the situation from another's perspective, they could move faster and make the right decision. Design stylists complain that others fail to grasp the gestalt, or entirety, of a design; when non-designers pick it apart and make changes to the pieces, they compromise the overall effect. Engineers argue about cost overruns and the inability to deliver on style without compromising performance quality. Manufacturing argues about the feasibility of maintaining tolerances given form complexity or material choices. Human factors and safety specialists constantly call for changes in engineering and styling to ensure a higher degree of safety. Cars are designed to be driven, but human-factors specialists are trained to think about when the car will fail. Marketing argues for details that stylists reject as incompatible with the new approach to style. In short, there are plenty of reasons to disagree. Kapur does not like to take sides; when he must, however, it is to ensure a successful outcome, and he strives to bring his team along with him. A persistent operating theme for him is "integrated execution!"

When Kapur started in automotive design, he was as fascinated with styling as he was with engineering. While directing the Truck Division at Ford, Kapur, along with marketers Bob Masone and Allison Howitt and head truck designer Pat Schiavone, was viewing an old two-seat roadster with saddle leather interior. The car exuded high class, and at the same time, the leather reminded him of the saddles cowboys used. And those cowboys happen to be customers of pickup trucks. Wouldn't it be great if a pickup had a similarly luxurious interior, one that still connected to the cowboy aura? That leap led to the development of a limited-edition F-150 pickup with saddle leather interior, co-branded with the King Ranch in South Texas.

The King Ranch accomplished a number of things inside Ford as well as with the F-150. The project not only made a strong brand statement of innovation for Ford, it also created a great working relationship with the whole team. Trucks and SUVs became the place where everyone wanted to be; it was where the action was. The new line of F-150s introduced in was a product of the team that brought you the King Ranch as well as the Harley Davidson F-150 (designed jointly by Gordon Platto and Willie G. Davidson himself). According to Kapur, "The name of the game is to continually change it." That is the focus of Kapur's view on innovation.

Yet Kapur's last assignment at Ford was to deal with the challenging problem of controlling costs in vehicle programs. Controlling costs by itself is not a difficult task—cut out all unnecessary parts, and cheapen *those that are integral. But that approach leaves the company with little to sell other than a low price. The challenge is to produce great products while meeting cost goals. More managers are needed who can handle both the creative innovation such as that in the King Ranch and the pragmatics of cost, because the combination of these two positions gives Kapur the ying and yang of what it takes to develop innovative products. Now, Kapur will see whether that same approach can help clarify and rebuild the International brand in the trucking industry.*

Kapur sums up his approach to managing innovation in three steps:

1. *Make innovation and boldness part of the culture—everyone needs to know what you stand for.*

2. *Role-model innovation as often and in as many forums as you can.*

3. *Institute a management process that fosters innovation.*

Kapur lives by the vision that "the future for society and the country is vibrancy in innovation." Kapur is a new breed of innovator.

You see, agile marketing, while a concept I am trying to help pioneer, is not new. How we choose to put it into action utilizing the two fundamental concepts that are the foundation to my ideas surrounding agile marketing is. Pragmatic innovation is the cornerstone idea of agile marketing. Your adoption of these thought processes that incorporate these ideas is fundamentally important and what I will be discussing in this book. So why isn't the book called obvious pragmatic innovation? First, because that will be my second book, but most importantly because the ideas are fundamental ideas and not a panacea.

Concepts are only concepts, but obvious pragmatic innovation is about your approach to things, not just processes and procedures but a *methodology*. Did I just say methodology? Yes, I did, and I certainly understand that the silver bullet that has been promised in the past was often not realized in the application of a methodology. So before you start rolling your eyes about that all-too-cumbersome catch phrase—methodology—and start recalling nightmares, please understand that I realize that anyone who has worked for any period of time in a corporation probably has thought of *the* worst methodology transformation that demonstrated limited results. Certainly fans of the movie *Office Space* recall the cover page that had to be put on top of the TPS report—which is an example of methodology implementation at its worst: doing things for the sake of what it says in the methodology vs. what may be practical. The fact that many of us can relate to this idea of an obviously silly requirement enforced for the sake of enforcement or adherence to a methodology demonstrates fully the need for obvious pragmatism in everything we do.

Now before this turns into a debate on the usefulness of methodologies, please be aware that I am a great proponent of organizations following, adopting, and implementing methodology to drive efficiencies in business processes as a foundation for standards and improvement for any organization. It is always in the practice of the methodology where things may fall outside of the goals (see Figure 1-1) that are trying to be met. More on methodology a little bit later.

Figure 1-1. Are your processes overly complex?[4]

Please recall that I am talking about pragmatism, so while I will be covering recommended organizational constructs, approaches to implementation, and driving effectiveness in process and procedures, the key is agile, so the agile process is nothing like the traditional rigid formal process with countless formalized steps and prescribed forms that have to be completed for something to be considered done. Also it is important to understand that the very nature of agile is flexibility and adoption. Okay, so I've touched on the subject of agile but have really not defined it. Nor have I explained how what is traditionally considered an application development approach fits into marketing and certainly not how we can market in an agile fashion. So first, yes, the terminology (pigs, chickens, scrum), approach, and methods in this book follow the same ideals that support agile software development. The reason for this is that agile closely matches in approach, process, and ideology how I have been able to drive successful pragmatic innovation.

For a little more on what agile is as a methodology, it is simply an approach to developing value, generally software, that meets a business need, and instead

---

[4] Mike Vizdos, *Implementing Scrum,* http://www.implementingscrum.com/section/blog/cartoons/. Used with permission.

of being an arduous waterfall process of project planning to dates, it looks to simplify things. It puts people first, trusting that, working together, they can find or build solutions in an incremental way, scrapping unnecessary design requirements for value delivered early. They are able to do this by, instead of working to a rigid project plan, putting together teams of people into what we will discuss later as scrum teams, which meet daily to take action together to solve challenges and come to solutions in an iterative fashion. Scrum is the concept of bringing people together in agile. As Figure 1.2 shows it's about freeing people of the unnecessary and not "jailing" them with the unnecessary. This concept, while it came out of technology development, can easily be applied to marketing and used as a framework. A little later on, we will examine a case study that demonstrates the who, what, where, and how.

Figure 1-2. Implementing scrums[5]

So back to the silver bullet. We are all seeking a comprehensive solution to whatever problems we face because we are looking for solutions tied most often to challenges of enormous complexity. No one would argue that marketing is not a complex challenge. There are so many components, and each one of them is moving at the speed of the Internet—they change faster than your 13-year-old can text. Gone are the days where marketing plans, goals, and objectives were set in years. In today's marketplace, a marketer needs the skills, competency, instincts, and processes to be nimble—agile.

Before we go much further, I think it is important that we try to define an elusive term for what we as professionals do every day. Let's look at what marketing is and how it is defined. The American Marketing Association (AMA) defines marketing as follows:

---

[5] Mike Vizdos, *Implementing Scrum*, http://www.implementingscrum.com/section/blog/cartoons/. Used with permission.

"The process of planning and executing the conception, pricing, promotion and distribution of ideas, goods and services to create exchanges that satisfy individual and organizational objectives." —*Marketing News*, March 1995

This definition does not really define what we as marketers do. It may seem more like a definition or description of sales. Well, yes and no. Sales is the facilitation of the exchange, most notably delivering goods for revenue; so sales is enabled by marketing, is a partner in marketing, but not marketing. Exchanges in marketing are between buyers and sellers, with money as the classical marketing method. Sales, depending on how you define it, is shorter-term focused, whereas marketing is longer-term and focused on the sense of enabling a customer experience. Understanding marketing is important so we can understand better how to employ innovation. No discussion about marketing would be complete without gaining from Al Ries and Jack Trout's argument that the market position of a product or service in the perception of the customer is "everything"; they have defined 22 "immutable" laws of marketing, which to them demonstrate this fundamental point.

The precept they employ aligns itself with their customer's perception of reality.

> "...To cope with the terrifying reality of being alone in the universe, people project themselves on the outside world. They "live" in the arena of books, movies, television, newspapers, and magazines. They "belong" to clubs, organizations, and institutions. These outside representations of the world seem more real than the reality inside their own minds."

One might consider that we tend to feel that reality is the world outside of the mind and our perceptions and that we are just one small component in this massive global perception, but I think it is probably quite the opposite; the only reality you can be sure about is in your own perceptions. We might be crossing into the realm of what you think is science fiction, à la the movie *The Matrix*, but it is an important precept for understanding behavior, perceptions, and ultimately Ries and Trout's approach to marketing—hence their "laws." Here is another quote from Ries and Trout, which is an extension of the philosophical idea of solipsism: "If the universe exists, it exists inside your own mind and the minds of others." This is the reality that marketing must deal with. According to Ries and Trout, the fundamental flaw in most marketing programs, and certainly why so many marketing mistakes are made, lies in the idea that you are competing in a battle surrounded by a product's characteristics based on having its roots in reality. It really makes little difference; "perception is reality" is something I say to my staff all the time. It is not what really happens; it is what people perceive has happened.

All the "immutable laws," I think perhaps somewhat correctly, are derived from that exact point of view or, forgive me, that reality.

Their 22 'laws' are as follows:[6]

1. *The law of leadership*: It is better to be first than it is to be better. "The basic issue in marketing is creating a category (i.e., a given type of product or service) you can be first in. It's the law of leadership. It's better to be first than it is to be better. It's much easier to get into the mind first than it is to try to convince someone you have a better product than the one that did get there first."

2. *The law of the category*: "If you can't be first in a category, set up a new category you can be first in."

3. *The law of the mind*: "It's better to be first in the mind than to be first in the marketplace. Although this may seem to contradict the "law of leadership," it is more of an additive component to leadership. The law of the mind modifies the law of leadership with the idea that leadership must also encompass the idea to be first in the prospect's mind, not exclusively of being first into the marketplace. Being first in the mind is everything in marketing. Being first into the marketplace is important only to the extent that it allows you to get into the mind first."

4. *The law of perception*: Marketing is not a battle of products; it's a battle of perceptions.

5. *The law of focus*: The most powerful concept in marketing is ownership of a word in the prospect's mind. Think of the word cola—probably the name Coke comes to mind. Also Kleenex is a facial tissue, and, even to this day, when there are so many more copiers on the market, most will think of Xerox.

6. *The law of exclusivity*: Two companies cannot own the same word in the prospect's mind.

7. *The law of the ladder*: The strategy to use depends on which rung you occupy on the ladder—each category has its own ladder or hierarchy, and where your product or service is in this hierarchy will determine your strategic options.

8. *The law of duality*: In the long run, every market becomes a two-horse race.

---

[6] Al Ries and Jack Trout, *The 22 Immutable Laws of Marketing* (New York: HarperBusiness, 1994). Used with permission.

9. *The law of the opposite*: If you're shooting for second place, your strategy is determined by the market leader.

10. *The law of division*: Over time, a category will divide and become two or more categories.

11. *The law of perspective*: Marketing effects take place over an extended period of time.

12. *The law of line extension*: "There's an irresistible pressure to extend the equity of the brand. One day a company is tightly focused on a single product that is highly profitable. The next day the same company is spread thin over many products and is losing money."

13. *The law of sacrifice*: You have to give up something in order to get something. "The law of sacrifice is the opposite of the law of line extension. If you want to be successful today, you should give something up. There are three things to sacrifice: product line, target market, and constant change."

14. *The law of attributes*: For every attribute, there is an opposite effective attribute. "Marketing is a battle of ideas. So if you are to succeed, you must have an idea or attribute of your own to focus your efforts around. Without one, you had better have a low price."

15. *The law of candor*: When you admit a negative, the prospect will give you a positive. "...it may come as a surprise to you that one of the most effective ways to get into a prospect's mind is to first admit a negative and then twist it into a positive."

16. *The law of singularity*: In each situation, only one move will produce substantial results.

17. *The law of unpredictability*: Unless you write your competitor's plans, you can't predict the future.

18. *The law of success*: Success often leads to arrogance, and arrogance to failure.

19. *The law of failure*: Failure is to be expected and accepted.

20. *The law of hype*: The situation is often the opposite of the way it appears in the press. "When things are going well, a company doesn't need the hype. When you need the hype, it usually means you're in trouble."

21. *The law of acceleration*: Successful programs are not built on fads, they're built on trends.

22. *The law of resources*: Without adequate funding, an idea won't get off the ground. "Marketing is a game fought in the mind of the prospect. You need money to get into a mind. And you need money to stay in the mind once you get there."

The laws outlined here are extracted from a book that at the least makes intriguing reading, and while it may not be revolutionary in what it presents, it most importantly goes against surmised perceptions and indeed perhaps the organizational constructs of marketing organizations. Written several years ago, these laws, and 22 laws on branding, which I will cover later, are often pointed to as some of the key reads for any marketing professional because of the counter-intuitive approach and contrarian stance on principal constructs of product development and therefore product marketing (for example, the idea that product attributes—the features and functions—do not by themselves matter, but the position of the product in the mind of the consumer is the important thing). Ironically the 22 "laws" are the basis used to cover every situation imaginable, so the book may seem more prescient than it actually is. It is arguably noted that without exception each of the immutable laws presented by Ries and Trout can be disputed and examples of contradictory success given as examples. This may state that the only truly immutable law of marketing is that there really are not any immutable laws of marketing. Remember perception is reality. So again, I present these concepts as being precepts or constructs to my overall ideology that anything that itself becomes the steadfast rule or guiding principle for how to conduct business is suspect if we do not look at true continual improvement. Continual improvement is a cyclical construct that allows for feedback to correct or adopt an existing process or procedure. Cyclical is fundamental to agile, and agile's primary objective is constant improvement.

One other note on the immutable laws: I suspect that it may be truly the only book most marketing professionals read because of its shortness and plain-speaking about what appears to be common sense, as it relates to the complexity of marketing. What I am not certain of is if it can be truly executed as it is fundamentally contrary to how successful companies are established—the producers create a product that in some way defines itself, creates a market, drives revenues, creates jobs, and is successful. This product then is the company in the mind of the company and in the mind of the consumer, and every construct that supports further consumption of the product rightly so becomes the cornerstone for the business. What the laws put in perspective is a realistic look at mistakes that are continually made unless the company is ready to disassociate in some way from what made it a company in the first place. Preservation of a market is not conducive to a growth strategy and certainly not a long-term survival strategy; the fundamental way to grow is to enter new markets. When we try to enter new markets, we must look beyond the founding product. Not to oversimplify the great marketing machine that is Apple Inc., they have successfully created a new market that extended their founding product (personal computers) into portable consumer products, which rely on the construct of the personal computer but are perceived as entertainment devices. This example, however, is often seen as an exception rather than a rule, and, in fact, one strong caution that comes from Ries and Trout is that the advice given in their book will probably not go over well with the senior management in your company, who, having tremendous loyalty invested in a particular brand, naturally see it as a key asset to be capitalized upon, and are thus tempted into the "line extension" folly.

Again, the 22 laws are a foundation to understand that application of anything requires obvious pragmatic innovation. Marketing transformation and indeed agile marketing will also meet with opposition from young and old "hotshot marketing types" who are eager to change things and make their mark on the organization. This warning, while it may be perceived as harsh, is often ignored and costs organizations millions and millions of dollars. Again, there are always exceptions, but, then again, those exceptions may be really aspects of taking an organization into new markets—but more on that a little later.

One key theme brought forth by Ries and Trout, and certainly one of their biggest areas of known vulnerability or traps, is the idea I touched on before as a proponent of defining what marketing is, and this is the concept of brand. Brand is the trumpet call of every marketing organization, by either creating a brand or keeping a brand alive in the mind of the consumers, because brand makes a company—or does it?

Let's go back to a couple of fundamental marketing ideas; buyers or consumers usually outnumber sellers or producers, and, in and of themselves, generally are just a receiver because we as individuals are single consumers. But every marketer knows the total power of all buyers together is what makes up market power, and market power can sway the market in their favor. Producers compete to sway buyers to them, and it is the goal of marketing to sway the buyers not only as a whole but also individually—hence the 22 laws and the discussion about perception.

We also have to realize or understand that the market and, therefore, the buyers and the producers are influenced not only by themselves, because of loyalty to a product or brand, but also by other buyers, other sellers, and things that have happened throughout the marketing process. So back to the silver bullet and resolving complexity with a unified solution—perhaps if we can understand the proper perspective and role of brand, we can better drive success for establishing a difference to the buyers, or defining a favorable perception, which is the goal of a brand. Let's take a look at brand.

Interestingly, the father-daughter team of Al and Laura Ries contradicts Ries' earlier marketing book, which implied that an extension of a brand is folly in their *The 22 Immutable Laws of Branding*. A brand name is a name (a proper noun, in fact) in the mind of the consumer that conveys a single proposition about a particular product or service. The power in a brand name lies in its ability to positively influence purchasing behavior. In an increasingly cluttered information society, a powerful brand image can act as a guidepost for the consumer in making a purchase decision as well as serve as a foundation for promotion of buying-related activity that directly or indirectly is tied to the product (a Miller Lite concert series, for example). So far and, not surprisingly, consistent with the 22 laws of marketing, it is about perception—so what is the relevance of brand as it relates to marketing and what does this have to do with agile marketing? Well, if we accept that brand is the ultimate mission of marketing, and marketing is the partner of sales and fundamental to business, then it is important that we understand the role of brand for a company and how it should but often does not fit in today's marketing organizations.

There tends to be an over-simplification of the consumer buying process and certainly an over-generalization of the important integration of the role of selling. This may be because, in a brand-conscious society, it can be surmised that a brand represents expectations, and consumers buy based on their expectation of the brand. I am not convinced, however, that this necessarily relates to business-to-business consumerism, especially with the changing dynamics of the business marketplace and, most importantly, the segmentation of those markets. On the contrary, a successful branding program should differentiate your product or service from all the similar products or services out there. Buying because of brand may be a safe call for consumers in a B2B space, but things are changing in the consumer space as cost pressures and a new social world means the customer experience a brand gives or doesn't give will become a more important aspect of brand programs. This branding program therefore is a core component of marketing because it is based on the concept of singularity. It creates in the mind of the prospect the perception that there is no product on the market quite like your product or that can give them the same level of service. Given that, a successful brand cannot appeal to everybody. In fact, because of the idea of singularity, brand itself makes certain that no one brand can possibly have a universal appeal. Does this then mean that brand as a singularity does not work for a multi-product company? In its simplest form, the answer is probably no, but let's see how the 22 laws of branding complement the 22 laws of marketing—we can, for the moment, accept the supposition that we can cite many examples of how the 22 laws of marketing hold true across innumerable product and service offerings. Continuing the theme that Ries has championed, they maintain that a major problem for companies is the temptation to extend a successful brand into other, sometimes only periph- erally related areas. (Two actual examples mentioned in the book are Harley-Davidson wine coolers and Heinz all-purpose cleaning vinegar.) Such brand extensions serve only to confuse the consumer and dilute the single message strength of the core brand.

Their 22 "laws" of branding are:[7]

1. *The law of expansion*: The power of a brand is inversely proportional to its scope. "Marketers constantly run branding programs that are in conflict with how people want to perceive their brands. Custom- ers want brands that are narrow in scope and are distinguishable by a single word, the shorter the better."

2. *The law of contraction*: A brand becomes stronger when you narrow its focus.

3. *The law of publicity*: The birth of a brand is achieved with publicity, not advertising—Ries and Ries maintain that advertising is best used to maintain a brand, but that it is very difficult and expensive to launch a new brand through advertising alone. The best way, they say, is to be first in a new product or service category, and reap the attendant publicity.

4. *The law of advertising*: "Once born, a brand needs advertising to stay healthy."

5. *The law of the word*: A brand should strive to own a word in the mind of the consumer, which was mentioned earlier and is really an extension of an immutable marketing law—the law of focus. Some examples they cite include: Mercedes = prestige; Volvo = safety; Kleenex = tissue; Xerox = copier; FedEx = overnight.

6. *The law of credentials*: The crucial ingredient in the success of any brand is its claim to authenticity, and the best claim to authenticity is being the leading product or service in your category, because con- sumers assume that if it is a leading seller, it must be good; this is an

---

[7] Al Ries and Laura Ries, *The 22 Immutable Laws of Branding* (Harper Paperbacks, 2002). Used with permission.

extension of the immutable marketing law of leadership. "Once you get on top, it's hard to lose your spot. A widely publicized study of 25 leading brands in 25 different product categories in the year 1923 showed that 20 of the same 25 brands are still the leaders in their categories today. In 75 years, only five brands lost their leadership."

7. *The law of quality*: Quality is important, but brands are not built by quality alone—in fact, as the authors point out, most people have no idea as to the "real" quality of a product or service. Is a Rolex really better at keeping time than a Timex? How do you know?

8. *The law of the category*: A leading brand should promote the product or service category, not the brand. This may seem counter-intuitive, but the authors argue here that the best way for the brand leader to build sales is to promote the category, not the specific brand. This is a more effective way to build up overall market awareness and interest, and the brand leader will naturally benefit to a greater degree than other competitors, by virtue of its larger market share. (And when the overall size of the market is built up, then the leader is in a good position to increase market share still further.)

9. *The law of the name:* In the long run, a brand is nothing more than a name.

10. *The law of extensions*: The easiest way to destroy a brand is to put its name on everything.

11. *The law of fellowship*: In order to build the category, a brand should welcome other brands—see rule #8.

12. *The law of the generic*: One of the fastest routes to failure is giving a brand a generic name. Generic names (i.e., names that describe the product or service category, such as "wine coolers") do not strongly position the product or service within the category, and are thus liable to confuse potential customers.

13. *The law of the company*: Brands are brands. Companies are companies. There is a difference. Brand names should almost always take precedence over company names. Consumers buy brands—they don't buy companies. So when a company name is used alone as a brand name (GE, Coca-Cola, IBM, Xerox, Intel), customers see these names as brands.

14. *The law of sub-brands*: What branding builds, sub-branding (i.e., brand extensions) can destroy. The name "Chevrolet" used to stand for something. Now, what is it? A large, small, cheap, expensive car or truck.

15. *The law of siblings*: There is a time and a place to launch a second brand. "The key to a family approach is to make each sibling a unique individual brand with its own identity. Resist the urge to give the brands a family look or identity. You want to make each brand as different and distinct as possible."

16. *The law of shape*: A brand's logotype should be designed to fit the eye—both eyes. The authors argue here that the ideal shape for a logotype or brand symbol is two and a quarter units wide and one unit high.

17. *The law of color*: A brand should use a color that is the opposite of its major competitors.

18. *The law of borders*: There are no barriers to global branding. A brand should know no borders.

19. *The law of consistency*: A brand is not built overnight. Success is measured in decades, not years.

20. *The law of change*: Brands can be changed, but only infrequently and very carefully.

21. *The law of mortality*: No brand will live forever. Euthanasia is often the best solution.

22. *The law of singularity*: The most important aspect of a brand is its single-mindedness.

Both these sets of laws are extremely important to keep in mind as a marketing professional, and even though we have all been down the path of violating these laws because of organizational influence and directives, we must each begin to ensure we actively drive some of these ideas as we think about our roles as individuals in the marketing organization, as well as what these ideas can do to influence the success of your company. Before going much further, I must clarify that I am a deep believer in brand and the importance of brand in the marketplace and in marketing. What I am not so convinced of is whether marketing can truly create the brand as defined in a classic sense and outlined in what I might call the 44 laws of marketing.

If we recall that perception is reality, indicative of some of my own perceptions as it relates to taking these laws at full face value—we simply cannot define a company's brand. Secondly, the guiding ideology I discussed before of obvious pragmatic innovation is applicable in evaluation of all illustrations I include. In other words, the laws and even some of the illustrations you will encounter throughout this book are not a panacea; they do, however, reflect obvious pragmatic innovation and how marketing can apply agile methodology; but I am getting ahead of myself. So getting back to the discussion, please know that I am a fan of branding and understand the distinct impact branding has on successful organizations. What is not so obvious, pragmatic, or innovative is not understanding the concepts of the combined immutable laws and seeing how they need to be considered as we enter a new program or campaign. A brand campaign on its own without an established brand, to me, is, at a minimum, possibly questionable.

What I am certain of is that if we are consistent with our representation to our customers and our symbols, terminology, and experience are consistently delivered, that there becomes a familiarization of a customer to that experience, and perhaps it establishes or influences an advantage for one product over another. Simply stated, I think we can accept at one level that brand then is an important goal of marketing. What I think happens is that there becomes a near obsession with brand establishment or its acquisition. If the goal of marketing is to enable the exchange of goods for revenue and we acknowledge that the ultimate way to accomplish that is with brand identity, then absolutely we must adhere to that identity. What I think can be detrimental is steadfast regulation over what does and does not represent a brand. Back to the idea of practical innovation—even if we have an established brand, markets are in constant flux and new markets are emerging constantly. This means that as the market changes, there has to be an adjustment to that market, which in some ways transforms a brand. It is important to appeal to the new markets while maintaining consistency with your existing markets, so you must innovate in order to keep the edge; it is important to be flexible. We must also consider at this point that marketing tends to relate to consumer goods and services—with very few exceptions, most branding is established at a consumer level, so certainly the same types of approaches to the market are going to vary depending on your products.

Again, consumer marketing is different in approach and process than one might consider for non-consumer or business-to-business marketing. There are certainly lessons learned from consumer marketing that can influence and drive the same or similar approaches to the business-to-business marketing because ultimately people make the decisions for the business. Most people have experience as consumers and would therefore have a level of expectation consciously or not on how things are sold to them as they represent the best interest of their companies. Any discussion of marketing and, in particular, "high-tech" marketing, although this author has marketing experience from organizations and businesses, would not be complete without acknowledging the impact and influence of Geoffrey A. Moore and his book *Crossing the Chasm.*[8] Published in 1991, Moore has built an industry around offering advice to high-tech companies on the marketing and selling of products to what he refers to as mainstream customers. The premise is that there are categorizations of customer types—markets that will adopt/ purchase technology innovation, sometimes for the sake of innovation (not very pragmatic)—that set false expectations on the company selling the technology of who else or what other markets can be tapped. Those false expectations are the stifling area where companies lose and fail—falling into a chasm and disappearing, never to be heard from again. What Moore advises is how to get across the chasm for survival and extend and expand into the promised markets. The foundation of this is his technology adoption life cycle, which I will cover a little later. As with everything else, Moore has turned his premise and understanding of the adoption of technology into more books and a boutique consulting organization.

As mentioned earlier, the underlying premise in the high-tech marketing world is based on what is widely accepted as the technology adoption life cycle. The model has five divisions, each representing a group of buyers to whom a product is sold during its life cycle. These groups of buyers in Figure 1-3 below—or markets if you will—are divided into five segments: Innovators, Early Adopters, Early Majority, Late Majority, and Laggards.

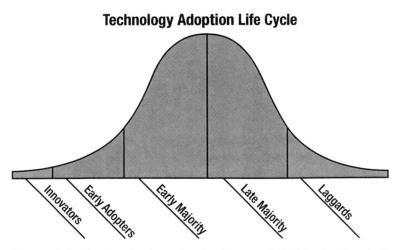

Technology Adoption Life Cycle

Figure 1-3. Classic technology adoption life cycle © 1991 by Geoffrey A. Moore

[8] Geoffrey A. Moore, Crossing the Chasm (New York: HarperBusiness, 1991). Used with permission.

Innovators are technology enthusiasts. They are very open to being the first to try out a new technology, but they represent just a small segment of the marketplace or small group within a company with limited influence for wide-scale adoption.

Early Adopters, also known as visionaries, are open to trying out new technologies too. They understand the potential value or competitive advantage a product can bring to their organization. These visionaries are a larger segment of the market, and they tend to have much more influence in an organization than do Innovators.

The Early Majority, also referred to as pragmatists, tend to buy in to new technologies only after they are convinced there is a reduced risk and there are many other successes and solid references. They are heavily risk-averse and represent the bulk of the technology market.

The Late Majority, or conservatives, are extremely risk-averse and cautious when making technology decisions. Conservatives want multiple proof points in their own environments, not just good references. They are also a very large portion of the market.

Laggards are skeptics who would prefer to avoid new technologies altogether. They will buy only if they really must.

The difficulty comes because the Early Majority, by their very nature, need good references before buying into a new technology, and Early Adopters do not make good references. The chasm then becomes a treacherous hazard indeed.

For the benefit of the reader, although I do not presume to do justice to Moore's book, I attempt to summarize key points here:

A market is defined as follows:

- A set of actual or potential customers
- For a given set of products or services
- Who have a common set of needs or wants, and
- Who reference each other when making a buying decision

To cross the chasm, Moore advocates that a company focus on a single market, a beachhead, win domination over a small, specific market, and use it as a springboard to adjacent extended markets to win. This is accomplished with a four-stage approach to crossing the chasm. He calls it the D-Day strategy, a reference to the Allied invasion of Normandy in World War II. The idea is to

1. Target the point of attack

2. Assemble the invasion force

3. Define the battle

4. Launch the invasion

These four steps allow an organization to successfully attract pragmatist buyers, and to build a significant market share for its new product.

Everything we have covered thus far relates to a fundamental component of knowledge that I feel is vital so we can better understand the challenges we as marketing professional face. While it may seem that on the journey we have taken thus far we are adding more and more variables and terminology, these ideas and concepts are the foundation of what marketing implies. What we have covered is, in essence, the ideology that describes a support mechanism for a customer or prospect to purchase goods from a company. Complementary to the immutable laws of marketing and branding are the illustrative examples covered in the ideas of *Crossing the Chasm*, which relates the real difficulties of participating in the marketplace of high tech. As I write this, I'm constantly thinking, "This can't be that complicated! Wouldn't a pragmatic, innovative approach to resolving what appears to be complex issue work here?"

I am not advocating revolution, but I certainly think that fundamentally what all the respected professionals in the field of marketing are proposing is obvious solutions to the various aspects of what one might call "marketing in action." What I mean by that is the immutable laws, *Crossing the Chasm*, one-to-one marketing, just-in-time marketing, or whatever the latest application is, all shouting to the world, "Look what we know and understand, look at how we think can assist in adjusting what you are doing to succeed more, look at how other guys have made mistakes and you are going to make the same mistake." What happens is with the steadfast trust of their own theories, in a sense each of them falls victim to their own vision of marketing.

So marketing as a discipline and certainly as a science is probably not as definable as we think, because when we talk about success, we point to market share, revenue, and brand, all of which at some level may have been "being at the right place at the right time" or hitting some intrinsic factor that was executed against—not a formula that can be applied to ensure success. The fallacy with a formula is that we are looking to understand something that at best is an inexact science but probably more of an art form. We can apply formulas to science; applying formulas to art is somewhat less tangible. Everything related to marketing is established to enable the delivery of that goal of marketing, which is the exchange of goods, but I would put forth the idea that marketing is a culmination of many aspects of the enablement of exchange. Decision-makers in those exchanges, even in non-consumer or business-to-business exchanges, are people. Therein lies another important element of agile marketing that has to be part of the thought processes and implementation of the ideas in this book.

The single most important factor to any success is the right people at the right place, with the right capability, the right capacity, the right influence, the right empowerment, and the right attitude. But more on that a bit later.

In school you're taught to get the four Ps of marketing (product, price, promotion, and place) right, and bam—you have success, but it's not always that simple, because what is success, after all, in marketing? The way to quantify success is not always black and white if you are not using only one promotion and one channel to get to market. Who is responsible for that success? Does marketing open the door and sales close it? Does the Internet and viral consumption spell success for your program, and who can claim victory or point a finger in your eye with defeat?

Success gets defined by a number of people, not just your boss and his or her boss, but the other departments, like sales, which depends on leads, and finance, which foots the bill, and let's not forget the customer, as they have expectations as well. Social media is also changing what success is for today's marketing departments. No longer is it enough to just sell your product but having the most friends, tweets, and crowdsourced ideas also indicates whether your programs are successful. At the center of all of this are the people marketing serves. Marketing needs a method to help bring all together, as the four Ps of marketing that they teach in school leave out the most important ingredient: people. There is a fifth P in the marketing mix that needs more thought than any of the other areas—it is people, the people who are your ultimate consumers, the people you service in your company that have expectations of your programs.

I will talk a lot about people and how you interact with them in order to define the other four Ps and success of your programs, your companies, and your own success metrics. People are the center of every idea and metric that is used to define success, and yet it is rare that marketing departments take a step back and think about the people they serve. Yes, I said the people marketing serves…marketing is a service business. Anyone who disagrees I encourage to spend some time in a B2B company, where dollars for programs are competed for within a business unit, and only the best ideas survive. If the marketing department has not delivered well in the past and given the services it has promised, i.e., leads, brand awareness, sales, etc., I can assure you the job will be more difficult. It is for this reason the first tenet of this book is about marketing needing a new method that puts people first and allows for a fundamental shift in how marketing views its job in a company and how you can use this to your own personal advantage. Marketing departments often think of themselves as the hotbed of innovation and forget that their real purpose is to provide a service to sales and their customers, helping to open doors and promote products others are busy creating or using.

Marketing as a service department may not be a new concept, but it does call for a new way to approach the work. When you view your work in marketing as a service, providing the best service and iterating on that over time becomes more important than a one-time flash in the pan marketing campaign. Marketing as a service is defined on the Web as a model of marketing deployment whereby a provider licenses its marketing resources to customers for use as a service on demand. If you think of your marketing department and yourself as being on loan to sales or the other stakeholders in your company, and your job is to make their job easier, your objective becomes easier, as you are no longer trying to constantly sell or market your programs to them, as you are then playing for the same team. I see this as one of the most fundamental issues in companies today, as marketing, product development, and sales are often more adversarial than on the same team fighting the external challenges, of which there are enough to go around.

Placing yourself as a marketer in a service role and as the consigliere of sorts not only enables you to better understand the needs of the different areas of the business, but also gives you permission to interact with the customer on behalf of your company's support arm or sales team and to bring teams together to win business. All this said, it is not easy to be recognized as a service if you haven't provided any lately. I say that tongue in cheek, but it is often the perceived case, as the business can resent high dollars spent on branding initiatives and other expensive advertising areas that take longer than 24 hours to show results. It may not be fair, as it does take time to make good marketing work, but it is fair to say that things have to be done to prove value in the meantime.

Values in your company may differ, but it generally starts with listening and saying yes instead of no to all the other departments' ideas. If you ever saw the Jim Carrey movie *Yes Man*, you have experienced already the power of what saying yes can bring. In the movie, Jim Carrey, a notorious negative Nelly who has a dead-end life, is brainwashed by a new-age mentor into believing that he has to say yes to every opportunity or something bad will happen. Because he does this, he is open to a world of new opportunity, dating new people and approving a bunch of micro-loans at his bank job that prove to be profitable, which no one in his company would have done. He ends up getting the girl and the promotion. I liken marketing to a service to allowing you to do this and open yourself up to new opportunities. After all, it is unlikely you are getting paid for just coming up with new marketing ideas but instead executing well the ideas that are there. Where they come from becomes less important, and the credit you can give to others will help to catapult you to new levels of career success, as you're able to make new alliances by helping others.

So you may be asking, what was the old marketing method and why doesn't it work? There are many different methods. They include direct marketing, relationship marketing, advertising, public relations, positioning, and my favorite bullshit marketing method, the holy grail of marketing buzz words, "integrated marketing." All these methods of communicating your message are important, and I'm not saying we should throw them all away, but I just believe there is a better way that doesn't rely on loosely linking now-related elements into a package and saying now I have an integrated program. Being integrated in pictures and words alone won't sell your products if they are garbage and don't solve a customer need or want. And worse yet, your ideas won't see the light of day because you can't convince your CMO, head of sales, or other important constituents that your program will work. So it can get funded, and, even worse still, once it does get executed and you are expecting them to give you the "atta boy," they don't because they don't believe the results, even when you show them the cold facts in leads and dollars and cents, because of channel conflict with where the lead truly originated from.

I have seen it time and time again that when all the parties in a company have not bought in, even a great program can and will fall on its face without collaboration from all the important parties, from those creating the product, those creating the messaging, those creating the program, and those ultimately having to close the deal. So why is this so hard? Because people (I will be talking more about people as a fifth P in the marketing mix of four Ps a little later on in this chapter) need to feel a part of something and to make it their own, in most cases, in order for them to be supportive of it. People have egos, and they must be fed all the way around. A lot of people might challenge me and say, but don't you think people want what is best for their company and won't they act altruistically? And to that I say yes, but they also generally think that they know the best way to do things, unless you work with a bunch of droids and unless you have already convinced them with perfect ideas and execution over many years. The chances of people just getting on the bandwagon of your latest campaign is not likely.

Ego also shouldn't be thought of as a bad word; pride of ownership is one of the biggest traits you can use to your advantage once you learn to be a marketing service to your colleagues. It also can be dangerous if you have too much pride of ownership and are not open enough to change. I am a big fan of Darwin, as I think he put it best when he said, "It is not the strongest of the species that survive, nor the most intelligent, but the one most responsive to change." Changes in business needs demand that we approach how we do our jobs with respect to ensuring and being open to change. The human element is the frailest component because each individual has a unique set of concerns that affect management of change. As a leader in a marketing organization, you must consider that there are unique personalities or behaviors that tend to be part of marketing organizations. These include the following:

- *"The Shampoo Super Genius Marketer"*: You may remember the antagonist cartoon character from the Warner Brothers Road Runner cartoons of yesteryear—Wile E. Coyote Super Genius. It seems he had a marvelous contraption for every occasion. Tenacity was never his downfall. Rather, it was the excessive creativity and thinking there was a buyable solution to every problem, whether that might be a favorite agency like "Acme" or repeating the same behavior— similar to shampooing your hair: wet, shampoo, rinse, repeat. One way or another, marketers have had success with a particular approach or solution, either from outside the company or from a different department, and that solution is what they bring to the table and all they are willing to try or know. Generally they recycle presentations over and over to prove their point.

- *"Produce or Perish"*: Another typical behavior is a direct result of the precarious times in which we live. With corporate downsizing, early retirement programs, layoffs, and the like, employees are apt to believe that if they do not give more than 100% they will be terminated. Analogous to success in academia, marketing professionals (and managers) that exhibit this "produce or perish" behavior approach to each campaign or marketing program as a means of survival. The typical reaction to marketing initiative requests reflects a focus on the delivery of the end product, not the process. When challenged with a short delivery time frame, the immediate reaction is to ignore the methodology and start producing the product without regard to improving quality through improving the process.

- *"A Room Without a View"*: Sometimes, marketing professionals feel that they operate best in isolation. This occurs when a campaign or initiative becomes a finite project performed in a vacuum rather than as part of an ongoing process. Often these folks have the perception of being so busy that they are unable to see their work as part of a continuous process. Consequently, they do not take the time to apply techniques or lessons they have learned. When the opportunities for improvement have not been institutionalized or at least formalized and recorded, the successes that occur are more often than not based on chance.

I certainly do not want to over-generalize, but have you identified behaviors that have to be considered as you look at your organization? It is important that everyone in your organization act, and be treated, like part of a team. Failure to do so will greatly impede the resultant quality of the system. A successful approach to initiating an attitude of teamwork can be achieved by following the 3C approach—communication, cooperation, and clarification.

Communicate effectively at all levels within the group, from the top down (managers to subordinates) and from the bottom up (subordinates to managers).

Stress that it is necessary for each member of the team to cooperate with one another. No member of any team can afford to say, "That is not in my job description." Of course, cooperation should not be viewed as a synonym for off-loading work to co-workers.

And finally, clarify all matters that are confusing. Do not blindly attempt to develop what you do not understand. Once again, clarification should be implemented in both directions—top down and bottom up.

By embracing the 3C approach, the "island unto myself" attitude can be eliminated and the foundation of adopting within and without organizational transformation to agile marketing will be easily laid.

Instituting a Flexible Methodology

I mentioned earlier my support of adopting methodology. I say that in the context of understanding that mandating what may be termed a "commercial methodology," which incorporates idealized procedures and methods, has proven to be ineffective and viewed as a nuisance by all participants. The need for procedures and structure is paramount to the success of any type of endeavor. What is of primary importance for the adoption of a methodology is an agreement on a basic philosophy that underlies and supports the motivational factors that drive the group. Additionally, it is important that strict adherence to the "written word" be absent from the methodology; a methodology must be flexible. The rigorous methodologies that are in place within most organizations are often not successful directly because of the rigor. Shifting the understanding of those who must adhere to the methodology is crucial. This shift cannot be achieved without accomplishing two objectives:

- Modify your methodology to make it less stringent. Most commercial methodologies are procedural in nature and require strict adherence to the letter of its processes.
- Educate your team on the methodology and the purpose for the methodology. Without stating a purpose, your methodology will usually fail regardless of how flexible it is, because those not familiar or aligned to something other than agile will view it as bureaucracy and a hindrance. With a noble goal, however, a flexible methodology has a chance to succeed.

Streamline the Perception

One key area of focus for a management group whose mission is to improve quality by moving to agile is to first establish an internal definition of achieving goals. While this may at first appear to be a simple task, the perception of what represents a goal vs. an achievable outcome from the perspective of a media buyer differs greatly from the perspective of a product marketing individual. This in turn will vary from the perspective of the CMO, the manager, the analyst, etc.

The Teamwork Resolution

In order to respond to the demands of the customer, both internal and external, a simple progressive process needs to be put into place. This will initiate an environment in which everyone works toward the common goal of reliability and quick problem resolution.

The individual, in this case, is the manager who can influence or direct teams with relative autonomy. When an individual makes a decision to travel down a particular path for self-improvement, goals and milestones are set to accomplish that achievement. Listed here are some suggestions for instituting process improvements that require minimal effort and reap significant benefits:

1. Implement process improvements as small-step, procedural changes that provide more structure to existing processes.

2. Empower members of the project team with responsibilities associated with the implementation of the application of "structure." Get the team involved in the process.

3. Establish and use project management tools to project and track tasks and resources associated with all or one particular phase of a project's life cycle. This will establish baseline statistics and improve estimates for future projects.

4. Institute task tracking by linking time-reporting to task completion through the use of individualized tasking sheets or spreadsheet links to project management tools.

5. Adopt metrics associated with establishing these techniques:

    1. Establish baseline measurement of an easily definable result of the process (i.e., end-user satisfaction qualified and measured by raw number of problem reports).
    2. Institute structured techniques, then measure and analyze results of the process.
    3. Share the measurements and results with the team.
    4. Evaluate applied structure and improve.

6. Establish a consensus understanding of quality products and results.

7. Encourage ideas for improvements from the team. There is much to be said for "pride of authorship."

These steps result in the application of procedures—a methodology to facilitate agile as a movement toward improvement of processes. In short, the basis for the success of any type of procedural/process improvement begins with the participants.

Agile Enabling Quality

One of the most important tools that can be used to promote the continuous improvement of the process associated with the application of the agile approach involves ensuring quality. Like everything else, things must be measured, and quality metrics provide a benchmark—feedback from end users and direction for improvement, not unlike requirements gathering via crowdsourcing (but more on the crowdsourcing topic in a later chapter).

Specifically, some attributes of quality that usually contribute most to corporate objectives relating to marketing are predictability, business impact, appropriateness, reliability, and adaptability.

- Predictability means knowing and controlling the risk factors involved, such as delivery date, cost, and resources needed.
- The business impact dimension of quality relates to whether a marketing initiative or campaign provides a significant benefit to the organization, usually in the form of leads but really revenue.
- An appropriate approach will provide a solution that is suitable to customers: extending relationships and meeting their needs by providing value.
- Reliability concerns whether there is a continual dialog with the marketplace and customers as a result of the perception of your brand.
- Adaptability means that the system and support are able to change cost-effectively to meet the evolving needs of the customer.

By breaking each of these quality issues down into their key components and then formulating a measurement system based on those components, managers can begin to get a handle on the agile application to the marketing process. The key, then, to an agile marketing program lies in whether it can be measured. This measurement is the foundation of the iterative nature of the agile approach. If a process cannot be measured, it cannot be understood, controlled, or improved.

Using Technology to Augment Quality

Although much of this discussion may seem to be railing against technology and more about process application, this is not the intent. Technology for technology's sake will never result in transformation. However, the appropriate adoption and adaptation of technology can provide an increase in the facilitation of a rapid adoption of agile.

As I said earlier, agility and adaptability are paramount to survival in life as well as marketing. If you hold too tightly to your ideas and are not open to seeing things differently and changing, I assure you will not survive regardless of how smart you are. The single best skill a marketer in today's world can have is agility.

The old marketing methods do not take into account the need for change and require rigorous planning for budgeting cycles that just can't meet the needs and demands of ever-changing business and market pressures. Think about it this way: let's say tomorrow your company decided it wanted to be in a new market with a new product, how long would it take you to get together all the right messaging and creative, buy the right ad words, create print advertising, update your web site, etc. with the new information? If you are like most companies, a six-month cycle would not be unrealistic, but this is just not fast enough if you are going to beat your competitors. If you wait six months, you risk falling into the "me too" scenario in the marketplace. For this reason, the old integrated marketing methods don't work…that is, unless you have an agile process that allows you to move much faster and to adapt to these marketing pressures on the fly where necessary. Some of you might say, "Isn't consistency of message going to be impacted if I can change so fast?" and to that I say yes, it might be, but while change is inevitable, the truth is having the ability to change is important. Actually changing everything 180 degrees often is unlikely, as people (that ever-important fifth part of the marketing mix) don't generally like to change that often. So while it may be a risk, it is not likely a great one, as the adoption curve will prevent the masses from seeing all the changes. Of course, if you experience a hit and it takes off, your risk is greater for making changes and showing the inconsistency, but if you already have an audience who loves something and is buying in droves, chances are you won't have the requirements for the changes.

Marketing today often is disconnected from the business in terms of what it can deliver and when. Every person I know has an opinion of how to market something. Marketing is, of course, not alone in this problem, but it is generally the most visible department in any company and one of the hardest to measure. Therefore, it is the most susceptible to ridicule internally as well as externally. That is the fundamental issue, in that marketing should not be a department's job but a whole company's job, as everyone needs to know how to tell the company story, succinctly and credibly. When you relegate that authority to a department and don't get all the other departments bought in, you lose. You cannot build a brand on one department; brands are built on people doing things consistently and in a positive matter. Colors, words, advertisements, events, etc.—they are only tools for doing this and alone cannot build a positive image. You need people who believe and live a message to make a good brand.

People collaborating are always what make things succeed or fail—everything else can be changed with enough money and resources. People and their opinions, however, take time and proof to gain trust and acceptance, so getting it right from the beginning makes it much easier. I'm not advocating you fire yourself or your marketing department if they haven't figured this out, as most haven't. Instead, change your model to become service-centric and lead by example by building agile marketing via cross-functional teams into every part of your business and extending it out to customers and prospects via crowdsourcing.

Now I want to review the next three models to get your internal house in order so you can reach customers and prospects effectively. By now you are starting to see that the silos companies set up (departments) are a fundamental cause of marketing being disconnected from the business in most organizations. Because it is acting as something outside the other core areas of the business, it is unable to truly understand changing objectives. While they may have agreed to plans six months ago or a year ago for budgeting purposes, new market pressures have come to bear, so that no budget is left to cover new events, advertising vehicles, or new social media channels where your customers are congregating. The business and often sales will scream loudest, saying they need more help in getting leads through these channels, but the non-agile marketing team can only look back at them and say, "But we made you this nice brochure and have these other events, ads, etc. planned." Everyone leaves the meeting dissatisfied, believing that no one understands the needs or the efforts that have been expended. Marketing is frustrated because they have worked hard to build to the requirements they had at the time, and sales is aggravated that marketing can't keep up. This battle is waged on a daily basis in conference calls and meeting rooms all over the world, but there is a solution if you can learn to be service-oriented and agile. This book is meant to help you to be able to do that.

A Look at Whom You Are Serving

First let's look at the fundamentals of whom marketing is supposed to serve. In the old paradigm, marketing was meant to serve the company as a whole, by providing a message that people could use to convey the company's value proposition on their products and services to prospects and customers. The message was to be consumed by the entire customer-facing parts of an organization but primarily sales, services, and support. If the company was publicly traded, the importance of communicating this to shareholders and the investment community was also added to the list of requirements, so add financial analyst relations to the list as well. If your marketing organization is like most, there likely is delegation of authority on things like field marketing, advertising, PR, creative services, web, corporate marketing, product marketing, etc. So oftentimes the customer might be the marketing department's own silos, as field marketing, for instance, needs to consume product marketing messaging to do field events, etc.

Marketing also serves important services as a channel to communicate back to product development what new trends are in the market and what customers are responding positively and negatively to, so add product development to the list of marketing's customers. Last but certainly not least, those very prospects and customers marketing is targeting its messages toward are some of the most important stakeholders, as they depend on honest and simple messaging to help them cut through the hype to the real value and help they can get from a company. Quickly you start to see that marketing serves everyone, but that isn't to say some customers aren't more important than others. Only you know your business, so look around carefully and understand your own organization's politics. Yes, I said politics, because it is a factor in your program's success and your success. Every organization, no matter how sophisticated or altruistic its people, has politics, and politics by its very nature is not negative. After all, the definition of politics is simply a process by which groups of people make collective decisions and form policy, which in itself is not a bad thing. Politics is ugly only when you are on the opposite side of the ruling authority. That's not to say your company wants a bunch of yes men and women creating group-think, but understanding who has power in your company for funding and blessing things is beneficial, and figuring out how to be a service to those people will, in fact, benefit everyone.

If those in power start to work with you and you start to serve their needs, you gain permission to help influence their beliefs, wants, and needs. It takes being humble enough to be able to listen and truly try to help the other person, not just serve your own interests. This is harder to do than you might think, as I have found that people love to say no to other people's ideas. In my own marketing department and for all my interactions, always, always, and let me stress always, start from yes if someone asks if you can do something, even if you think the idea is the worst idea you've ever heard. And here's my reasoning: just about anything can be done, and if a person comes to you and you shoot them down right off the bat, you have already put them in a defensive posture, and they are unlikely to hear anything you say after. If you start from yes, you bring down the person's guard to talk about the how, and that is where everything really starts to happen. The how might need to include more money or resources, but then you are working with that person to achieve an objective. You may even be able to make a recommendation of how, given "their idea," they might be able to do it even better. Yes is the strongest word you have in your marketing dictionary, and I ask you use it as often as you can, as it will open more doors for your marketing programs than any other ideas or actions you can bring to bear. This is how you can make politics in your organization work for you by influencing others through helping them make their ideas a reality. Then once you've done this a time or two, you earn the trust and respect to introduce them to your own ideas and can get them to help you get whatever it might be that you need to prove your initiative successful.

Right now I suggest that we acknowledge that the marketing profession and, indeed, marketing as a whole are not easily definable, as there are numerous ideas about what marketing means to various people. Simply stated, if we take the best of what the industry presents to us as ideas to support our own implementation, then I know you will succeed, and certainly it has been a mainstay in my life. A colleague of mine once said, "I eat from many tables." This too is what this book will help define, as it relates to your success as a professional marketer as well as suggestions on transforming your organization for success. Most importantly, the ideas within this book should become part of how you think and approach your role in a marketing organization. As I write about your role in an organization, I am reminded of one of the precepts in how I approach my interaction with colleagues, customers, and associates—it is well known that everyone who works for a company represents that company, so that every interaction should be guided by the idea that everyone is in sales and, to that end, everyone is in marketing—every interaction is important, every interaction is vital, every interaction is key to your success and the success of the organization, both internally and externally.

The Four Ps and the Marketplace

Since we have at some level determined that we cannot easily define marketing, what may be easier to understand rather than the definition of marketing is what a market is and how it is presented. Classically, there are many influences on the market, but at their core, they are the four Ps: product, price, place, and promotion. These four Ps define classic marketing. Each component has a very strong and complex construction in and of themselves. Deciding what product to make, defining that product, pulling together the cooperation of departments to produce that product, the facilitation of what that product is and how it is perceived in the marketplace, deciding how to be competitive with respect to the product, taking into account product cost, price, and the competition, and considering the promotion of the product all require marketing. We tend to think of all of these in a classical marketing sense. All steps are followed in a linear order to create one big product, with a big launch and a lot of hullabaloo.

So a market is where we deliver our solutions or where there is a potential consumer for our solution. With this classic marketing or traditional marketing method, we find ourselves as marketers asking these questions: How do I get knowledge about what my customers want? How do I target my customers? How do I get my product to market? What outlets are available to me or my company? What combination of direct and indirect outlets do I need to work? How do I gain the outlets I need and manage conflicting outlets? How do I manage the customer's perception of the product in the marketplace? And many more...

In today's constantly evolving marketplace, how can asking these questions within a classical marketing process help you and your business to succeed? Let's think about the classical marketing model a bit more. When marketing acts within a very traditional set of processes, a lot of times it has trouble keeping up with the marketplace and the needs of the business, and oftentimes loses sight of what the customer wants.

Think about it: Do you understand your customers today? Are you able to articulate in a valid and relevant way to them why your products and services meet their needs best in today's marketplace? Do you understand what the business needs, or requirements, are? Do you understand what the market demands are? Can you change and adapt your programs and campaigns in order to meet their changing needs/requirements?

Setting up the product, price, place, and promotion marketing mix shows it requires a lot of skill and effort, careful and thoughtful selection of the marketplace, especially in today's changing markets. Oftentimes, it's an easy thing to conceptualize, but very difficult to do. As markets become more fragmented and more specialized, traditional marketing processes simply cannot keep up. Oftentimes, by the time marketing programs and campaigns are developed and ready for deployment, they are already out of date. Marketing therefore needs a new method in order to reach these newly segmented groups of the market and of customers in order to ensure the business succeeds. So now that we have reviewed some of the precepts to marketing and examined marketing as a discipline, and I have shared so many of my personal beliefs, we are going to focus on examining some of the current processes of marketing and develop ideas as to how we can evolve these processes to be in line with the always changing marketplace today.

Marketing Processes

Let's take a look at one conceptualization of the marketing process.

Implementation

This is the actual task of getting the job done. So beyond conceptualization and planning and beyond strategy and development, we have what is seemingly the most pragmatic component of marketing—the actual implementation. This includes programming and allocating budget, development of short-term programs focused on integrated approaches for different products, allocation of resources, sales promotion, sales enablement, sales incentives, product development, and time across various products and functions. It also includes knowledge of customers, acquisition of customer information, analysis and research, acquisition of quantitative and qualitative data, channel knowledge, routes to market, online marketing, marketing system integration, partnerships, event planning and execution, promotion, etc. This is certainly a lot to think about without even identifying all of the components—the differentiating factor is a holistic approach to ensure there is a common way of doing things throughout the marketing process. The best way to enable that holistic approach is to ensure the proper integration of leadership across the various organizations, all marching to the same goal of success. That success must be defined the same way for everybody—revenue. As I mentioned before, the measure of success is based on a continued sustainable growing influence in the market through branding as well as increasing revenue and market share.

Sales and marketing have always been tied together as they are integral to mutual objectives and success. Where there tends to be a disconnect is where the organizations are of different purposes. Getting back to the complexities of implementation, each of the factors across the organization must be working in synch, otherwise there will be a lot of fingerpointing and blame across the organization. Earlier I suggested that the most important criteria for a successful marketing organization is people—this I feel can be defined as the most important P and is a critical factor when relating to the classic four Ps of product, promotion, price, and placement.

Marketing Planning

Development of long-term plans with a stronger impact is a goal of many organizations but can be impossible when revenue goals are short-term. Agile gives an opportunity to bridge that fundamental gap. Marketers may have a three- to five-year plan overall, but have shorter-term components, which enable them to meet overall plans or goals or objectives. This is different from strategy, which enables marketing to support the business. Oftentimes, there tends to be a disconnect here, as the business is interested in more short-term goals rather than long-term goals, whereas marketing strategy is traditionally aligned with longer-term objectives. Monitoring and auditing: keeping track of what's going on and requires analysis and review of programs put in place, plans, and strategies. These measurements and analysis allow marketers to make informed decisions about their programs. They can put more funding behind programs or campaigns that are succeeding, and can halt ones that are not. This piece really allows marketing to be flexible and dynamic, and helps to make great strides in keeping up with the changing marketplace, the business, and customers. It is imperative that marketers are able to adjust processes and marketing as a whole, always keeping in mind what is important: the five Ps.

Marketing's purpose is very important because marketing is meant to separate customers or potential customers from their money in exchange for services from the organization. Marketing can't live up to its mission the way it is currently doing things. It's a combination of improving processes, knowing and understanding what marketing is and that it does exist for its own purpose, but that it risks failure in the siloed separateness that it always had in the past.

The Changing Market and New Demands on Marketing

There is a perception that marketing seems to be at war with those it is meant to serve. I don't believe it's at war, but that marketing has had the difficult task of trying to bring together shorter-term and longer-term objectives into quarter-by-quarter results. Sales has quarterly objectives and is in the customer's face constantly. They have an immediate need to respond to every need of the customer and to what is going on in the street for a quarterly time period. Because we want to be sure of some objectives that marketing has in planning and strategy, we, as marketers, aren't reacting quickly enough to what those changes on the street are. This may be because of a traditional process we have in place for the development of a marketing strategy for the enablement of an organization's objectives. Maybe marketing's longer-term goals of three to five years break down into 18–24-month cycles, and then teams can build within that time frame with increased flexibility.

So when we say that marketing is at war with those it's meant to serve, we're talking about the perception of marketing—that it reacts to the market, to the demands of the business, and is at sales' beck and call. This is obviously always in conflict with the marketing objectives of product development, placement, and promotion, where marketers think products fit in the marketplace and what consumers are thinking or wanting. It's not a bad thing—marketing is all about strategy and planning and trying to hear the market. But the other organizations within the business often complain that marketing does not react fast enough to what the customers are really saying—even if that's what the customer is saying for a short period of time. This is why marketing can't live up to the expectations of sales, customers, or the business with the current way of doing things. There has to be nimbleness, flexibility, and strategy. Marketers have to be agile.

Marketing seems to be removed not only from the business but also from customers. If we look at a traditional marketing organization, one of the components within the confines of product knowledge is that marketers think they know what customers are going to want. I like to call this *product pride*. We, as marketers, tend to think that we know what is going to be important to customers. This can be great—if you guess right. But if you guess wrong, you're trying to put features and functions or bells and whistles that are, in the marketplace, meaningless and not consumable. To the business, this means marketing is wasting money—again.

On the other side of that same coin is to hold back, and not react to anything happening in the marketplace. We treat everything like a trend. Again, we may be right, or we may be wrong. But without the correct information, all we can do is guess. So it's a difficult mix between people who are trying to support product marketing, as well as providing value to the customer. Based upon that, there is a high degree of pride that comes across. Oftentimes, it's easier to hear what you want to hear, and forget the rest. This can mean listening only to a small segment of customers, or to one sales guy that needs x-y-z for his customer. Without doing the proper level of research and understanding, marketing is flying blind.

The Solution: Agile Marketing

But all of this research takes time, and in today's market, there is no time. Marketers need to listen and understand what is really happening out there, then apply this knowledge and thought leadership to a process that will churn out the most important pieces for success in the marketplace.

This is where agile marketing comes in: it is critical that marketing get up to the speed of the business, the market, and customers. Agile marketing is the ability to outpace your completion in the marketplace by being nimble enough to realign resources as necessary.

What agile marketing isn't: It's not changing your strategy every time someone new comes into your office, and it's not allowing you not to plan. Planning for change is the paramount rule of agile marketing. Now you're saying, Michelle, you are crazy. How can you plan for change? What money, people, and tools can you choose to do this if you don't know what the change might be? And while it might seem paradoxical, that is exactly what you must do, and, trust me, planning for change might seem hard to do, but not planning for it will make your job far harder. For instance, if you use traditional marketing planning methods and you divide your spend and your resources completely among today's business needs, what happens tomorrow when your competitor acquires or builds the new killer app or your biggest customer goes bankrupt and you now have to compete in a new market? You are no longer able to turn on a dime, and now you have to go back to the business and say there is no money to execute the new program or idea because you are already forced down a path to failure. So how do you plan for change? You put into your marketing strategy that change is a constant, and you need to start planning by looking at what your long-term company strategies are and what the constant of change will demand.

You will always need people, processes, and tools to get things done, and you're likely to never have enough regardless of the methodology you use. By employing agile, you will be able to go farther, because, instead of setting in stone from the start what your programs will be and building every requirement at the most granular level, you will start with the end states you want to accomplish, and you can create key performance indicators around them, such as a goal to generate four times the number of inquiries that you have today for a specific product area or x dollars in revenue. By starting with the objective and goal and then starting to scrum with the right folks in the various groups in your business, you can gain acceptance to help you in executing an agile marketing plan. Who is not going to agree or want to be a part of contributing to revenue or improving customer experience? Start with the high-level vision and not the tactics of how to get there—this is the first rule of success in agile marketing. This means giving up preconceived notions of what works and doesn't, as each participant in the scrum will have a role and place to provide feedback into the process. As a scrum master, you will need to learn that listening and being open-minded are the keys to success for agile marketing and, more importantly, for all successful business dealings.

So you have a marketing idea and you want to put it into action using an agile methodology. Does that mean you should just jump right in and do everything yourself in a vacuum, as it is the most expedient approach? Only if your hope is to fail miserably and be burned in effigy for your dumb ideas that wasted company money, and produced no revenue; this is not the fastest way to success if you ask me. Even the best ideas in the history of a marketing department will fail without the proper buy-in, so what kind of team structure do you need to be successful? Easy for you to say, but how do I get all the people I need from all the different departments, who will surely want to shut me down or drag this out until it isn't even a good idea anymore? I've found success by starting with sharing your idea at the top of the food chain in your company with the individuals who have power. I'm not talking about just those folks who sit in the C suite, but you know that manager down the hall from you who has the C-level suite's ear. That is all it takes to start. If you can sell one key person on getting started, the rest will follow, as you can build a program structure that will help. And as I mentioned before, start with a broad vision instead of the exact program and vendors you want to run with. Everyone wants to increase revenue and make relationships better; not everyone wants to do an advertising campaign or golf event. The broader your initiative, the more room for change to be able to be planned for effectively. Agile marketing says, let's take the agile project management method, and apply it to the processes within a marketing organization in order to ensure it can respond to the market, the needs of the business and, most important, the needs of the customer.

How do you understand the analysis? How do you get others in the organization to focus with the marketing organization on how to best get to these groups? How do you get distributors or channels to believe that what you're trying to sell takes a better method than what exists now? In agile marketing, the four Ps of traditional marketing are still important—but in addition to this, a fifth P comes into play: people. As we will see, it's often people who make the biggest difference.

Especially in an agile context, marketing is meant to serve, to facilitate the entire organization and components within the organization, both in a short-term and long-term context. In planning and strategy, we must make sure that we include the objectives of the organization; then, in context, define what planning and strategy are. This will allow marketers to make sure they establish and enable their channels to the market, promotion to the market, and other components that are going to support the business objectives.

In the project management sense, agile was developed in order to deal with changing requirements from multiple stakeholders. Agile offers an organized process that enables teams to succeed in constantly changing environments. This seems to be just what marketing needs! But before we dive deeper into agile marketing, let's take a look at the classic "Pigs and Chickens" story to give us some context (Figure 1-4).

Figure 1-4. Scrum roles[9]

This story is meant to illustrate the important roles within the agile processes: pigs and chickens. Pigs are the hard workers—those that are totally invested in the project or program or campaign. Chickens are the folks that strut around, giving orders, but are not necessarily completely invested.

Pigs and chickens work closely together throughout the agile process, from planning to completion. Agile marketing managers need to adopt a shared or participative leadership style in order for the process to succeed. They need to communicate vision to chickens and pigs, who can then develop the appropriate tactics to achieve the project/program/campaign vision. It is important to have teams of pigs and chickens with cross-functional abilities. Agile marketing managers keep both an external focus—their hand on the pulse of the market—and an internal focus—their hand on the pulse of the project/program/campaign's success.

Agile marketing requires a sharp and constant focus on reaching objectives/goals successfully, with the highest quality, and as completely as possible in the time allowed. This focus on success encourages fast failures. We'll talk more about this later, but the purpose of this is to harness change to enable the business to have a competitive advantage.

Throughout the agile marketing process, there should be a constant priority on business values, and meeting what the market, the business, and customers demand. Agile marketers follow a process of plan, iterate, fail, and succeed to keep them in line with these demands—ensuring successful projects/programs/campaigns.

---

[9] Mike Vizdos, *Implementing Scrum,* http://www.implementingscrum.com/section/blog/cartoons/. Used with permission.

A Practical Case for Using Agile Methods

In this chapter, we will look at how, in a recession economy, a large software company with multiple product lines successfully delivered greater value to the business while reducing its marketing staff and budget by more than 50%. This case study will examine the application of an agile approach for organizational alignment, process transformation and optimization, and managerial leadership. We'll look at how agile uses planning, iteration, and failures to ultimately succeed. We'll also start with looking at how a software company took the Agile Manifesto and created the new Agile Marketing Manifesto:

- People working together for a common goal over processes and tools
- Campaigns that deliver vs. the same old marketing plans
- Customer collaboration through crowdsourcing not through guesswork
- Taking action over talking

All companies need to deliver their products and services faster, with more quality, and with fewer resources. These three components are key to ensuring success for any organization as everyone is driving to streamline for efficiency. The difference is in the ideology around how to streamline. As I pointed out in the previous chapter, agile is significantly more than just doing things in a faster fashion. It is the precept of adapting engineering concepts based on the agile method into the fabric of organization, process, and people functionality. This requires a dramatic transformation of marketing to a new state to support agile. The mission statement here demonstrates that objective—to achieve maximum return and figure 2.1 illustrates that journey.

■ **Mission Statement for Transformation** Creating, implementing, and sustaining changes in behavior, processes, and tools required to build long-term, sustainable relationships with customers, manage costs, stay ahead of the competition, create demand, and maintain profitable growth.

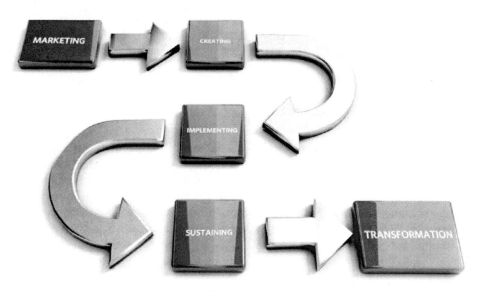

Figure 2-1. Streamline processes © 2010 by CA, Inc.

Trying to transform a product or an organization is no easy feat. Anyone who has tried to make a meaningful transformation of any sort will know the difficulty. There are many different symptoms that drive the need for change in an organization or product. Figure 2-2 lists some of the common challenges or opportunities.

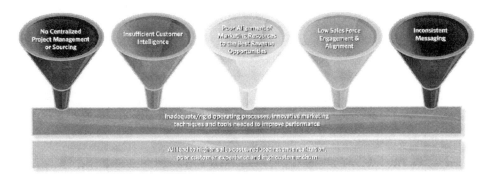

Figure 2-2. Marketing challenges © 2010 by CA, Inc.

At a basic level, the business has, at a minimum, requirements to maximize margins. This can be visualized in the model called the "iron triangle." The "iron triangle" represents the relationship between time, cost, and scope within a project. When one parameter increases or decreases, the others are affected. More recent project management theory acknowledges that quality is affected by all three sides of the iron triangle, and therefore all aspects of the triangle must be taken into account, as illustrated in Figure 2-3.

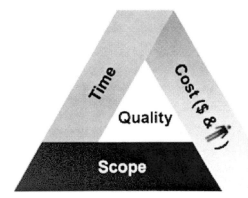

Figure 2-3. From the classic PMO model, the "iron triangle" is key to success in any management process. © 2010 by CA, Inc.

Another factor that drives transformation and cannot be ignored is that a disproportionately aligned marketing organization fails to deliver revenue to targets and is not entwined enough with sales despite excessive spending, as indicated in Figure 2-4.

■ Marketing Spending

■ Marketing Driven New Product Revenue

Disproportional Spending to Realized Product PNCV

Figure 2-4. Disproportional spending to realized product—PNCV © 2010 by CA, Inc.

As Figure 2-4 demonstrates, PNCV or Product New Contract Value, in relation to measurable comparable marketing spend, shows little return. So if we apply the "iron triangle" to agile marketing, it shows that any one thing that you change affects the central goal. So to equate the four elements of the precepts I discussed earlier, the correlating elements of marketing are as follows:

Constructs:

- *Collaboration*: People working together for a common goal in regard to processes and tools
- *Customer input*: Customer collaboration through crowdsourcing not through guesswork
- *Execution*: Taking action over talking

Objective: The goal of the program and key performance indicators you need to have in place to define yourself as successful.

Revenue: Campaigns that deliver vs. old-hat, cumbersome marketing plans

The ability to deliver all three aspects can be daunting. Most project management methodologies, and organizations in general, recommend picking the two on the triangle that are most important to the project and using them as the main constraints. I tend to think we can do better. This gives marketing departments a new way to attack their projects or their organizational challenges. Borrowing from the methodological "iron triangle," Figure 2-5 illustrates the same approach in the agile world. Our three biggest constraints in marketing are *collaboration*, *execution*, and *customer input*. Revenue is affected by all of these. Therefore, the basic reality is that if any two of the three suffer, revenue suffers. And if we acknowledge that revenue is the true measurement of marketing success, then we, as marketers, need to make sure our iron triangles are healthy.

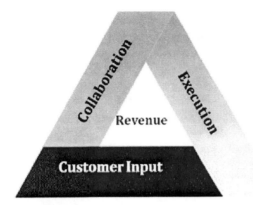

Figure 2-5. Agile marketing iron triangle © 2010 by CA, Inc.

Figure 2-5 demonstrates an "iron triangle" for agile as it relates specifically to marketing. As with the project management iron triangle, the agile marketing triangle shows that any one thing that you change affects the central goal. Ultimately, without successful marketing, revenue suffers. While sales may be tasked with bringing in the revenue, the road to that revenue is directly and indirectly related to successful marketing in the form of everything from branding to campaigns. For the purpose of the illustration, campaigns refer to anything marketing delivers that drives revenue.

We can discuss other metrics for marketing success, but the final objective when it is all said and done is to increase revenue. So how do we make this happen? What are some examples of going from our siloed organization to the cooperative aspects of agile? What are the steps in the process and procedures we must follow to be successful? These are probably some of the questions that have come to mind as you read this, and I will address some of the specifics in the coming chapters.

Let's first take a look at a real-life example of something I was able to deliver with the application of the components of agile to what I would argue is the most important aspect of media and interaction—the online experience. A little later on, I will discuss the importance of this route to market, but suffice it to say the realization of the capability, ability, and pervasiveness of what one might call Web 2.0 is the most exciting aspect of marketing implementation that the marketing industry has seen in years. I am talking about the perceived second generation of web development and design that aims to facilitate communication, secure information sharing, interoperability, and collaboration on the World Wide Web. In other words, Web 2.0 is about all the new ways we are using the Web.

So today's marketing must take into account the ways marketing is being practiced with Web 2.0 concepts and tools. While these new ways are particularly evident in marketing communications (how sellers and buyers talk to one another), they are affecting the entire practice of marketing as a whole. Two key areas of focus from an interaction perspective are concerned with what one might call "tailored interaction." This idea is defined as implementation of a "persona," where a persona is a group of specialized interactions of someone known or unknown. The second aspect of this transformed and important marketing reality is the idea of social networking.

The techniques for social networking are changing constantly, but here is a list of the major social networking platforms today:

- Blog (personal; easily updated web sites plus blogging aggregators, e.g., Twitter)
- Online communities (e.g., Facebook, MySpace, LinkedIn, private)
- Podcasting and videocasting (e.g., YouTube)
- Virtual worlds (e.g., SecondLife)
- Widgets and wikis (e.g., Wikipedia)
- Online games and contests
- RSS feeds (means "really simple syndication")

Given that there are so many diverse platforms for interacting and that our overall objective is to drive revenue, the *how* continues to be the difference. You as a marketing professional can manage it all.

As an example, let's talk about how we do it at CA Technologies. Six months prior to the launch of the first phase of our agile marketing application, we realized we had both an internal issue and a customer facing issue. The internal issue was a personnel issue, and the external issue was a promise we made to customers 12 months earlier to create an integrated online experience. Commitments to customers are paramount to the success of any organization and were of particular significance in this instance. The commitment we had made to our customers 12 months earlier, an improved online experience, was about to fail to be delivered. One of the key areas that we were not delivering as promised was the community aspect of our online experience.

Figure 2-6 shows the "to be" state we were striving for in customer interactions.

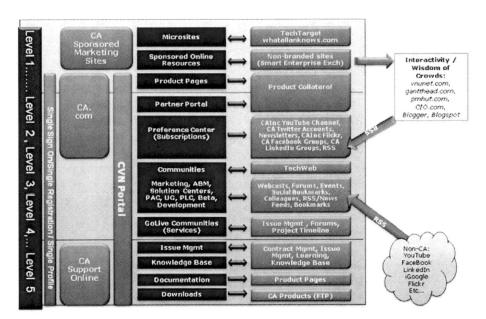

Figure 2-6. "Future state" for CA Technologies' customer online experience © 2010 by CA, Inc.

This aspect as part of the social networking capability mentioned earlier was a path to market that had direct interaction with existing customer communities. We ran the risk of falling short on the promise of management, integrations, improving the voice of our company to our customers, and facilitation of the marketing idea of Word of Mouth (WOM). We had stark options before us: not to live up to our promise or to become agile. We chose to be agile.

Given that decision, we realized we had to overcome a number of obstacles, but saw these as opportunities for improvement. One of these areas was to mobilize multiple parties with differing roles. Here is a list of the engagement folks who we had to take into consideration:

- *Systems integrators (SI)*: Infosys, Accenture, project management office
- *Agency partners*: Digitas, User experience, Lippincott, corporate brand
- *Internal information service*: Project management, development, testing/QA, business readiness resources, and technology infrastructure
- *Business single point of contacts (SPOCs)*: Business process optimization

- *Software partners/vendors*: CA Technologies, Baynote, Coveo, Microsoft, Liferay, Sitecore, Informatica, and SalesForce.com (SFDC)

First we partnered with the business. Our key SIs identified what we needed to be able to accomplish in our "to be" state. We established workstreams that had business SPOCs as strategic partners and created a detailed Requirements Traceability Verification Matrix (RTVM). Critical to the RTVM is a standardized format. Figure 2-7 shows a sample of the master template utilized for the RTVM. Specifically aligned to deliver value to the business and marketing objectives, Figure 2-8 shows call-outs tied to the requirement, which help determine planning for an initiative. This example is tied to engineering, but it can be applied easily to marketing objectives like campaign components, advertising, etc. Definitions of the components follow the grid sample from the RTVM in Figure 2-9.

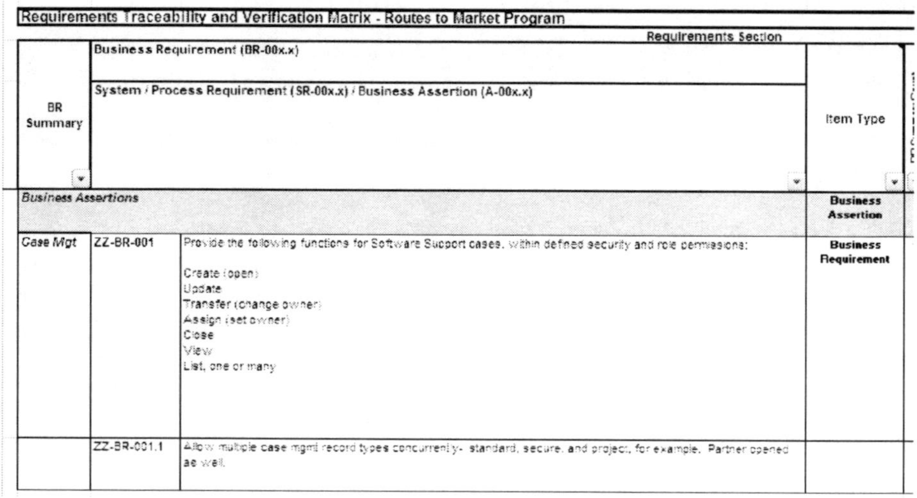

Requirements Traceability and Verification Matrix - Routes to Market Program

		Requirements Section	
BR Summary	Business Requirement (BR-00x.x) / System / Process Requirement (SR-00x.x) / Business Assertion (A-00x.x)		Item Type
Business Assertions			**Business Assertion**
Case Mgt	ZZ-BR-001	Provide the following functions for Software Support cases, within defined security and role permissions: Create (open) Update Transfer (change owner) Assign (set owner) Close View List, one or many	**Business Requirement**
	ZZ-BR-001.1	Allow multiple case mgmt record types concurrently- standard, secure, and project, for example. Partner opened as well.	

Figure 2-7. Master template columns—RTVM © 2011 by CA, Inc.

Value					Strategic Priorities				
Increase Sales Efficiency and Effectiveness	Increase Customer/Partner Satisfaction and Loyalty	Expand Ideation	Improve Business Intelligence	Increase Operational Efficiency And Effectiveness	Accelerate Growth	Delight Customers	13K Acting as 1	Innovate (Technology Though Leader)	Compliance/Regulatory

Figure 2-8. Value and strategic priorities call—RTVM © 2011 by CA, Inc.

RTVM				
	Requirements Section			
B	BR Summary	A Short (preferably under 10 words) summary of a group of requirements.		Optional
C	Requirement Number			Mandatory
D	Business Requirement or System/Process Requirement or Business Assertion	A _Business Requirement_ defines a request at a business level, satisfying one or more Business Objectives, and does not solution. A _System/Process Requirement_ defines the project, application and / or manual process that need to be accomplished in order to meet the need of the Business Requirement. There will be 1- many System/Process requirements to further refine the Business Requirement. A system requirement does not solution. A _Business Assertion_ is a statement that clarifies what should continue without change or a statement of what is not in scope. It is intended to be clarification so that a reader does not make a false interpretation.		Mandatory
E	Item Type	Business Requirement, System/Process Requirement, or Business Assertion. Used for filtering.		Optional
F	BR Summary Count	A count of the number of Business Requirements in the document. Place a 1 in this column for each business requirement.		Optional
G	BR Detail Count	A count of the number of Business Detail Requirements in the document. Place a 1 in this column for each business detail requirement.		
H	SR Count	A count of the number of System Requirements in the document. Place a 1 in this column for each System requirement.		Optional
I	BR Priority	Business Requirement Priority defines the business need for the business requirement. Since System requirements define the detail to meet the Business requirement, priority is only at the Business Requirement Level. • Critical - The solution will not be acceptable unless the business requirement is delivered • non-Critical - The solution can be accepted without these requirements, typically nice to haves.		Mandatory
J	Touch Point	Tied to System Requirement. Lists the responsible application, process area or project responsible for delivering the System Requirement Solution.		Mandatory
K	Touch Point Contact	Tied to System Requirement. Lists the responsible person who owns the deliverable for the touch point.		Mandatory
L	Requirement SME	Subject Matter Expert for the requirement.		Mandatory

Figure 2-9. Requirement definition—RTVM © 2011 by CA, Inc.

The elements associated with the RTVM requirements in these figures are defined here:

BR Summary: A short (preferably under ten words) summary of a group of requirements

Business Requirement: A business requirement defines a request at a business level, satisfying one or more business objectives, but not the solution.

System/Process Requirement: A system/process requirement defines the project, application, and/or manual process that need to be accomplished in order to meet the need of the business requirement. There will be many system/process requirements to further refine the business requirement. A system requirement does not contain the solution.

Business Assertion: A business assertion is a statement that clarifies what should continue without change or a statement of what is not in the scope. It is intended to be a clarification so that a reader does not make a false interpretation.

Item Type: Business requirement, system/process requirement, or business assertion; used for filtering

BR Summary Count: A count of the number of business requirements in the document; place a 1 in this column for each business requirement.

BR Detail Count: A count of the number of business detail requirements in the document; place a 1 in this column for each business detail requirement.

SR Count: A count of the number of system requirements in the document; place a 1 in this column for each system requirement.

BR Priority: Business requirement priority defines the business need for the business requirement. Since system requirements define the detail to meet the business requirement, priority is only at the business requirement level.

- *Critical*: The solution will not be acceptable unless the business requirement is delivered.
- *Non-critical*: The solution can be accepted without these requirements; typically nice to have.

Touch Point: Tied to system requirement; lists the responsible application, process area, or project responsible for delivering the system requirement solution

Touch Point Contact: Tied to system requirement; lists the responsible person who owns the deliverable for the touch point

Requirement SME: Subject matter expert for the requirement

process if the system requirement involves a process or an IT change

Geo/Country: Geo (APJ, EMEA, NA, LA, or WW) or country-specific change; country takes precedence over the GEO.

What is important to note about these figures is the matrix of complexity for just one functional area and the column headings that facilitated the traceability function of the matrix. RTVM as a functional management tool for requirements documentation, in conjunction with a sophisticated project management facility, proved instrumental in tracking the project. We utilized our own project management solution to do the job.

So armed with our Software as a Service (SaaS) solution, we created an integrated project plan with all resources aligned across all of our external and internal resourcing as well as our external and internal service providers. This facilitated full cross-functional and integrated time/resource management in line with the complexity of the requirements. We employed two methodologies:

1. A customized version of Accenture's ADM Waterfall Dev methodology for the data architecture and security aspects of the project

2. Agile project management for all other components of the project—most importantly, new agile development (see Figure 2-10)

Using CA Clarity, we were able to align agile development sprints with the internal waterfall releases. This enabled us to build a very dynamic online experience *on time and on budget*. The project was divided into two phases, with most of the work of establishing project components being integrated and managed for the first phase launch. Figure 2-11 illustrates the elements involved in the Phase I and Phase II implementation and roll-out.

Solution Delivery Methodology

- Hybrid Agile (Scrum) (four-week design; two four-week build/test sprints)
  - o **Advantages:** (1) Full requirements translated into designs prior to development sprints starting (lower requirements volatility risks); (2) more time to mobilize Agile/Scrum teams and fine-tune methodology and internal capabilities (important for new Agile implementations)
  - o **Risks:** Fewer development/test sprint cycles potentially impact overall quantity of features delivered

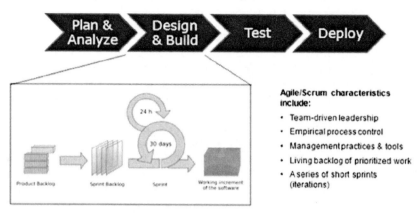

Figure 2-10. Solution delivery with hybrid agile © 2010 by CA, Inc.

We stuck pretty closely to the traditional agile methodology (see Figure 2-10), with a backlog, 30-day sprints, daily scrum meetings, and releases. We produced live, working pieces of the overall project within those 30 days, and we were able to prioritize the backlog across workstreams, allowing us to deploy the right pieces at the right time. It also helped us to develop a cadence that folks on the project quickly and easily adapted to.

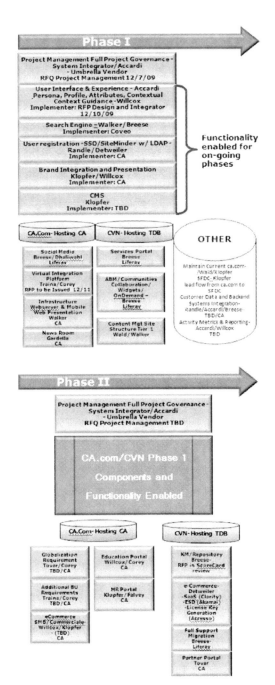

Figure 2-11. Project Beacon Phase I and II overview © 2010 by CA, Inc.

We used Phase I of the project as a time to set ourselves up for Phase II. What that means is that we enabled the right functionality that would be needed in subsequent phases, we made sure we had the right infrastructure and software, and we made sure we were integrated with other systems and business processes where we would need to be down the line.

The project had additional complexities, as we had multiple portals internally and externally and some new community portals. Most importantly, we needed to move quickly to meet our customers' expectations. Figure 2-12 shows the complexity of the deployment environment in the "to be" state for the online experience for our customers.

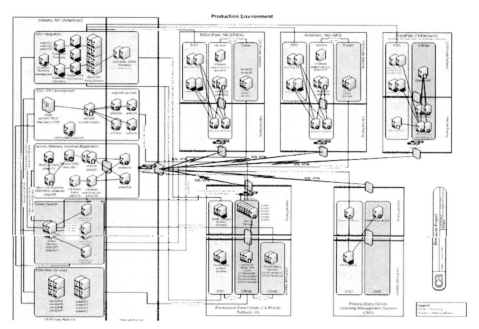

Figure 2-12. Technical infrastructure complexity © 2010 by CA, Inc.

Managing a single identity through strong authentication across multiple portals with some of the architecture being Software as a Service (SaaS), some on premise, and managing to build a core business service from creation through ongoing support with 99.999% of availability is no small task in less than two months. But we proved it was possible.

Figure 2-13 shows the type of meeting schedule needed to support the aggressive timeline for the project—note the timeline objectives based on the accelerated delivery.

Mission to May

January 2010						
S	M	T	W	T	F	S
					1	2
3	4 △	5△	6△	7	8	9
10	11	12	13	14	15 ●	16
17	18	19	20	21	22 ●△	23
24	25	26	27	28	29 ●△	30
31						

February 2010						
S	M	T	W	T	F	S
	1	2	3	4	5 ●	6
7	8	9	10	11	12	13
14	15	16	17	18	19	20
21	22	23	24	25	26	27
28						

March 2010						
S	M	T	W	T	F	S
	1	2	3	4	5 ●	6
7	8	9	10	11	12	13
14	15	16	17	18	19	20
21	22	23	24	25	26	27
28	29	30	31			

April 2010						
S	M	T	W	T	F	S
				1	2	3
4	5	6	7	8	9 ●	10
11	12	13	14	15	16 ●	17
18	19	20	21	22	23	24
25	26	27	28	29	30 ●	

May 2010						
S	M	T	W	T	F	S
						1
2	3	4	5	6	7	8
9	10	11	12	13	14	15
16	17	18	19	20	21	22
23	24	25	26	27	28	29
30	31					

June 2010						
S	M	T	W	T	F	S
		1	2	3	4	5
6	7	8	9	10	11	12
13	14	15	16	17	18	19
20	21	22	23	24	25	26
27	28	29	30			

Weekly Program Leadership Team (PLT) meetings

Weekly status reports published by Program Manager

Bi-weekly Sponsor meetings

Project Teams meet daily or at otherwise defined intervals

● Program Deadlines (est. critical path)

△ **January Planning and Analysis Milestones**

1. Program Mobilization (Accardi, Sawyer)
2. Governance & Program Ops Meetings
3. Detailed Scoping & Workstream Requirements
4. Detailed Cross-Workstream Requirements
5. Detailed Use Case Analysis

Figure 2-13. Accelerated project timeline sample © 2010 by CA, Inc.

CA Technologies can do all these things today because we leveraged a marketing team and a technical team driving together for the good of the company. Now the real question is, where can deploying agile help you make this kind of impact and what roles are the most critical to its success?

Establishing a strong program leadership team, while time-consuming up front, was what made the difference between failing and organizational success. Initially there were many questions about how such a diverse and cross-functional team could work together. We utilized very crisp and clear communications to bring together the team. Figure 2-14 is a practical example of an initial communication that went out to motivate and move the team together toward success.

Program Charter & Leadership Welcome

As you know, *Insert company name here* is undertaking a major *Insert Initiative Name Here* in advance of this *Insert Compelling event you are driving to.* Our objectives in implementing this transformation are ambitious: the new *Insert Initiative Name Here* will set the stage for a new era of relationship our customers and prospective customers have with *Insert company name here*, ultimately translating into strategic market share, customer loyalty, and revenue growth for the company.

Because of our focus on offering an *Insert Initiative Name Here*, we are now looking for a name for the project and will be launching a team contest to arrive at that name.

In order to accomplish the aggressive timelines established of *Insert timeframe here*, the Executive Leadership Team, program sponsors, and the Program Leadership Team all agreed that there is one critical dependency to realizing the vision: a team of can-do leaders within the company who can collaboratively build this *Insert Initiative Here*. There are many important organizations involved in realizing the vision, including the *List Departments Here.*

You are receiving this communication because you have been identified as one of those can-do leaders from within these organizations!

Please spend time reviewing the table shown at the bottom of this e-mail that lists your leadership assignment in the capacity of either Workstream Lead or Workstream Project Manager. The sections immediately following provide a high-level recap of responsibilities for each of these roles. All roles will coordinate with the program release manager.

Workstream Lead Responsibilities

- Scope the functionality, identify interdependencies, and clear impediments to achieving workstream scope delivery objectives
- Drive delivery of the features of the workstream against identified timelines
- Lead the workstream team
- Ensure ongoing alignment within workstream to include resourcing, project management, development leadership, test management, user education collateral, post-production sustainability

Workstream Project Manager Responsibilities

- Interface with program management to establish and manage project workstream cadence through recurring project meetings
- Own surfacing of visibility and reporting through communicating project status, issues, risks, and escalation at recurring meetings
- Own resolution of project workstream impediments

Be prepared to hold your cross-divisional teams accountable to the workstream deliverables of the initiative. To ensure that you are equipped with the necessary awareness to begin this transformation, we are scheduling a series of kick-off sessions over the next few days to provide you with a briefing on overall program organization, your workstream objectives and scope, role, technology design standards and agile methodology, resources, meeting cadence, and the initial blueprint for mobilizing your workstream.

The **Workstream Lead** and **Project Manager Kick-Off** session will be held *Insert Date time Here*. You will receive a meeting invitation from me later today for applicable session(s).

Implementing the *Insert Initiative Here* is not without risks, especially our Phase I release, *Insert Date Here*. Offsetting this risk, however, is a significant level of commitment and support from our company's senior executive leadership team in providing you and your fellow program leaders with resources and clearing hurdles necessary to realize our shared objectives.

If you have questions prior to attending the upcoming kick-off sessions noted earlier, please contact your immediate supervisor.

Thank you,

(Insert Name of Overall Program Lead)

Figure 2-14. Sample welcome message © 2010 by CA, Inc.

Next we set out to assign roles, with each workstream having a workstream lead and a project manager as seen in Table 2.1.

Table 2-1. Workstream Lead and Project Manager Assignments

Workstream Lead and Project Manager Assignments		
Workstream Name	Workstream Lead	Project Manager
1. Content Lifecycle Strategy & Architecture		
2. Web Content Management		
3. Communities Portal Infrastructure and Interfaces		
4. User Experience: Personas, Scenarios, Flow, Branding, Design		
5. Single Sign-on: ca.com, CSO, CVN, On-Demand, Education		
6. Search Engine Marketing: Knowledge Management		
7. Social Media Communities: User Groups, Forums, Blogs (optional), On-Demand, ABM (optional), Go Live (services-beta)		
8. Community Analytics		
9. Business Application Gadgets with Web Services		
10. On-Demand Specific Enhancements		
11. System Integration & Implementation		
12. External Projects		
13. Technical Architecture (program level)		
14. Testing (program level)		
15. Move to Production (program level)		
16. Release/Program Manager (program level)		

The Release Delivery Manager role defined in Figure 2-14 is vital to the success of agile implementation. At a program level, the Release Delivery Manager role will help the team to do the following:

- Remove "roadblocks" and disruptions that may distract the project team from the day-to-day work effort (e.g., resolve issues, communicate those issues to PMO so that they can be documented and brought up in PLT so we can clear issues where the release manager alone is unable)
    - Work with workstream leads and PLT members to clear impediments
    - Track impediments and document interventions/resolutions via clarity risk/issue log entries
- Articulate and review key project deliverables
    - Develop deliverables matrices and communicate to program team members
    - Approve and track ongoing changes to deliverables requirements
- Monitor and manage the delivery of business results assigned to the release
    - Work with workstream teams to ensure traceability from requirements through to testing
    - Issue weekly reports on traceability per stage of development
    - Report to PLT on requirements coverage in all testing activities (i.e., unit, assembly, integration, system, UAT, performance, availability)
    - Construct baselines with PLT, and communicate to the program what the "definition of done" is per phase gate
    - Monitor and report on current status of "definition of done" per construction phase
    - Construct, implement, and manage a comprehensive and integrated deployment management framework (configuration, technical release, technical change management), resource the plan, and ensure continuous optimization of the plan
    - Monitor, develop, and sustain staffing and organizational capability with respect to all phases of development and release manage-

ment; maintain appropriate management systems to ensure continuous PLT visibility into this process

- Manage the release design, development, and deployment effort within schedule and budget
  - Work closely with Workstream Portfolio Leads (WPLs) in the following activities that produce the related deliverables
    - Establish and manage compliance with the integrated design management framework (including design tools); resource the plan, communicate with and educate development community, monitor ongoing compliance with the same
    - Lead construction of integrated deployment management framework (including deployment management tools); resource the plan, communicate with and educate development community, monitor ongoing compliance with the same
    - Establish multi-release roadmap management process/ system; implement the system in advance of Release I to ensure appropriate capture of scope slated for post-Release I
- Review and intervene based on continuous monitoring of status/progress for projects within a release
  - Construct and continuously operate a solution development health status report that communicates solution stage of readiness for release
  - Together with workstream leads and PLT, construct and execute intervention plans for out-of-boundary project status
  - Escalate issues that cannot otherwise be resolved at the workstream level
- Utilize the latest methodology and customize documents (tasks, deliverables for each project included in the release); educate project managers on the methodology and ensure continuous compliance with methodology requirements (i.e., code review templates, unit test documentation, etc.)
- As a member of PLT, communicate program objectives, policies, standards, procedures, and processes to project managers; verify compliance
- Reinforce the communication that the workstream lead has given concerning roles and responsibilities to project manager

- Communicate the release/cross-project view to project managers at weekly WSL/PLT meeting; this "view" should ideally visualize the current completion status of both the cross-program technical standards and the degree of functional workstream compliance with cross-program standards.
- Help the workstream lead to maintain team morale across projects within the release
- Provide deployment leads with applicable standards, tools, policies/procedures, and time frames; escalate as necessary to PLT
- Work with Digitas, the marketing web team, and technical architect to ensure the integration of projects within and across releases
- Monitor, at a detailed level, work plans, timelines, and milestones for projects within the release
  - Proactively uncover, document, and manage issues, risks, and escalations
  - Work closely with each project to ensure the foregoing deliverables are completed
- Identify and track cross-project dependencies as a function of the overall integrated requirements management plan
- Identify scope changes (e.g., changes that may affect the release budget, timeline, or performance outcomes), and resolve/escalate them per scope change control guidelines (as articulated in the Configuration Management Plan)
- Balance the need to minimize risk to release schedule, cost, and benefit with the need to accommodate changing customer needs
  - Work with all impacted stakeholders to understand and document the economics
  - Present a business and technical case to the PLT for consideration
  - Communicate PLT change decision to requesting entity
  - Work with entity to assist in designing resultant changes (if approved) or workarounds (if change request is denied)
- Facilitate the resolution of project team and cross-project team issues
  - Use issue and risk tracking and informal systems to identify intervention needs

- Plan interventions with appropriate stakeholders and decision-makers
- Conduct intervention with applicable stakeholders
- Document results of intervention
- Follow up periodically after intervention to ensure resolution has taken root

- Identify issues and risks that may affect the release budget, timeline, or performance outcomes or other releases and cannot be resolved by teams; report issues to Program Management Office, and escalate them as specified in the issue management process
- Identify risks and develop mitigation plans (i.e., potential future issues), and report them to Program Management Office

The significance of simplified communication also had to be communicated in a somewhat simplified form. Figure 2-15 shows what we affectionately called the "house diagram." This diagram served to show everyone involved as well as interested parties: pigs and chickens in the agile vernacular, the who and what of the project. This construct also remained as the guidepost for communication for the second phase of the project, which was initiated immediately after implementation. Both phases of the project and indeed the current development and management methodology reflect the application of the agile method and adherence to the agile marketing triangle. Due to the success that was demonstrated through the adoption of agile in Phase I of the project, we were able to be less dependent on old waterfall components in Phase II.

Figure 2-16 shows the Phase II "house diagram." Figure 2-17 relates how we aligned our agile planning into sprint deliverables and milestones.

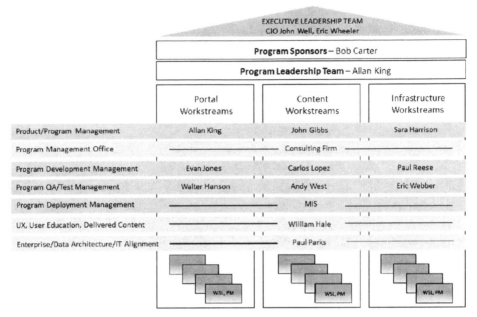

Figure 2-15. Phase I agile iteration of "house diagram" © 2010 by CA, Inc.

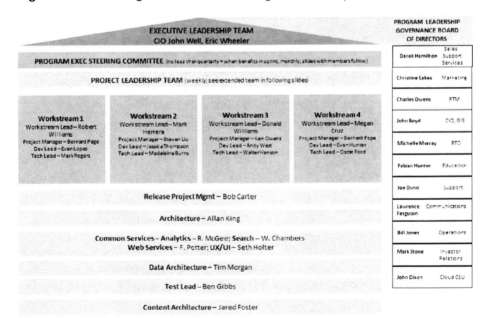

Figure 2-16. Phase II agile iteration of "house diagram" © 2010 by CA, Inc.

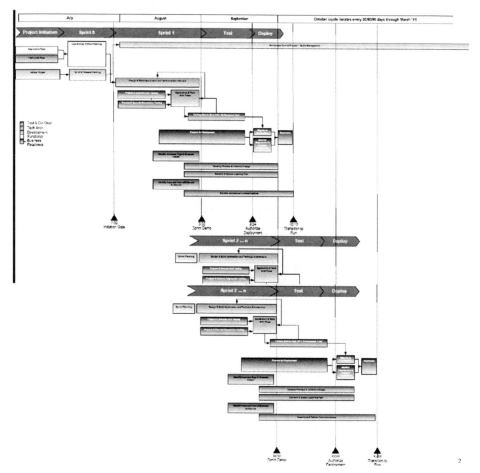

Figure 2-17. Phase II timeline—note the overall agile methodology to the milestone task and delivery cycle. © 2010 by CA, Inc.

Personal Development

While not specific to the system development process, the agile method was applied to the various inputs to the constructs of the customer experience through the application of applied research and customer input (part of the iron triangle). As the objective of the experience was to personalize, if you will, the engagement for the users of our online sites, we applied the idea of personas guided for interaction. The development of the persona types themselves utilized an agile approach (see Figure 2-18).

If we look at the persona development process, we note that the iterative nature of the development is a recurring mechanism utilizing a feedback loop that continually improves the user's experience. Simply stated, the proponent of the process of persona creation is continually updated as the customer feeds online interactions.

Figure 2-18. Persona development cycle © 2010 by CA, Inc.

Persona Types

If we examine the types of personas developed as a result of the agile development process applied as a feed mechanism to the overall project, we see that we started with two primary persona types. Figures 2-19 to 2-20 show the primary types we deployed for the first release of the project.

Figure 2-19. Persona Beth Big Picture © 2010 by CA, Inc.

Figure 2-20. Persona Freddy Fact Finder © 2010 by CA, Inc.

Further Persona Development

As we gauged the success of the implementation of the personas in Figures 21-23, we also evaluated three other persona types for incorporation into other aspects of our customer experience. These personas are illustrated later and reflect roles for differing types of what I might term market segmentations. Important to this as it relates back to agile marketing adoption, and a key element of the case study, is that the application of these personas was driven by customer behavior.

Going back to the "iron triangle"—time, cost, scope, quality—we based our implementation on our customer interaction. Personas were the way we grouped our customer interactions—as a customer, were you a troubleshooter? A fact finder? A big picture executive? Who are you, and what are you looking for on our site? With the inputs we received, based on our personas, we were able to more clearly define, and redefine as the project went on, our time (fixed), cost, scope (fixed), and the overall quality of the project. This, combined with the collaborative environment for the project and the aggressive timeline, facilitated taking action vs. spending time planning and not executing. The persona types that follow also reflect the diversity of the consumers of our information. Each of these interactions fed an overall streamlined collection point for iterative improvements to the customer experience.

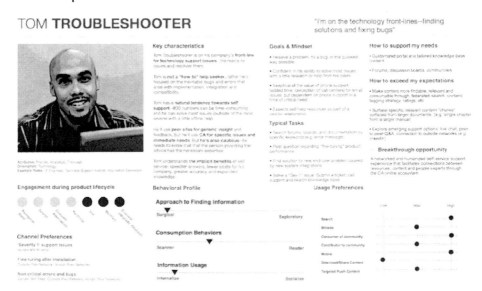

Figure 2-21. Persona Tom Troubleshooter © 2010 by CA, Inc.

Figure 2-22. Persona Ted Tracker © 2010 by CA, Inc.

Figure 2-23. Persona Sam Sage © 2010 by CA, Inc.

Analytics Strategy

Another important component to the implementation of the project in the first and ongoing phases was the idea of cyclical analytics. Once again we were looking at an overall implementation of an iterative approach coupled with improved functionality through customer interactions. Customer input was adjusted as each phase of the project progressed.

This is a further example of the incorporation of a collaboration of the inputs to the process that allow the functional implementation to be adjusted based on a progressive agile implementation. Scrums result in business supporting customer inputs showing successes and failures of the parts of a system implementation. These are adjusted "on the fly" for further phases of development. The analytics also show inputs to our execution objectives. One can also look at analytics as a trending mechanism. Our approach to the project shows a progressive implementation of analytical inputs as seen in Figure 2-24.

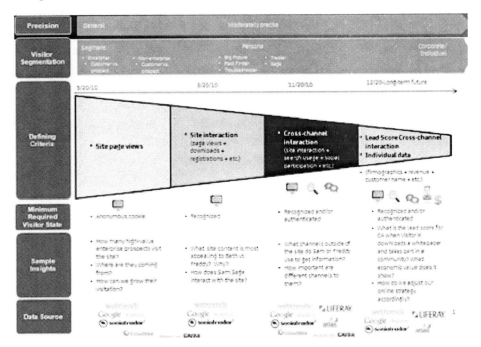

Figure 2-24. Analytics evolution timeline © 2010 by CA, Inc.

Functional Delivery

Finally, for this case study, I think it is important to point out that the over-all objective of the agile marketing triangle is to meet revenue goals. Revenue is developed from the lead process, which is delivered through customer interactions. As noted earlier, the application of sophisticated customer engagement programs through persona developments, customer inputs through analytics, and perhaps most importantly delivery of "leads" to the business is the goal of any marketing interaction. Figure 2-25 shows the lead process from the customer's online experience.

The "scoring model" in Figure 2-25 has been implemented in conjunction with the continual improvement paradigm for customer interactions. This implementation of the agile marketing approach for the accelerated delivery of what was originally planned to be a 12-month implementation project in the space of four months helped to shrink the original timeline to one third of its original amount, without sacrificing the customer promise.

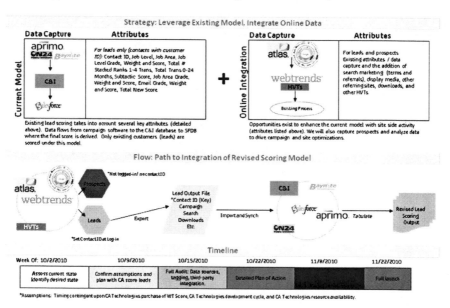

Figure 2-25. Scoring model for analytics adoption © 2010 by CA, Inc.

The project utilized the capabilities of the Web 2.0 functional road to market. Truly this is a shining example of the application in practice of the agile method for marketing. It utilized inputs to the project facilitated by agile application through analytics, persona development, and ultimately lead generation. At the time of this writing, the customer feedback has been tremendously positive and has altered the perception of the company's stance in the market. The overall measure of revenue impact continues to be analyzed. Certainly both internal and external customers of the experience and supporting suppliers are well satisfied. Most importantly, this case study is a testimony to a practical application of agile marketing in a typically siloed environment.

Collaborative Leadership

Aligning Resources, Sales, and Other Frenemies: The Making of the Marketing Garden of Eden

Marketing and sales always seem to be at odds. Ever wonder why? No, it's not because salespeople are egomaniacal jerks who think they know everything, or because marketing folks are a bunch of lazy, good for nothing, ivory-tower stuffed suits (though I have seen some organizations where those generalizations could stick). It's because their missions are not aligned. Sales is tasked with bringing home the bacon on a month-to-month, quarter-by-quarter basis. Marketing has a longer time threshold with awareness, thought leadership, demand generation, and lead nurturing metrics being measured over a much longer time period. After all, brands are not built overnight. So how can a sales organization that loves its marketing department when it is doing well and hates them when times are slow ever really get out of being accused of being corporate backstabbers, when marketing may be a quarter behind them in delivering the leads they need today? Can there ever be peace in the Garden of Eden with snakes lurking around every corner? The truth, and starting at the very beginning, can set you free.

Just like any addiction recovery program or quite frankly any improvement process, the first step is admitting you have a problem. Collaborative leadership through transparency between teams tends to be the hardest thing to overcome, as well as the most important step. Today most marketing organization plans are made 6 to 18 months in advance. People believe their mission is to begin completing programs directly as planned. Variation is seen as failure as opposed to addressing new opportunities. In some even worse cases, all budget dollars are committed with little ability to make changes and new opportunities are simply lost.

While planning clearly is a good thing (we will talk more about that in later chapters), the ability to improvise and ensure room is in the budget if marketers need to make changes is vital. It is also important to deal with disruptions in the market caused by new competition, the exit of a competitor in the market, or even other external events that simply cannot be predicted. Having an agile marketing organization dedicated to researching and executing small programs and taking advantage of new opportunities can foster new life in 18-month-old plans. This is clearly an advantage that not only boosts the results of campaigns, but also garners the attention of the market, as it perceives a potential sleeping giant has awakened.

But what does it take to have an agile marketing team? It takes a business that wants to be agile. Becoming agile requires people who want to be agile. That is the first question you need to ask yourself: are you ready for the demands of being agile? Is your team? Your sales org and the rest of your business? It is very different than the old stick-to-the-plan marketing of yesterday. People wanting to adopt an agile methodology are one of the most important keys to having success with any kind of agile development, whether you are engineering a new product or designing a marketing campaign. You can't do agile by yourself, but you can be the change agent for it in your organization.

A large challenge many companies face is continually striving to execute the best possible marketing campaign instead of wanting to just get to market. Unfortunately a marketing organization too focused on wanting to always put forward the "best" marketing program fails to execute anything because too much time elapses as people continually tweak the message. It is better to take an iterative approach and break marketing strategies into smaller subtactics that can be delivered on and improved over time. You simply need to take the high-level requirements, use them as the broad framework, and get the team to have full buy-in. Now you may feel that getting buy-in is the most difficult part and takes a significant amount of time. This can be true. But I think you should consider that buy-in is one of the most critical components of a marketing plan. Certainly, there is a significant amount of time and money that is wasted in a perfectly planned and executed campaign that has no buy-in.

The answer to this issue starts from the premise of having collaborative leadership. How can one get collaborative leadership when often the goals of the teams are not aligned? The answer requires that you explore putting some hard work in up front to get alignment. You can execute without it and pray your results are somehow good enough to be accepted, but I don't recommend this. The latter approach seems to be what I have seen happen in most unsuccessful companies. The most successful do what agile marketing advocates suggest: get teams collaborating from the start.

The first premise of agile development in technology is that teams have to have users involved in developing. The same is true for agile marketing. If sales or the customer is the end user or benefactor of your campaign or program, it only seems right to get them involved up front. It may not always be possible to have an end customer involved, and when that is the case, the next best thing might be to have your best salespeople and/or their management and/or your customer support team involved to give you insight. By doing this, you ensure not only that you have campaign requirements that everyone understands and have a business priority, but also that you have a team available to help reprioritize as you learn new things through the iterative design and execution of your programs. As the market changes and new requirements come into play, having this collaborative team's daily work in scrums can enable you to react more quickly, while ensuring you aren't out there on your own, making decisions where you won't be backed up.

As you continue to work and deliver, you can bring your product or campaign to your scrum team and ensure it meets demands or includes what changes might be made to make it better and easier for the end customer. You are also giving your partners in the business some skin in the game and visibility into the level of intensity that goes into bringing something to market. This visibility allows your new partners to best see you and your entire marketing team's commitment as your marketers work in the role of campaign development, taking the daily feedback and continually iterating for better success. The campaign developers are wholly accountable for their actions to the team, and utilizing the level of transparency between groups ensures alignment on what is delivered. Sales can no longer say to marketing, "The copy you used in the advertising sucked" because they now share in the responsibility, as it was a joint team effort to build from the start. All issues about what goes into a campaign, be it a feature, timing, or offer, are made in the scrums, and decisions can be made at that time as they come up to deal with them.

The really good news about this is that the responsibility, whether for success or failure, is shared. I once read a sign in a theater that said, "Team means never having to take the blame alone," and I often joke that many agile teams begrudgingly start at this same premise in the beginning, but find success because they have done the hard work of becoming collaborative up front and truly take the sharing of responsibility seriously. Agile projects can fail just like any other project can fail, but the difference is all failure in agile projects is learned by a broader team. So you will therefore be less likely to repeat the failures of your past. Where there is shared pain, people generally learn to move on fairly quickly, whereas in non-agile approaches and non-collaborative environments, witch hunts can go on from weeks to months to years, with teams throwing arrows at one another, all the while not delivering on what they promised sales.

Finding Your Way to the Marketing Garden of Eden with ADAM and EVE

I think we are all familiar with the idea of a Garden of Eden as an ideal place, because there was peace, prosperity, harmony, and happiness. It is with this ideal that we begin our discussion on the strength of collaborative leadership. I want to emphasize that this is about a practical application of what I feel are some key approaches to bring what seems like a simplistic and perhaps often talked about idea into fruition.

I think everyone talks about being agile, but few are really succeeding in implementing it because of what may be termed dysfunctional agile application. Yes, I said dysfunctional, and what I mean by dysfunctional is the siloed approach that organizations tend to have, especially in the realm of marketing. We are siloed because we are all trying to show everyone that what we are doing extends and outreaches what other folks in the organization are doing—not only for the advancement of individuals within the silos, but also so a silo will continue to exist.

Since we are talking about marketing as the subject of this book, let's take a look at marketing in organizations. One of the most interesting things about marketing organizations is that they are often very skilled at devising multifaceted marketing campaigns. But the real question is: are marketing activities getting the company anywhere? Are the prospects of an organization listening? And if they are listening, do they get the message?

As an example, if we look at major campaigns for an organization for something like a product launch, one might expect that for this launch the company will reach out to as many as six separate internal marketing groups and an equal number of external specialty agencies. Typically, the groups or agencies are responsible for separate aspects of the campaign—mass advertising, direct response, online promotions, and so on. They use different methods for developing, managing, and evaluating their parts of the program. For whatever reason, and it may be as simple as "that is just how it is done," everyone assumes that these independent efforts can only reinforce each other.

But while they may succeed individually according to their own performance measures, they often fail as a whole to support the broader business objective. In fact, the efforts can directly undermine each other. You may recall the huge long-distance battles that were going on in the telecom industry. All the major players launched mass advertising campaigns to build brand awareness and differentiate their services. They also rolled out national direct-mail programs that concentrated single-mindedly on generating responses. They simply mailed out checks to get customers to switch. The response rates were high—after all, getting a check in the mail is always a good thing—and by the measure of the high response rates, the switching campaigns were successful. But the programs did not include any type of messaging that reinforced brand preference or differentiated the companies. High spending on mass media got people to pay attention to long distance. But at the same time, a blizzard of indistinguishable checks told consumers that there were no real differences between the competitors. In essence, the telecom industry spent hundreds of millions of dollars to decommoditize then recommoditize their category. Soon customers were ricocheting from one carrier to another, cashing the checks with little regard for their source. All the competitors suffered massive margin erosions due in large part to these counterproductive campaigns. Given this example, let's discuss the important components of the Garden of Eden in marketing.

Here I outline an overview of the four-step ADAM process I have developed that can make sales or any other frenemies you may have into true allies for your sanity and your businesses success.

The Four-Step Process

- **A**dmitting you have a problem
- **D**efining and agreeing on what the problem is
- **A**ssigning both sales and marketing (or any appropriate department for that matter) resources to fix the problem
- **M**easuring the result and iterating on the success or failure of the teams

As I said earlier, admitting you have a problem between teams is often the hardest hurdle to overcome, as oftentimes executives feel like admitting there is an issue somehow means they personally are at fault. No one likes to have fingers pointed at them, and there is a great and obvious way to help yourself not be the target of this fingerpointing. You yourself need to not fingerpoint. No, this doesn't mean you never communicate issues in other areas or departments; but just like my mother told me, "It's not what you say, it's how you say it" that matters most.

When I see major issues in other groups, I try to not bring them up in a mixed group but first always call the person or head of the department of the area that is causing or is part of the roadblock that surrounds resolution to an issue. It is always important that you create an atmosphere of cooperation, *not* confrontation. So I tend to communicate tactfully what I perceive the issue to be by saying something to the effect of, "I am coming to you in confidence so that I can understand and have you address what seems to be an issue or roadblock to moving forward. Perhaps you can better explain the reason. You see, I noticed that by your team doing this, it seems to be having this (insert issue here) effect. Is this the intended result you are hoping for? If so, I'll say no more. If not, I was thinking we could try x to get a different result." Or I'll ask how I might be able to help the person to change the perception.

Most times, after perhaps an initial defensiveness, the executive is happy you have brought the issue to him or her so that he or she can consider and fix it. Or I am then informed that actually they have a method to their madness that I can then help to better communicate to bring teams together. At the very least, even if the problem is not solved, you've proven to be an ally who at least tried to bring both sides together, when you do get everyone together.

I have always found, though, that the easiest way to keep yourself from being the target of arrows from your various other departments is to address any weaknesses head-on and own them regardless of whether they are yours. Perception is the reality, and if others think it is your problem, it is your problem. I know what you are thinking—but what about when the issue is not something I have direct control over? How can I own the problem then? The answer is through collaboration and communication and not fingerpointing and passing the buck. After all, you will fail if someone doesn't stand up and take ownership, so you have nothing to lose if you take the blame up front and schedule the calls to get all the right people on the phone or in the meeting to come up with an action plan to solve the issues.

You can turn a bad situation around simply by taking ownership and driving conversations with the teams who can make an impact—especially if you take a big issue and are able to turn it around. In this way, you are taken into confidence by all the various teams. Being the consigliere of sorts to various departments can help you stay out of harm's way, as it gives you a top-level perspective of people's individual as well as business motives. The way to best do this is to follow the path to either success or failure quickly, using what I call the EVE principle—if followed, the EVE principle will help you know which fruits in the business garden to avoid and which to take a bite out of and execute on. So here are the components of the EVE principle.

- **E**valuate whether the issue is a real issue for your company and your options. Be concerned first with business impact, and then consider personal impact as well as business gain to gather the right team of people to start solving the problems. From this, create a program vision and charter, and assemble your proposed leadership team.
- **V**alidate the information with your program leadership governance board—do others see the vision? If they do, then you may want to march forward.
- **E**xecute quickly and with key performance indicators that you put in place with part of the ADAM process in mind, so that if it isn't working, you know when best to abandon ship and try something new or, better yet, if successful, to start showing the results to the rest of the company.

In every organization, there is a yin-and-yang relationship between sales and marketing. While some organizations seem to be better at balancing the political and financial landscapes of both, in many cases the balance is less than harmonious. As we have discussed, sales forever wants to see more qualified net new leads and relationship-building events and marketing is continuously claiming to have provided them. Spreadsheets and ROI models abound. However, the missing link in many cases is the agility required to meet what seems to be ever-changing demands.

In many companies, process improvement programs within marketing aimed at improving ROI have created an almost overly structured view of workers being relegated to a specific function with very little autonomy to look beyond their singular task or department. This approach can be useful as it relates to improving results on a specific program or initiative. It may also be a dangerous approach, as often it can cause companies to fail to recognize opportunities for new markets, products, and services that would benefit the customer and, of course, the selling organization. So how can a company succeed at providing both the focus needed to run success-ful campaigns and the foresight to see the next big thing while helping to accelerate sales? The answer to this question is twofold: first you have to change the mission of marketing to be customer-focused, both internally and externally. I have often seen this happen with organizations as an initia-tive or mantra, but nothing changes internally. Often marketing does not realize that sales is as much a customer of their services as the end user of the product is. In fact, I would venture to say that at some level, marketing services are more critical for sales than the external customer, as sales is the foundation of the relationship that the customer has with the supplier. This is especially true in the B2B market, but also the consumer market or for large-ticket items like automobiles.

So, a dedicated marketing team that understands sales needs is as important as one that understands the customer itself. This requires an agile group of marketers that are empowered to influence and change course in a previ-ously planned program, or execute new "incubation" programs to help sales meet the demands of the inevitably changing competitive environment. Al-lowing this team the ability to test-run new incubation plans often requires new innovative approaches leading to a breakthrough in product or cam-paign improvement and can occur with little disruption to the core market-ing engine of a company—creating even larger dividends.

There you have it—ADAM and EVE and the marketing Garden of Eden. In-cidentally, as I am writing this, I am reminded of the wonderful Pixar picture with the robots called *WALL-E*. The main characters are two robots that "fall in love," and their primary role is the establishment of a new world, a new Garden of Eden. Rather than being thrown out of one, they do make a new world, similar to what we are doing here: overcoming obstacles and us-ing good old-fashioned tenacity. This is especially significant because this author's current husband is named Wally (Walter), and we too had to cre-ate our own Garden of Eden from siloed adversities—but that is a whole other book.

As I said before, in virtually every organization there is a yin-and-yang rela-tionship between sales and marketing. Interestingly enough, product de-signers and development engineers in the software industry learned years ago that they'd save time and money if they consulted with their colleagues in manufacturing rather than just throwing new designs over the wall. The collaboration for technical engineering with systems like PIM and special-ized manufacturing demonstrates the mutual goal of achievement with sup-pliers and consumers of manufactured goods—whether those goods are tangible, like a hard-drive head, or non-tangible, like software. The two functions realized it wasn't enough to just coexist—not when they could work together to create value for the company and for customers. You'd think that marketing and sales teams, whose work is also deeply interconnected, would have discovered something similar—hence the writing of this book on agile marketing.

As a rule, though, sales and marketing do exist in silos because they're separate functions within an organization, and, when they do work together, they don't always get along. When sales are disappointing, marketing blames the sales force for its poor execution of an otherwise brilliant rollout plan. The sales team, in turn, claims that marketing sets prices too high and uses too much of the budget, which instead should go toward hiring more salespeople or paying the sales reps higher commissions—sound familiar? More broadly, sales departments tend to believe that marketers are out of touch with what's really going on with customers. Marketing believes the sales force is myopic—too focused on individual customer experiences, insufficiently aware of the larger market, and blind to the future. In short, each group often undervalues the other's contributions. This lack of alignment ends up hurting corporate performance. Time and again, during research and consulting assignments, we've seen both groups stumble (and the organization suffer) because they were out of sync. Conversely, there is no question that when sales and marketing work well together, companies see substantial improvement on important performance metrics: sales cycles are shorter, market-entry costs go down, and the cost of sales is lower.

That's what happened when a major software organization integrated its sales and marketing groups to create a new function called *Channel Enablement*. Before the groups were integrated, the company's senior executives reported that sales and marketing operated independently of one another. Salespeople worried only about fulfilling product demand, not creating it. Marketers failed to link advertising dollars spent to actual sales made, so sales obviously couldn't see the value of marketing efforts. And, because the groups were poorly coordinated, marketing's new product announcements often came at a time when sales was not prepared to capitalize on them, or, as is often also the case, the current sales cycle they were in was disrupted because there was a new version of the product that the customer now wanted. This disconnect happens continuously between sales and marketing, and I have to tell you I have been through countless re-orgs, alignments, new models, and department integrations to know that to succeed you have to investigate and identify best practices; you have to remove the roadblocks that are hampering progress, and find answers that could help enhance the joint performance and overall contributions of these two functions and, most importantly, fix the dysfunction. As I mentioned, as part of the ADAM process, we must make sure we understand the constituents. This may be accomplished in the form of surveying or interviewing the chief marketing officer and sales executive leadership to capture their perspectives. Also important in the ADAM approach is to examine in depth the relationship between sales and marketing.

Let's examine some different types of organizations. My research, done with a broad spectrum of a logistical company, a cosmetic company, a financial services firm, a medical provider systems company, an energy company, an insurance company, a high-tech electronic products company, and a public service company, demonstrates these findings:

- The marketing function takes different forms in different companies at different product life cycle stages—all of which can deeply affect the relationship between sales and marketing.
- The strains between sales and marketing fall into two main categories: economic and cultural.
- It's not difficult for companies to assess the quality of the working relationship between sales and marketing. See Figure 3-1 as one way I have done so.
- Companies can take practical steps to move the two functions into a more productive relationship, once they've established where the groups are starting from.

Target the Silos

Okay, so what can my organization do? you may ask. Simply stated, you have to adopt a management structure that eliminates silos. This allows you to apply some of the same results-oriented systems engineering concepts that engineers, and many executives, routinely draw on to address complex problems. In the highly competitive "chip" industry, engineers designing a more powerful or efficient chip to attempt to "beat" their competitor will define overarching goals at the outset and then design and assemble the subsystems to achieve them. In much the same way, you can "systems engineer" new product launches and other marketing initiatives, treating each marketing discipline as a subsystem within an overall plan.

So this is an integrated approach that defines a campaign and organizational structure. Once again, I have always suggested the adoption of agile methodologies and pulling from many sources to apply toward your goal and objectives, and, while this is an obvious best practice, the key idea is that a systems approach sometimes requires that each component be compromised to better serve the needs of the whole. For the common good and ultimately the good of the company, compromises have to be made. This is one of my precepts of the pursuit of a marketing Garden of Eden, whose ADAM and EVE components are the key. Believe it or not, in some fields, such compromise is readily accepted...okay, maybe not readily, but perhaps out of necessity.

One example is the idea of taste and appeal in the fast food industry. Teams of tasting engineers score according to their preferences, but they are more willing to give alternatives from what their ideal is a try if they feel it will give the company profitability. It can be argued that, because of the subjectivity of taste, this paradigm is more necessary; however, that subjectivity is applicable in all markets and demands. In traditional marketing, though, the siloed specialists reject the approach or even the idea of compromise. Certainly an ad firm or agency will never willingly modify a commercial to help its client's other agencies do a better job, and vice versa. Each focuses on its performance in isolation.

Fixing this silo problem starts with a customer-centric approach coupled with agile methodology. Let's take a look at a marketing campaign. I suggested earlier that the key to a successful marketing campaign should borrow from our engineering colleagues in structure and agile approach and appoint a systems architect. This systems architect is one person with broad responsibility for all aspects of a marketing campaign. The architect must understand the campaign's overall business objective, have a solid grasp of the marketing disciplines at his or her disposal, and wield "buck stops here" authority to manage the program.

The architect's first job is to assemble a lean and tight-knit marketing team—an agile team. For the same reasons that forward-thinking software companies keep core development teams as small as possible, efficient marketing programs are best developed and run by small, cohesive, cross-functional groups. Team members have a common goal that eliminates the focus on narrow marketing objectives and defuses the turf wars so common in multi-siloed programs. This is agile.

OLD APPROACH   NEW APPROACH

Old Approach	New Approach
Product Profitability	Client Profitability
Current Sales	Client Lifetime Value
Brand Equity	Client Equity
Market Share	Client Equity Share

Figure 3-1. Marketing transformation © CA, Inc. 2010

Make Agile a Priority

Let's take a look at an example I have researched. This is not specifically a case study, as we will examine later, but based specifically in the package delivery industry. Some years ago, as part of expanding to compete with overnight delivery companies, the US Postal Service engaged in an agile application and approach to marketing. The Postal Service's Priority Mail objective was to expand its market share in the expedited-delivery business. You may remember there was a mass advertising campaign that used the tagline "What's Your Priority?". This campaign utilized an engineering approach, even in the consolidation of the marketing team to one location. Resultant from this approach, Priority Mail's annual growth rate expanded from 2% to 12%, representing a 10% growth in incremental revenue of reportedly $300 million the first year. For the next three years, that growth was sustained—and revenue compounded—by an increasingly sophisticated series of interrelated iterative marketing programs. Each arm of the campaign—television, print, online, direct, and other advertising—was assigned a subordinate messaging goal. And the core development team ensured that all the pieces worked together to create a more compelling sequence of messages.

This approach succeeded well with targets like small business owners and catalog shipping managers. As with all things, you have to re-vamp, re-examine, and re-look, and be iterative in your marketing efforts, because the markets are changing and the needs of the clients are changing. As your competition expands into new arenas, you have to make the decision to follow, lead, or not compete in new markets.

One area where the Postal Service decided to lead was the online retail market. The challenge for the agile marketing team was changing perception. Online retailers had the perception that the Postal Service lacked the supporting technology to perform in the online world and therefore went to perceived technology-savvy organizations like FedEx and UPS. The Priority Mail team had to change some minds—and, more importantly, behavior. They were successful because of the iterative and integrated nature of their messaging to the online retail industry. Yes, pricing was a factor; however, the people, that fifth P, made all the difference. Priority Mail revenues rose over $1.5 billion during the three-year campaign, $1.3 billion of which was attributed to new marketing efforts. The agile approach, which is the adoption of engineering principles, isn't just for rocket scientists—it's a matter of common sense. But it's rarely seen in marketing because siloed bureaucracies will not willingly dismantle themselves. If companies want to reap the benefits of efficient, coherent, business-objective-driven marketing, borrowing applications from systems thinking must be mandated from the top.

At a recent meeting with top marketing executives from businesses ranging from consumer products to biotechnology and all the way to massively multiplayer online games, I was stunned to hear the games SVP say that 90% of her 2008 budget was earmarked for traditional TV advertising. Let's take a look at the market the gaming industry is trying to reach. This is a terminally hip, youth-oriented, net-dependent offering. In this Web 2.0-capable marketplace, why set aside so little for web-based alternatives, event marketing, and word-of-mouth campaigns? It turns out that, in this situation, it was because of the siloed approach and doing what they had always done. They were not being agile and not able to meet the demands of the consumer. We've all heard about a wholesale shift to alternative channels—and yet it keeps not happening. But here's a prediction: a perfect storm is brewing for network advertising, and it will be gigantic for having been pent up so long.

The shift has already begun: digital advertising is growing far faster than other categories—by 31% in 2009, according to Carat, compared with 8% for advertising overall. Alternative channels, which tend to cost less, have attained legitimacy. The Internet has become a place to reach mainstream customers; marketers' experience with it has expanded; and organizations that help companies pioneer new approaches have grown, along with methods of gauging the effectiveness of targeted, permission-based marketing. These new measurement capabilities feed management's increasing insistence on proof of marketing's ROI. By now it's clear—to many marketing executives, at least—that emerging options such as mobile advertising, community building, word-of-mouth campaigns, and new point-of-purchase techniques are more easily measurable, and more effective, than the mass media. But despite that clarity, change has been slow. The reason lies in one word: inertia. One can see the huge potential in alternative media, based on the results of programs such as product placement in other games and a high-profile tournament for players, but my SVP friend and most of my industry colleagues concur that most senior executives resist giving programs like this a larger share of the budget. "They're just not ready," the consumer products executive said to the group. Across the wide range of companies at the meeting, the marketers all agreed.

So the capability is building, and the people responsible for results see increased ROI if they use it, but a high-level dam is holding back the flood. That said, I think this will soon all change, and possibly the turn will be happening by the time of publication of this book. Think about it. During economic crunch times, marketing budgets are almost invariably slashed; they are among the few major discretionary items available to CEOs desperate to protect profits. Faced with painful cuts, marketing chiefs quickly look for bargains, hoping to avoid a commensurate loss of impact in the marketplace. Suppose the games CFO demands a budget cut of 15%. If the marketing SVP announces that she can sustain the level of impact despite the cut, will her bosses be ready to listen? Probably. Here is an approach you may consider: you could cut TV in half, from 90% to 45% of the original budget, and return the requested 15% to the CFO. That would leave 30%—enough to quadruple the 10% previously allocated to the media. That would probably be a better channel anyway. Invariably, though, you can imagine a brand manager sitting in an office, developing a marketing strategy for her company's new sports drink identifying her marketing mix . She identifies which broad market segments to target, sets prices and promotions, and plans mass media communications. The brand's performance will be measured by aggregate sales and profitability, and her pay and future prospects will hinge on those numbers.

What's wrong with this picture? This company, like my friend in the games business—like too many—is still managed as if it were stuck in the 1960s, an era of mass markets, mass media, and impersonal transactions. I am a great fan of *Mad Men*, as it reflects a bygone era of my profession, but I can imagine what Don Draper could do today. Never before have companies had such powerful technologies for interacting directly with customers, collecting and mining information about them, and tailoring their offerings accordingly. And never before have customers expected to interact so deeply with companies, and each other, to shape the products and services they use. To be sure, most companies use customer relationship management and other technologies to get a handle on customers, but no amount of technology can really improve the situation as long as companies are set up to market products rather than cultivate customers. To compete in this aggressively interactive environment, companies must shift their focus from driving transactions to maximizing customer lifetime value. That means making products and brands subservient to long-term customer relationships. And that means changing strategy and structure across the organization—and reinventing the marketing department altogether.

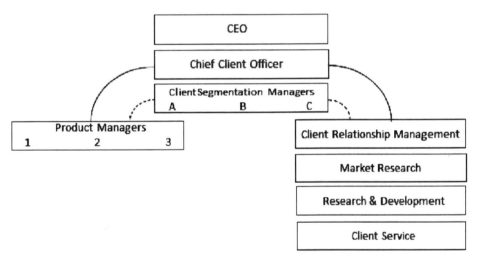

Figure 3-2. Building relationships: CCO model © CA, Inc. 2010

Cultivating Customers

Not long ago, companies looking to get a message out to a large population had only one real option: blanket a huge swath of customers simultaneously, mostly using one-way mass communication. Information about customers consisted primarily of aggregate sales statistics augmented by marketing research data. There was little, if any, direct communication between individual customers and the firm. Today, companies have a host of options at their disposal, making such mass marketing far too crude. Figure 3-2 shows where many companies are headed, and all must inevitably go there if they hope to remain competitive.

The key distinction between a traditional and a customer-cultivating company is that one is organized to push products and brands, whereas the other is designed to serve customers and customer segments. In the latter, communication is two-way and individualized, or at least tightly targeted at thinly sliced segments. This strategy may be more challenging for firms whose distribution channels own or control customer information—as is the case for many packaged-goods companies. But more and more firms now have access to the rich data they need to make a customer-cultivating strategy work. B2B companies, for instance, use key account managers and global account directors to focus on meeting customers' evolving needs, rather than selling specific products. Large B2B firms are often advanced in their customer orientation, and some B2C companies are making notable progress. Increasingly, they view their customer relationships as evolving over time, and they may hand off customers to different parts of the organization, selling different brands as their needs change.

For instance, from conversations I've had with marketing personnel at Tesco, a leading UK retailer, I am aware of the importance of investments in analytics that have improved customer retention. Tesco uses its data-collecting loyalty card (the Clubcard) to track which stores customers visit, what they buy, and how they pay. This information has helped Tesco tailor merchandise to local tastes and customize offerings at the individual level across a variety of store formats—from sprawling hypermarts to neighborhood shops. Shoppers who buy diapers for the first time at a Tesco store, for example, receive coupons by mail not only for baby wipes and toys but also for beer, according to a *Wall Street Journal* report. Data analysis revealed that new fathers tend to buy more beer because they can't spend as much time at the pub.

In the services arena, I talked with a division manager of a large credit card organization that actively monitors customers' behavior and responds to changes by offering different products. The firm uses consumer data analysis and algorithms to determine the customers' next best product according to their changing profiles and to manage risk across cardholders. For example, the first purchase of a upper-class airline ticket on a Gold Card may trigger an invitation to upgrade to a Platinum Card. Or, because of changing circumstances, a cardholder may want to give an additional card with a specified spending limit to a child or a contractor. By offering this service, the credit card organization extends existing customers' spending ability to a trusted circle of family members or partners, while introducing the brand to potential new customers.

Credit card companies also leverage their strategic position between customers and merchants to create long-term value across both relationships. For instance, the company might use demographic data, customer purchase patterns, and credit information to observe that a cardholder has moved into a new home. Credit card organizations capitalize on that life event by offering special rewards on purchases from merchants in its network in the home furnishings retail category. One insurance and financial services company I know of also proved adept at tailoring products to customers' life events. Customers who lose a spouse, for example, are flagged for special attention from a team that offers them customized products. When a checking account or credit card customer gets married, she's a good cross-selling prospect for an auto or home insurance policy and a mortgage. Likewise, the firm targets new empty nesters with home equity loans or investment products and offers renter's insurance to graduating seniors.

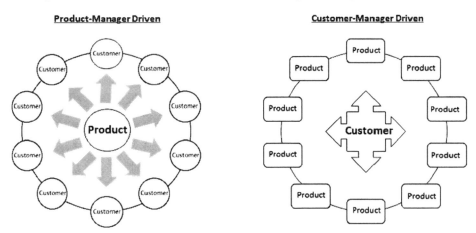

Figure 3-3. Comparative traditional product vs. customer-driven management © CA, Inc. 2010

Reinventing Marketing

These shining examples aside, boards and C-suites still mostly pay lip service to customer relationships while focusing intently on selling goods and services. Directors and management need to spearhead the strategy shift from transactions to relationships and create the culture, structure, and incentives necessary to execute the strategy. What does a customer-cultivating organization look like? Although no company has a fully realized customer-focused structure, we can see the features of one in a variety of companies making the transition. The most dramatic change will be the marketing department's reinvention as a "customer department." The first order of business is to transform the traditional CMO with an expanded role—one that includes the r. esponsibilities of a chief customer officer (CCO) to keep track of what is trending in the marketThe CCO role is becoming increasingly common in companies worldwide.

Companies as diverse as Chrysler, Hershey's, Oracle, Samsung, Sears, United Airlines, Sun Microsystems, and Wachovia now have roles that represent CCOs. But too often the CCO is merely trying to make a conventional organization more customer-centric. In general, it's a poorly defined role—which may account for CCOs' dubious distinction as having the shortest tenure of all C-suite executives. To be effective, the CCO role *must* be part of the CMO's role. Where better to align the responsibility of the integration of marketing objectives with those of the customer-facing functionality?

There are those who think a CCO is necessary as a separate role, and most have failed because the creation of the role does not in any way solve the problem. This executive is responsible for designing and executing the firm's customer relationship strategy and overseeing all customer-facing functions. This, in turn, must be a role in marketing and therefore a function of the CMO. A company, not a role, promotes a customer-centric culture and removes obstacles to the flow of customer information throughout the organization. This includes getting leaders to regularly engage with customers.

A colleague of mine has talked with peers at the insurance and finance organization USAA. Their top managers spend two or three hours a week on the call-center phones with customers. This not only shows employees how serious management is about customer interaction but also helps managers understand customers' concerns. Likewise, Tesco managers spend one week a year working in stores and interacting with customers as part of the Tesco Week in Store (TWIST) program. As managers shift their focus to customers, customer information increasingly drives decisions. Organizational structures that block information flow must be torn down. The reality is that, despite large investments in acquiring customer data, most firms under-utilize what they know. Information is tightly held, often because of a lack of trust, competition for promotions or resources, and the silo mentality.

Different Roles for Marketing

Before we look closely at the relationship between the two groups, we need to recognize that the nature of the marketing function varies significantly from company to company. Most small businesses (and most businesses are small) don't establish a formal marketing group at all. Their marketing ideas come from managers, the sales force, or an advertising agency. Such businesses equate marketing with selling; they don't conceive of marketing as a broader way to position their firms. Eventually, successful small businesses add a marketing person (or persons) to help relieve the sales force of some chores. These new staff members conduct research to calibrate the size of the market, choose the best markets and channels, and determine potential buyers' motives and influences. They work with outside agencies on advertising and promotions. They develop collateral materials to help the sales force attract customers and close sales. And, finally, they use direct mail, telemarketing, and trade shows to find and qualify leads for the sales force. Both sales and marketing see the marketing group as an adjunct to the sales force at this stage, and the relationship between the functions is usually positive.

As companies become larger and more successful, executives recognize that there is more to marketing than setting the four Ps: product, pricing, place, and promotion. They determine that effective marketing calls for people skilled in segmentation, targeting, and positioning. So that fifth P is again a key part of success. Once companies hire marketers with those skills, marketing becomes an independent player. It also starts to compete with sales for funding. While the sales mission has not changed, the marketing mission has. Disagreements arise. Each function takes on tasks it believes the other should be doing but isn't. All too often, organizations find that they have a marketing function inside sales, and a sales function inside marketing. At this stage, the salespeople wish that the marketers would worry about future opportunities (long-term strategy) and leave the current opportunities (individual and group sales) to them.

Once the marketing group tackles higher-level tasks like segmentation, it starts to work more closely with other departments, particularly strategic planning, product development, finance, and manufacturing. The company starts to think in terms of developing brands rather than products, and brand managers become powerful players in the organization. The marketing group is no longer a humble ancillary to the sales department. It sets its sights much higher. The marketers believe it's essential to transform the organization into a "marketing-led" company. As they introduce this rhetoric, others in the firm—including the sales group—question whether the marketers have the competencies, experience, and understanding to lead the organization.

While marketing increases its influence within separate business units, it rarely becomes a major force at the corporate level. There are exceptions: Citigroup, Coca-Cola, General Electric, IBM, and Microsoft each have a marketing head at the corporate level. And marketing is more apt to drive company strategy in major packaged-goods companies, such as General Mills, Kraft, and Procter & Gamble. Even then, though, during economic downturns, marketing is more closely questioned—and its workforce more likely to be cut—than sales.

Why Can't They Just Get Along?

There are two sources of friction between sales and marketing. One is economic, and the other is cultural. The economic friction is generated by the need to divide the total budget granted by senior management to support sales and marketing. In fact, the sales force is apt to criticize how marketing spends money on three of the four Ps—pricing, promotion, and product. Take pricing. The marketing group is under pressure to achieve revenue goals and wants the sales force to "sell the price" as opposed to "selling through price." The salespeople usually favor lower prices because they can sell the product more easily and because low prices give them more room to negotiate. In addition, there are organizational tensions around pricing decisions. While marketing is responsible for setting suggested retail or list prices and establishing promotional pricing, sales has the final say over transactional pricing. When special low pricing is required, marketing frequently has no input. The vice president of sales goes directly to the CFO. This does not make the marketing group happy.

Promotion costs, too, are a source of friction. The marketing group needs to spend money to generate customers' awareness of, interest in, preference for, and desire for a product. But the sales force often views the large sums spent on promotion—particularly on television advertising—as a waste of money. The VP of sales tends to think that this money would be better spent increasing the size and quality of the sales force. When marketers help set the other P, the product being launched, salespeople often complain that it lacks the features, style, or quality their customers want. That's because the sales group's worldview is shaped by the needs of its individual customers. The marketing team, however, is concerned about releasing products whose features have broad appeal.

The budget for both groups also reflects which department wields more power within the organization, a significant factor. CEOs tend to favor the sales group when setting budgets. One chief executive told me, "Why should I invest in more marketing when I can get better results by hiring more salespeople?" CEOs often see sales as more tangible, with more short-run impact. The sales group's contributions to the bottom line are also easier to judge than the marketers' contributions. The cultural conflict between sales and marketing is, if anything, even more entrenched than the economic conflict. This is true in part because the two functions attract different types of people who spend their time in very different ways. Marketers, who until recently had more formal education than salespeople, are highly analytical, data-oriented, and project-focused. They're all about building competitive advantage for the future. They judge their project's performance with a cold eye, and they're ruthless with a failed initiative.

However, that performance focus doesn't always look like action to their colleagues in sales because it all happens behind a desk rather than out in the field. Salespeople, in contrast, spend their time talking to existing and potential customers. They're skilled relationship builders; they're not only savvy about customers' willingness to buy but also attuned to which product features will fly and which will die. They want to keep moving. They're used to rejection, and it doesn't depress them. They live for closing a sale. It's hardly surprising that these two groups of people find it difficult to work well together. If the organization doesn't align incentives carefully, the two groups also run into conflicts about seemingly simple things—for instance, which products to focus on selling. Salespeople may push products with lower margins that satisfy quota goals, while marketing wants them to sell products with higher profit margins and more promising futures.

More broadly speaking, the two groups' performance is judged very differently. Salespeople make a living by closing sales, full stop. It's easy to see who (and what) is successful—almost immediately. But the marketing budget is devoted to programs, not people, and it takes much longer to know whether a program has helped to create long-term competitive advantage for the organization. So ultimately the organization must create incentives that eliminate these counterproductive mindsets for increasing the profitability of the firm's customers, as measured by metrics such as customer lifetime value (CLV) and customer equity, as well as by intermediate indicators, such as word of mouth (or mouse).

Client managers as a role play a significant part in a customer-focused organization. Customer and segment managers identify customers' product needs; brand managers supply the products that fulfill those needs. This requires shifting resources—principally people and budgets—and authority from product managers to customer-focused client managers. This structure is common in the B2B world. In its B2B activities, Procter & Gamble, for instance, has key account managers for major retailers like Walmart. They are less interested in selling, say, Swiffers than in maximizing the value of the customer relationship over the long term. Some B2C companies use this structure as well; foremost among them are retail financial institutions that put managers in charge of segments—wealthy customers, college kids, retirees, and so forth—rather than products.

In a customer-cultivating company, a consumer-goods segment manager might offer customers incentives to switch from less profitable Brand A to more profitable Brand B. This wouldn't happen in the conventional system, where brand and product managers call the shots. Brand A's manager isn't going to encourage customers to defect—even if that would benefit the company—because he's rewarded for brand performance, not for improving CLV or some other long-term customer metric. This is no small change. It means that product managers must stop focusing on maximizing their products' or brands' profits and become responsible for helping customer and segment managers maximize theirs.

Customer-Facing Functions

As the nexus of customer-facing activity, CRM (customer relationship management) has been increasingly taken on by companies' IT groups because of the technical capability CRM systems require, according to a Harte-Hanks survey of 300 companies in North America: 42% of companies report that CRM is managed by the IT group, 31% by sales, and only 9% by marketing. Yet CRM is, ultimately, a tool for gauging customer needs and behaviors—it is not the Garden of Eden, but perhaps a tree of knowledge. It makes little sense for the very data required to execute a customer-cultivation strategy to be collected and analyzed outside a collaborative environment in the marketing organization. Of course, bringing CRM into the mix means bringing IT and analytic skills in, as well as market research.

The emphasis of market research changes in a customer-centric company. First, the internal users of market research extend beyond the marketing department to all areas of the organization that touch customers—including finance (the source of customer payment options) and distribution (the source of delivery timing and service). Second, the scope of analysis shifts from an aggregate view to an individual view of customer activities and value. Third, market research shifts its attention to acquiring the customer input that will drive improvements in customer-focused metrics such as CLV and customer equity. When a product is more about clever engineering than customer needs, sales can suffer. For example, engineers like to pack lots of features into products, but we know that customers can suffer from feature fatigue, which hurts future sales. To make sure that product decisions reflect real-world needs, the customer must be brought into the design process. Integrating R&D and marketing is a good way to do that.

One example of this from my research is Nokia in Asia, where its market share exceeds 60%. In an industry where manufacturers must introduce scores of new offerings every year, the group's ability to translate customer input about features and value into hit product offerings is legendary. Among its customer-focused innovation tools is Nokia Beta Labs, a virtual developer community that brings users and developer teams together to virtually prototype new features and products, inviting even "wacky ideas" that may never make it to the marketplace. (Nokia adopted a different strategy in the United States, using far less customer input, and has seen its market share slide.) Examples abound of companies that create new value through the collaboration of users and producers: Mozilla's Firefox in the web browser category, P&G's Swiffer in the home cleaning category, and International Flavors and Fragrances' partnership with B2B customers like Estée Lauder in the perfume market. It's a new world in which the old R&D–driven models for new product development are giving way to creative collaborations like these.

Customer Service and Support

This function should be handled in-house, not only to ensure that the quality of service is high but also to help cultivate long-term relationships. Delta Airlines, for example, recently pulled out of its call centers overseas because cultural differences damaged the airline's ability to interact with North American customers. Delta concluded that the negative impact on the quality of customer relationships wasn't worth the cost savings. Now, when customer service gets a call, a representative immediately identifies the caller's segment and routes her to a customer-service specialist trained to work with that segment. The interaction is captured in the customer information system and used, in turn, by the customer department to divine new customers' needs and create solutions. If customer service must be outsourced, the function should report in to a high-level internal client manager, and its IT infrastructure and customer data must be seamlessly integrated with the company's customer databases.

A New Focus on Customer Metrics

Once companies make the shift from marketing products to cultivating customers, they will need new metrics to gauge the strategy's effectiveness. First, companies need to focus less on product profitability and more on customer profitability. Retailers have applied this concept for some time in their use of loss leaders—products that may be unprofitable but strengthen customer relationships. Second, companies need to pay less attention to current sales and more to customer lifetime value. A company in decline may have good current sales but poor prospects. The customer lifetime value metric evaluates the future profits generated from a customer, properly discounted to reflect the time value of money. Lifetime value focuses the company on long-term health—an emphasis that most shareholders and investors should share. Although too often the markets reward short-term earnings at the expense of future performance, that unfortunate tendency will change as future-oriented customer metrics become a routine part of financial reporting.

An international movement is underway to require companies to report intangible assets in financial statements. As leading indicators such as customer-centered metrics increasingly appear on financial statements, stock prices will begin to reflect them. Even now, savvy analysts are pushing firms to understand customer retention rates and the value of customer and brand assets. Third, companies need to shift their focus from brand equity (the value of a brand) to customer equity (the sum of the lifetime values of their customers). Increasing brand equity is best seen as a means to an end, a way to build customer equity (see "Customer-Centered Brand Management," *Harvard Business Review*, September 2004). Customer equity has the added benefit of being a good proxy for the value of the firm, thereby making marketing more relevant to shareholder value.

Fourth, companies need to pay less attention to current market share and more attention to customer equity share (the value of a company's customer base divided by the total value of the customers in the market). Market share offers a snapshot of the company's competitive sales position at the moment, but customer equity share is a measure of the firm's long-term competitiveness with respect to profitability. Given the increasing importance of customer-level information, companies must become adept at tracking information at several levels—individual, segment, and aggregate.

Different strategic decisions require different levels of information, so companies typically need multiple information sources to meet their needs. At the individual customer level, the key metric is customer lifetime value; the marketing activities tracked most closely are direct marketing activities; and the key sources of data are customer databases that the firm compiles. At the segment level, the key metric is the lifetime value of the segment (the lifetime value of the average customer times the number of customers in the segment). The marketing activities tracked most closely are marketing efforts targeted at specific customer segments, sometimes using niche media. Key sources of information are customer panels and survey data. At the aggregate market level, the key metric is customer equity. The marketing activities tracked most closely are mass marketing efforts, often through mass media. Key sources of information are aggregate sales data and survey data. Obviously, firms will typically have a portfolio of information sources.

Clearly, companies need metrics for evaluating progress in collecting and using customer information. How frequently managers contribute to and access customer information archives is a good general measure, although it doesn't reveal much about the quality of the information. To get at that, some firms create markets for new customer information in which employees rate the value of contributions. Like any other organizational transformation, making a product-focused company fully customer-centric will be difficult. The IT group will want to hang onto CRM; R&D is going to fight hard to keep its relative autonomy; and most important, traditional marketing executives will battle for their jobs. Because the change requires overcoming entrenched interests, it won't happen organically. Transformation must be driven from the top down. However daunting, the shift is inevitable, and will soon be the only competitive way to serve customers.

Four Types of Relationships

Given the potential economic and cultural conflicts, one would expect some strains to develop between the two groups. And, indeed, some level of dysfunction usually does exist, even in cases where the heads of sales and marketing are friendly. The sales and marketing departments in the companies I have researched demonstrate four types of relationships. Much like a Capability Maturity Model (CMM aligned with the Software Engineering Institute research of a few years ago), the relationships change as the companies' marketing and sales functions mature. The groups move from being unaligned (and often conflicted) to being fully integrated (and usually conflict-free), though we've seen only a few cases where the two functions are fully integrated.

Undefined

When the relationship is undefined, sales and marketing have grown independently. Each is preoccupied largely with its own tasks and agendas, and each group doesn't know much about what the other is up to—until a conflict arises. Meetings between the two, which are ad hoc, are likely to be devoted to conflict resolution rather than proactive cooperation.

Defined

In a defined relationship, the two groups set up processes—and rules—to prevent disputes. There's a "good fences make good neighbors" orientation; the marketers and salespeople know who is supposed to do what, and they stick to their own tasks for the most part. The groups start to build a common language in potentially contentious areas, such as "How do we define a lead?" Meetings become more reflective; people raise questions like "What do we expect of one another?" The groups work together on large events like customer conferences and trade shows.

Aligned

When sales and marketing are aligned, clear boundaries between the two exist, but they're flexible. The groups engage in joint planning and training. The sales group understands and uses marketing terminology such as "value proposition" and "brand image." Marketers confer with salespeople on important accounts. They play a role in transactional, or commodity, sales as well.

Integrated

When sales and marketing are fully integrated, boundaries become blurred. Both groups redesign the relationship to share structures, systems, and rewards. Marketing—and to a lesser degree sales—begins to focus on strategic, forward-thinking types of tasks (market sensing, for instance), and sometimes splits into upstream and downstream groups. Marketers are deeply embedded in the management of key accounts. The two groups develop and implement shared metrics. Budgeting becomes more flexible and less contentious. A "rise or fall together" culture develops. I designed an assessment tool that can help organizations gauge the relationship between their sales and marketing departments. (See Figure 3-4.) I originally developed this instrument to help me understand what I was seeing in my research, but the executives at the places I was studying quickly appropriated it for their own use. Without an objective tool of this kind, it's very difficult for managers to judge their cultures and their working environments.

The Relationship Is...	If Sales and Marketing...
Undefined	• Focus on their own tasks and agendas unless conflict arises between them. • Have developed independently. • Devote meetings between them to conflict resolution, not proactive collaboration.
Defined	• Have rules for preventing disputes. • Share a language for potentially contentious areas (i.e. defining a 'lead'). • Use meeting to clarify mutual expectations.
Aligned	• Have clear but flexible boundaries: salespeople use marketing terminology; marketers participate in transactional sales. • Engage in joint planning and training.
Integrated	• Share systems, performance metrics, and rewards. • Behave as if they'll 'rise and fall together'.

Figure 3-4. How well do sales and marketing work together? © CA, Inc. 2011

Moving Up

Once an organization understands the nature of the relationship between its marketing and sales groups, senior managers may wish to create a stronger alignment between the two. (It's not always necessary, however. Figure 3-4 can help organizations decide whether to make a change.)

Moving from Undefined to Defined

If the business unit or company is small, members of sales and marketing may enjoy good, informal relationships that needn't be disturbed. This is especially true if marketing's role is primarily to support the sales force. However, senior managers should intervene if conflicts arise regularly. As I noted earlier, this generally happens because the groups are competing for scarce resources and because their respective roles haven't been clearly defined. At this stage, managers need to create clear rules of engagement, including handoff points for important tasks like following up on sales leads.

Moving from Defined to Aligned

The defined state can be comfortable for both parties. "It may not be perfect," one VP of sales told us, "but it's a whole lot better than it was." Staying at this level won't work, though, if your industry is changing in significant ways. If the market is becoming commoditized, for example, a traditional sales force may become costly. Or if the market is moving toward customization, the sales force will need to upgrade its skills. The heads of sales and marketing may want to build a more aligned relationship and jointly add new skills.

To move from a defined relationship to an aligned one, you need to encourage disciplined communication. When it comes to improving relations between any two functions, the first step inevitably involves improving communication. But it's not as simple as just increasing communication between two groups. More communication is expensive. It eats up time, and it prolongs decision-making. We advocate instead for more disciplined communication. Hold regular meetings between sales and marketing (at least quarterly, perhaps bimonthly or monthly). Make sure that major opportunities, as well as any problems, are on the agenda. Focus the discussions on action items that will resolve problems, and perhaps even create opportunities, by the next meeting. Salespeople and marketers need to know when and with whom they should communicate. Companies should develop systematic processes and guidelines such as, "You should involve the brand manager whenever the sales opportunity is above $2 million," or "We will not go to print on any marketing collateral until salespeople have reviewed it," or "Marketing will be invited to the top ten critical account reviews." Businesses also need to establish an up-to-date, user-friendly "who to call" database. People get frustrated—and they waste time—searching in the wrong places for help.

As your functions become better aligned, it's important to create opportunities for marketers and salespeople to work together. This will make them more familiar with each other's ways of thinking and acting. It's useful for marketers, particularly brand managers and researchers, to occasionally go along on sales calls. They should get involved with developing alternate solutions for customers early in the sales process. And they should also sit in on important account-planning sessions. Salespeople, in turn, should help to develop marketing plans and should sit in on product-planning reviews. They should preview ad and sales promotion campaigns. They should share their deep knowledge about customers' purchasing habits. Jointly, marketers and salespeople should generate a playbook for expanding business with the top ten accounts in each market segment. They should also plan events and conferences together. Appoint a liaison from marketing to work with the sales force. The liaison needs to be someone both groups trust. He or she helps to resolve conflicts and shares with each group the tacit knowledge from the other group. It's important not to micro-manage the liaison's activities.

One of the marketing respondents in my study described the liaison's role this way: "This is a person who lives with the sales force. He goes to the staff meetings, he goes to the client meetings, and he goes to the client strategy meetings. He doesn't develop product; he comes back and says, 'Here's what this market needs. Here's what's emerging,' and then he works hand-in-hand with the salesperson and the key customer to develop products." Co-locate marketers and salespeople. It's an old and simple truth that when people are physically close, they will interact more often and are more likely to work well together. One bank I studied located its sales and marketing functions in an empty shopping mall: different groups and teams within sales and marketing were each allocated a storefront. Particularly in the early stages of moving functions toward a more closely aligned relationship, this kind of proximity is a big advantage.

Most companies, though, centralize their marketing function, while the members of their sales group remain geographically dispersed. Such organizations need to work harder to facilitate communication between sales and marketing and to create shared work. Improve sales force feedback. Marketers commonly complain that salespeople are too busy to share their experiences, ideas, and insights. Indeed, very few salespeople have an incentive to spend their precious time sharing customer information with marketing. They have quotas to reach, after all, and limited time in which to meet and sell to customers.

To more closely align sales and marketing, senior managers need to ensure that the sales force's experience can be tapped with a minimum of disruption. For instance, marketing can ask the sales VP to summarize any sales force insights for the month or the quarter. Or marketing can design shorter information forms, review call reports and CRM data independently, or pay salespeople to make themselves available to interviewers from the marketing group and to summarize what their sales colleagues are thinking about.

If the current relationship is...	And...	Then move the relationship to...	By...
Undefined	• Sales and marketing have frequent conflicts and compete over resources • Effort is duplicated, or tasks fall between the cracks	Defined	• Creating clear rules of engagement, including hand-off points for important tasks (such as lead follow up)
Defined	• The market is becoming commoditized or customized. • Product lifecycles are shortening. • Despite clarified roles, efforts are still duplicated or tasks neglected.	Aligned	• Establishing regular meetings between Sales and Marketing to discuss major opportunities and problems. • Defining who should be consulted on which decisions (e.g. 'involve the brand manager in $2 million + sales opportunities). • Creating opportunities for Sales and Marketing to collaborate, e.g. planning a conference together or rotating jobs.
Aligned	• The business landscape is marked by complexity and rapid change. • Marketing has split into upstream (strategic) and downstream (tactical) groups).	Integrated	• Having downstream marketers develop sales tools, help salespeople qualify leads, and use feedback from Sales to sell existing offerings to new market segments. • Evaluating and rewarding both teams' performance based on shared important metrics. For instance, establish a sales goal to which both teams commit. And defined key sales metrics - such as number of new customers and closings - for salespeople and downstream marketers.

Figure 3-5. Do we need to be aligned? © CA, Inc. 2010

Moving from Aligned to Integrated

Most organizations will function well when sales and marketing are aligned. This is especially true if the sales cycle is relatively short, the sales process is fairly straightforward, and the company doesn't have a strong culture of shared responsibility. In complicated or quickly changing situations, there are good reasons to move sales and marketing into an integrated relationship. Figure 3-5 outlines the issues you'll want to think through. This means integrating such straightforward activities as planning, target setting, customer assessment, and value-proposition development. It's tougher, though, to integrate the two groups' processes and systems; these must be replaced with common processes, metrics, and reward systems. Organizations need to develop shared databases, as well as mechanisms for continuous improvement. Hardest of all is changing the culture to support integration. The best examples of integration I found were in companies that already emphasized shared responsibility and disciplined planning that were metrics-driven, that tied rewards to results, and that were managed through systems and processes. You can see where you are on the scale by using the survey questions shown in Figure 3-6.

	Strongly Disagree 1	Disagree 2	Neither 3	Agree 4	Strongly Agree 5
Our sales figures are usually close to the sales forecast.					
If things go wrong, or results are disappointing, neither function points fingers or blames the other.					
Marketing people often meet with key customers during the sales process.					
Marketing solicits participation from sales in drafting the marketing plans.					
Our salespeople believe that collateral supplied by Marketing is a valuable tool to help them get more sales.					
The sales force willingly cooperates in supplying feedback requested by Marketing.					
There is a great deal of common language here between Sales and Marketing.					
The heads of sales and marketing regularly confer about upstream issues such as idea generation, market sensing, and product development strategy.					
Sales and Marketing work closely together to define segment buying behavior.					
When sales and marketing meet they do not need to spend much time on dispute resolution and crisis management.					
The heads of sales and marketing work together on business planning for products and services that will not be launched for two or more years.					
We discuss and use common metrics for determining the success of Sales and Marketing.					
Marketing actively participates in defining and executing the sales strategy for individual key accounts.					
Sales and marketing manage their activities using jointly developed business funnels, processes, or pipelines that span the business chain - from initial market sensing to customer service.					
Marketing makes a significant contribution to analyzing data from the sales funnel and using those data to improve the predictability and effectiveness of the funnel.					
Sales and Marketing share a strong 'We will rise and fall together' culture.					
Sales and Marketing report to a single chief customer officer, chief revenue officer, or equivalent C-Level executive.					
There is significant interchange of people between sales and marketing.					
Sales and marketing jointly develop and deploy training programs, events, and learning opportunities for their respective staffs.					
Sales and Marketing actively participate in the preparation and presentation of each other's plans to top executives.					
TOTAL					

Scoring
20-39 Undefined
40-59 Defined
60-79 Aligned
80-100 Integrated

Figure 3-6. Survey checklist sample © CA, Inc. 2010

	Undefined	Defined	Aligned
Don't make any changes if...	• The company is small. • The company has good informal relationships. • Marketing is still a sales support function.	• The company's products and services are fairly-cut-and-dry. • Traditional marketing and sales roles work in this market. • There is no clear and compelling reason to change.	• The company lacks a culture of shared responsibility. • Sales and Marketing report separately. • The sales cycle is fairly short.
Tighten the relationship between sales and marketing if...	• Conflicts are evident between the two functions. • There's duplication of effort between the two functions; or tasks are falling through the cracks. • The functions compete for resources or funding.	• Even with careful definition of roles, there's duplication of effort between the functions; or tasks are falling through the cracks. • The market is commoditized and makes a traditional sales force costly. • Products are developed, prototyped, or extensively customized during the sales process. • Product lifecycles are shortening, and technology turnover is accelerating.	• A common process or business funnel can be created for managing and measuring revenue-generating activities.

Figure 3-7. Transformation guide © CA, Inc. 2010

The main rationale for integrating sales and marketing is that the two functions have a common goal: the generation of profitable and increasing revenue. It is logical to put both functions under one C-level executive. Companies such as Campbell's Soup, Coca-Cola, and FedEx have a chief revenue officer (CRO) who is responsible for planning for and delivering the revenue needed to meet corporate objectives. The CRO needs control over the forces affecting revenue—specifically, marketing, sales, service, and pricing (see Figure 3-7). This is similar to the CCO discussion earlier in the chapter with the added component of sales as a revenue center. Whatever the model, one must define the steps in the marketing and sales funnels. Sales and marketing are responsible for a sequence of activities and events (sometimes called a funnel) that leads customers toward purchases and, hopefully, ongoing relationships. Such funnels can be described from the customer's perspective or from the seller's perspective. (A typical funnel based on the customer's decision sequence is shown in Figure 3-8.)

The Buying Funnel

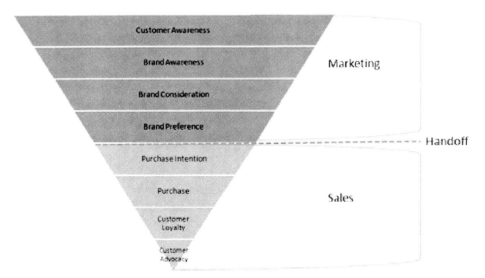

Figure 3-8. The buying funnel © CA, Inc. 2010

Marketing is usually responsible for the first few steps—building customers' brand awareness and brand preference, creating a marketing plan, and generating leads for sales. Then sales executes the marketing plan and follows up on leads. This division of labor has merit. It is simple, and it prevents marketing from getting too involved in individual sales opportunities at the expense of more strategic activities. But the handoff brings serious penalties. If things do not go well, sales can say that the plan was weak, and marketing can say that the salespeople did not work hard enough or smart enough. And in companies where marketing makes a handoff, marketers can lose touch with active customers. Meanwhile, sales usually develops its own funnel describing the sequence of selling tasks. Funnels of this kind—integrated into the CRM system and into sales forecasting and account-review processes—form an increasingly important backbone for sales management.

Unfortunately, marketing often plays no role in these processes. Some companies in my study, however, have integrated marketing into the sales funnel. During prospecting and qualifying, for instance, marketing helps sales to create common standards for leads and opportunities. During the needs-definition stage, marketing helps sales develop value propositions. In the solution development phase, marketing provides "solution collateral"—

organized templates and customized guides so salespeople can develop solutions for customers without constantly having to reinvent the wheel. When customers are nearing a decision, marketing contributes case study material, success stories, and site visits to help address customers' concerns. And during contract negotiations, marketing advises the sales team on planning and pricing. Of course, marketing's involvement in the sales funnel should be matched by sales' involvement in the upstream, strategic decisions the marketing group is making. Salespeople should work with the marketing and R&D staffs as they decide how to segment the market, which products to offer to which segments, and how to position those products. There's a strong case for splitting marketing into upstream (strategic) and downstream (tactical) groups.

Downstream marketers develop advertising and promotion campaigns, collateral material, case histories, and sales tools. They help salespeople develop and qualify leads. The downstream team uses market research and feedback from the sales reps to help sell existing products in new market segments, to create new messages, and to design better sales tools. Upstream marketers engage in customer sensing. That is, they monitor the voice of the customer and develop a long view of the company's business opportunities and threats.

The upstream team shares its insights with senior managers and product developers—and it participates in product development. It may set shared revenue targets and reward systems. The integrated organization will not succeed unless sales and marketing share responsibility for revenue objectives. One marketing manager told us, "I'm going to use whatever tools I need to make sure sales is effective, because, at the end of the day, I'm judged on that sales target as well." One of the barriers to shared objectives, however, is the thorny issue of shared rewards. Salespeople historically work on commission, and marketers don't. To successfully integrate the two functions, management will need to review the overall compensation policy. Integrate sales and marketing metrics. The need for common metrics becomes critical as marketing becomes more embedded in the sales process and as sales plays a more active role in marketing. "In order to be the customer-intimate company we are," says Larry Norman, president of Financial Markets Group, part of the Aegon USA operating companies, "we need to be metrics-driven and have metrics in place that track both sales and marketing performance."

On a macro level, companies like General Electric have "the number"—the sales goal to which both sales and marketing commit. There is no escaping the fact that, however well-integrated sales and marketing are, the company will also want to develop metrics to measure and reward each group appropriately. Sales metrics are easier to define and track. Some of the most common measures are percent of sales quota achieved, number of new customers, number of sales closings, average gross profit per customer, and ratio of sales expense to total sales. When downstream marketers become embedded in the sales process—for example, as members of critical account teams—it's only logical to measure and reward their performance using sales metrics. But then how should the company evaluate its upstream marketers? On the basis of the accuracy of their product forecasting, or the number of new market segments they discover? The metrics will vary according to the type of marketing job.

Senior managers need to establish different measures for brand managers, market researchers, marketing information systems managers, advertising managers, sales promotion managers, market segment managers, and product managers. It's easier to construct a set of metrics if the marketers' purposes and tasks are clearly outlined. Still, given that upstream marketers are more engaged in sowing the seeds for a better future than in helping to reap the current harvest, the metrics used to judge their performance necessarily become softer and more subjective. Obviously, the difference between judging current and future outcomes makes it more complicated for companies to develop common metrics for sales and marketing. Upstream marketers in particular need to be assessed according to what they deliver over a longer period. Salespeople, meanwhile, are in the business of converting potential demand into today's sales.

As the working relationship between sales and marketing becomes more interactive and interdependent, the integrated organization will continue to wrestle with this difficult, but surely not insurmountable, problem. Senior managers often describe the working relationship between sales and marketing as unsatisfactory. The two functions, they say, undercommunicate, underperform, and overcomplain. Not every company will want to—or should—upgrade from defined to aligned relationships or from aligned to integrated relationships. But every company can and should improve the relationship between sales and marketing. Carefully planned enhancements will bring salespeople's intimate knowledge of your customers into the company's core. These improvements will also help you serve customers better now and will help you build better products for the future. They will help your company marry softer, relationship-building skills with harder, analytic skills. They will force your organization to closely consider how it rewards people and whether those reward systems apply fairly across functions. Best of all, these improvements will boost both your top-line and bottom-line growth.

While some organizations seem to be better at balancing the political and financial landscapes of both, in many cases the balance is less than harmonious. Sales forever wants to see more qualified net new leads and relationship-building events, and marketing is continuously claiming to have provided them. Spreadsheets and ROI models abound; however, the missing link in many cases is the agility required to meet what seem to be ever-changing demands. Survival in the volatile marketplace requires that some level of transformation has to take place, and the mechanism to facilitate that transformation can even be applied in an iterative fashion itself—this is the promise of agile.

Plan, Fail, Iterate, Succeed

Failing to Plan Is a Plan to Fail

Some think that agile means not having a plan, but that is the same as saying that the marketing or sales person pursuing Sam (from *Green Eggs and Ham*) is not persistent. Not so coincidentally, agile is based on persistence and, most importantly, planning; perhaps just not in the typical areas you might think. Unlike more traditional approaches to project management or any task methodology you might adopt, agile methodology may not come into the project with neatly aligned objectives and requirements, but you still must plan. This includes what your project management governance model will be, who you will have on your program leadership team, and how you will interface with your stakeholders to get their buy-in along the way. This takes planning, but unlike in-depth requirements gathering for a product, the planning required in agile is program planning.

The premise of the agile approach to marketing borrows from a development process that exists because of the need to improve productivity in application development (Figure 4-1). It's no different with marketing. I know, I know—you believe that marketing is not like other areas of the business; it is an art as much as a science, so you cannot apply a process. If you believe that, I think you have to take a look at the progress that is being made in all aspects of the marketing role and the integration of all types of marketing activities across marketing outlets. Again, agile marketing is not a replacement, but an adaptation to new outlets.

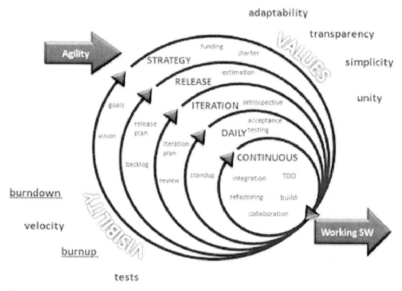

Figure 4-1. Agile software development © 2009 by CA, Inc.

As discussed before, evolving means including the progress in communication mechanisms centered around the traditional objectives of getting the marketing messages and branding to your customers. Yes, there is an artistic as well as a scientific aspect to "the what" of marketing. But beyond the nuance of this unique business activity, you have to take into account the new social world of marketing and selling. There is always a process that a buyer goes through to decide to buy things, and marketing needs to plan how it is going to facilitate that process to get the buyer to a decision point. Just as manufacturing is in a constant state of improvement, so must marketing be. Take, for instance, software development, which must continually meet the demands of the market, and some common agile and traditional development techniques. Notice throughout each of these agile methodology processes that the underlying design is the allowance of iterative reviews toward short-term objectives and the flexibility to "adjust as you go," as shown in Table 4-1 through Table 4-12.

Table 4-1. Agile Software Development: Agile Marketing © 2010 by CA, Inc.

Technique: Active Stakeholder Participation	
Description:	Stakeholders (users, managers, support people, ...) are actively involved with the modeling effort, using inclusive techniques to model storm on a just in time (JIT) basis
Feedback Period:	Hours. A stakeholder will describe their requirement(s), then the developer spend several hours, or perhaps day or two, implementing them to produce working software which they can then show to the stakeholder(s).
Marketing Acceptable	Yes – ADAM & EVE

Table 4-2. Agile Software Development: Agile Marketing © 2010 by CA, Inc.

Agile Model Driven Development (AMDD)	
Description:	AMDD is the agile version of Model Driven Development (MDD). With an AMDD approach, at the start of a project you do some high-level, initial requirements envisioning and initial architecture envisioning. During development you model storm on a just in time basis
Feedback Period:	Hours. With model storming, you explore a requirement with your stakeholder(s) or a technical issue with other developers and then spend several hours or days implementing working software
Agile Marketing Acceptable	Yes adoption of marketing process

Table 4-3. Agile Software Development: Agile Marketing © 2010 by CA, Inc.

Big Design Up Front (BDUF)	
Description:	With a BDUF approach, a comprehensive design document is developed early in the project life cycle which is used to guide the implementation efforts.
Feedback Period:	Months. It is typically months, and sometimes years, before stakeholders are shown working software which implements the design.
Agile Marketing Acceptable	Yes marketing planning

Table 4-4. Agile Software Development: Agile Marketing © 2010 by CA, Inc.

Big Requirements Up Front (BRUF)	
Description:	With a BRUF approach, a comprehensive requirements document is developed early in the project life cycle which is used to guide the design and implementation efforts .
Feedback Period:	Months. It is typically months, if not years, before stakeholders are shown working software which implements their requirements.
Agile Marketing Acceptable	Yes marketing strategy

Table 4-5. Agile Software Development: Agile Marketing © 2010 by CA, Inc.

Code Inspections	
Description:	A developer's code is inspected by her peers to look for style issues, correctness, etc.
Feedback Period:	Days to weeks. Many teams will schedule reviews every Friday afternoon where one person's code is inspected, rotating throughout the team. It may be weeks, or even months, until someone looks at the code that you've written today.
Agile Marketing Acceptable	Yes planning review

Table 4-6. Agile Software Development: Agile Marketing © 2010 by CA, Inc.

Continuous Integration	
Description:	The system is built/compiled/integrated on a regular basis, at least several times a day, and ideally whenever updated source code is checked into version control. Immediately after the system is built, which is often done in a separate "project integration sandbox" it is automatically tested.
Feedback Period:	Minutes. You make a change to your code, recompile, and see if it works.
Agile Marketing Acceptable	Yes feedback loop into process

Table 4-7. Agile Software Development: Agile Marketing © 2010 by CA, Inc.

Independent Parallel Testing	
Description:	The development team may opt to deploy their system on a regular basis, at least once iteration, to an independent test team working in parallel to the development team(s) that focuses on trying to discover where the system breaks. This is an agile testing strategy.
Feedback Period:	Days to weeks. Depends on how often the development team deploys their current working build into the test environment and how long it takes for the test team to get around to testing it (they are likely supporting several teams).
Agile Marketing Acceptable	Yes campaign testing

Table 4-8. Agile Software Development: Agile Marketing © 2010 by CA, Inc.

Model With Others	
Description:	Pair programming, you work with at least one other person when you're modeling something.
Feedback Period:	Seconds. You're discussing the model as you're creating it, and people can instantly see a change to the model made by someone else.
Agile Marketing Acceptable	Yes cooperative campaign or marketing initiative with sales

Table 4-9. Agile Software Development: Agile Marketing © 2010 by CA, Inc.

Model/Documentation Reviews	
Description:	A model, document, or other work product is reviewed by your peers.
Feedback Period:	Days to weeks. A work product will be created, the review must be organized, materials distributed, and so on. The implication is that it can be weeks, or even months, before the item is reviewed.
Agile Marketing Acceptable	Yes

Table 4-10. Agile Software Development: Agile Marketing © 2010 by CA, Inc.

Pair Programming	
Description:	Two developers work together at a single workstation to implement code.
Feedback Period:	Seconds. You're working together to develop the code, the second coder is watching exactly what the person with the keyboard is doing and can act on it immediately.
Agile Marketing Acceptable	Logically co-located marketing initiative work product development

Table 4-11. Agile Software Development: Agile Marketing © 2010 by CA, Inc.

Test Driven Development (TDD)	
Description:	With TDD, you iteratively write a single test then you write sufficient production code to fulfill that test.
Feedback Period:	Minutes. By implementing in small steps like this, you quickly see whether your production code fulfills the new test.
Agile Marketing Acceptable	Yes

Table 4-12. Agile Software Development: Agile Marketing © 2010 by CA, Inc.

Traditional Acceptance and System Testing	
Description:	Acceptance testing attempts to address the issue "does the system do what the stakeholders have specified". System testing, including functional, load/stress, and integration testing, attempts to address the issue "does the system work". With traditional testing the majority of testing occurs during the testing phase late in the lifecycle. Testers will write test cases, based on the requirements, in parallel with implementation.
Feedback Period:	Months. By waiting until the system is "ready for testing", the testers won't see the system until months after the requirements are finalized.
Agile Marketing Acceptable	Yes with advertising agencies

In the context of application development, the code you develop for a given cycle is reviewed for meeting objectives and if necessary changed through iteration. Therefore, as it relates to an adaptive marketing process that can respond to the realities of the business, such as pressure from Wall Street, changes in the marketplace, or redefining a need, there is usually a short-term analysis and alteration of the business strategy, whether executed through sales channels or organizational initiatives, and marketing must keep up and perhaps proactively be ready for these changes. This is one of the fundamental constructs of agile as it relates to application development and must be applied to marketing. As a typical and traditional business strategy becomes unsynchronized from even the shorter-term goals of the marketing process, those short-term objectives are generally reflective of longer cycles than the needs of the business, which may be quarter to quarter. The reason they are longer is that the traditional marketing planning ideology relies on underlying strategic goals. Relying only on this has proven to bring about costly failures.

Holding to an objective or defined strategy set in place without the ability to be agile in both a reactive and proactive manner will limit your ability to succeed. Process advancements and improved capability output to support the ultimate objective of the business in an agile fashion, whatever the impediments, will ensure greater productivity. The key point here is that the improvement to this process is the continual monitoring and auditing of what's going on, which requires analysis and review of programs put in place, plans, and strategies. These measurements and analysis allow marketing professionals to make informed decisions about their programs and make adjustments to the needs of the business. Practically applied, as a marketing decision-maker in response to trends or in anticipation of leading a market, you can proactively put in place mechanisms that allow for more funding behind programs or campaigns that are succeeding, and can halt ones that are not. This piece really allows marketing to be flexible and dynamic, and helps to make great strides in keeping up with the changing marketplace, the business, and customers. It is imperative that marketing professionals are able to adjust processes and marketing as a whole, always keeping in mind what is important: the five Ps (the fifth P is People as discussed earlier).

We have briefly touched on the adoption of the elements found in the agile development process as a way to improve what marketing is doing, as well as shown that when marketing is traditionally and necessarily tied to the strategy of a company, failure becomes more common than success. It is important that marketing improve. Let's look a little closer.

Marketing's purpose is very important because marketing is meant to separate customers or potential customers from their money in exchange for services from the organization. Marketing can't live up to its mission the way it is currently doing things. It's a combination of improving processes, and knowing and understanding what marketing is and that marketing or marketing organizations do not exist for their own purpose. Most importantly marketing cannot exist in the siloed separateness that it always has in the past.

Previously, we talked a bit about a disconnect between the business objectives of an organization and the marketing objectives and that these are symptoms of a siloed, non-flexible segmentation of marketing priorities with business goals. This drives a perception within a significant number of organizations that marketing seems to be at war with those it is meant to serve. I don't believe it's at war, but I do believe marketing has had the difficult task of trying to bring together shorter-term and longer-term objectives into quarter-by-quarter results. Sales has quarterly objectives and is in the customer's face constantly. It has an immediate need to respond to every need of the customer and to what is going on "on the street," usually in a quarterly time period. Because we want to be sure of some objectives that marketing has in planning and strategy, we, as marketing professionals, aren't reacting quickly enough to what those changes on the street are. This may be because of a traditional process we have in place for the development of a marketing strategy for the enablement of an organization's objectives. Maybe marketing's longer-term goals of 3–5 years break down into 18–24-month cycles, and then teams can build within that time frame with increased flexibility. That is not to say that long-term goals and objectives cannot be established, but perhaps focusing on more iterative short-term objectives as elements of the marketing process would drive the proper level of resolution to the apparent disconnect between marketing and other functional organizations within a given company. That's where agile is different. In agile, need sets the tone and the objectives. It does not push out methods or processes for reaching these objectives. Management allows those closest to the market to decide how to best reach those goals.

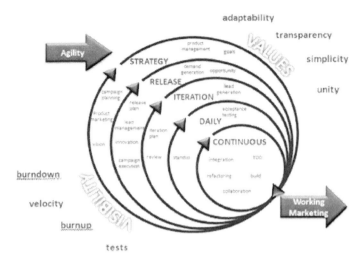

Figure 4-2. Agile marketing development framework © 2010 by CA, Inc.

Once management's objectives are set (which, by the way, can and probably will change over time), we can start to listen to the market to see how we can aid the business in meeting its needs. This will help us define what is most important to the market, and which of management's objectives we will be able to meet. With this information, we can build cross-organizational teams consisting of pigs and chickens that will enable us to meet the project or program's goals, and give everyone a say in the outcome of the project/program/campaign. Let's look at how this actually works.

Step 1: Plan

As mentioned at the beginning of this chapter, in the agile process, planning is paramount to success. Once you have direction from management and the market, it is imperative to know your budget, define your scope, sell your project/program/campaign idea to sponsors (and get the budget you need), and select a cross-organizational and cross-functional team that will enable you to reach your project/program/campaign goals.

I recently read a report from Scott W. Ambler, one of the industry analysts, where a group of respondents was asked to respond to what agile developers were actually doing at the beginning of agile projects and compare it with what's being talked about or is assumed about agile planning.[1]

---

[1] Ambler, Scott W., 2009 Agile Project Initiation Survey. Used with permission.

Some findings included the following:

- On average, agile teams spend 3.9 weeks on project initiation efforts.
- 89% do some sort of up-front modeling, or have initial requirements models given to them, or use reference models.
- 86% do some sort of up-front architecture/design modeling or have initial architecture/design models given to them or use reference models.
- 8% of agile teams produce no initial estimate at all, 73% create an initial high-level estimate, and 18% create an initial detailed estimate.
- 8% of agile teams produce no initial schedule, 77% develop a high-level schedule, and 12% develop a detailed schedule.
- The majority of agile teams work with legacy assets in some way. Legacy systems analysis and legacy data are apparently an important skill for agilists.
- 69% have a wide range of stakeholders.
- 30% are in regulatory compliance situations.
- 46% are co-located in a single room.
- 47% have a firm delivery date, and another 28% have promised an end date, although it may change.
- 56% have to produce a vision document.

So how, in reality, do you plan in agile marketing? First, you do your best to get the high-level objectives from your sponsors and stakeholders. Next, you try to make sure that the people on your team are willing to try, smartly, to reach those goals and objectives. From a budget perspective, you need someone leading the team that can make educated assumptions based on what is needed for the project/program/campaign. Look at how much you need and how much budget you have. What budget you do have will likely determine your shorter-term scope. What is important is that you deliver on that budgeted scope.

Another piece to keep in mind is that there are often times internal resources that you can tap into. Use them to make your project/program/campaign more valuable across the business or throughout the company. Look broadly across the organization to find the right people for your project/program/campaign to make it as successful as possible, and to include everyone that needs to be included to reach your objectives/goals. More on this later.

Selling to sponsors is one of the single most important things you'll do during your project/program/campaign. It boils down, really, to winning dollars for the project/program/campaign. Getting budget for a project/program/campaign may seem new to you. Once upon a time, marketing professionals were handed programs to run, with set budgets. Now, things are different. You can plan a project/program/campaign to spectacularly reach management objectives, but if they don't have the money to fund you, your plans won't matter. You'll probably be competing with other organizations for the same money. And who wins? The one who delivers to the business what it needs, when it needs it. That's where agile comes in. You can say to your sponsors, "We've done things like x in the past, but they never worked. Here's how we'd like to try it moving forward. Here's the budget we'll need. If it succeeds, here's how we'd like to take it to the next level." They'll have a level of expectation that gives you some flexibility in making sure your plans work for the business.

Oftentimes, your budget will define your scope, although it is important to keep in mind that not everything need be implemented at once—only those things that are critical to the business's success. Here's where you need to pick and choose those items and, later on, show the most ROI.

Some might think it may be harder to get time and resources for an agile marketing project/program/campaign. Quite the contrary. With the iterative nature of the project/program/campaign, it is easy for stakeholders or sponsors or management to either give more budget dollars to projects that succeed, or shut down projects that are no longer relevant or do not meet their business objectives.

Agile marketing professionals need to ask their sponsors and stakeholders what objectives they want them to meet. Then they need to come back with what kind of resources it will require. Agile marketing professionals may find early on that the way they were going to meet the objective isn't going to be effective, and they need to be open to try new things: new methods or ideas for reaching stakeholder and sponsor objectives. This can be a struggle in agile. People tend to be very regimented and to follow the status quo. Here, agile becomes difficult because you now need to start to get people to think and act differently, out of their comfort zone. They need to be open to change, and that's no easy thing. Your plan and project/program/campaign sponsorship now become incredibly important. It's also imperative to include everyone, especially those leery of change, in the process. We'll talk about that next.

As an agile marketing manager, picking a team is another very important piece of the puzzle. This is the fifth "P" we've talked about before as part of the marketing paradigm and one of *the* most important factors. Selecting a cross-organizational and cross-functional team will help you to reach your project/program/campaign goals. You need to set ground rules and expectations about how the team is to work together. The best place to do this, as well as give an overview of the project, is at the kick-off meeting. During this important piece, we can quickly understand exactly who does what—who will become the pigs and who will be chickens, when they can meet and who they can interact with, as well as ask questions of stakeholders and sponsors. It is important to give each member of the team this visibility, in order to get buy-in for the project/program/campaign. You'll want to define roles, keeping in mind who will be pigs and who will be chickens. Make sure you set expectations for both. It's good to have everyone together, so they know who will be working on what and can collaborate easily and effectively throughout the project.

After the meet and greet, here is where your sprint planning will begin. The project/program/campaign is usually broken into sprints, based on the needs of the business. The first sprint, or sprint 1, should include all those tasks/features/functions that will help meet the most important needs of the business. The entire team should be a part of this planning, especially the pigs, who will be able to estimate hours needed to complete any one task/feature/function. Chickens should be there to make sure that all of the correct tasks/features/functions are selected to meet those important business goals.

As you can gather, it is imperative to bring everyone together, for the sake of the project/program/campaign. I don't know how many projects/programs/campaigns I've seen start off without involving everyone. When it gets to the last hour, and everything is ready, some department stands up and says, "We can't do this." If they would have been involved at the beginning, and had their say in the project, this probably could have been avoided. It might be a headache to bring them in to begin with, but it will save the project/program/campaign from being shelved or killed—and you'll be able to deliver to the business.

If needed, it is also important to think about bringing in any agencies or vendors. Be sure to pick one that is familiar with agile and can adapt to your working environment.

It is also important to decide how you will document the project/program/campaign, as well as to set clear goals and key performance indicators (KPIs). In an environment where the market is rapidly changing, these will help you define project/program/campaign success.

Clear planning is necessary at the beginning of the project/program/campaign, in order to ensure you're meeting business objectives.

Step 2: Iterate

Let's get moving! Getting the work done is what really makes or breaks the project/program/campaign. Sure, you can plan it, but can you build it? The rules and expectations that you set at the beginning of the project should help to guide the team's everyday grind. Iterations make up the heartbeat of your project/program/campaign.

Your team should use the project/program/campaign documents to guide their everyday tasks. In agile, it is important to get working pieces of a project/program/campaign out the door quickly and with quality, so that the team can then build on those. Quickly and with quality can mean different things to different people. It is imperative to have defined measurements and KPIs going into your first sprint (and every sprint after). If driven from the market, these will define true success for your project/program/campaign.

Requirements gathering should be done in an iterative fashion, with stakeholders and constituents being engaged throughout the process. Development is iterative and goes hand in hand with requirements gathering. For example, once the first round of approved requirements is gathered, development starts on them. When a first useable draft or product is produced, it is taken back to the business, which validates that it is still what they need. During this process, testing is very important. It will help to show if you are measuring up to your time and quality goals throughout the project/program/campaign iterations.

The first iteration of a project/program/campaign is oftentimes the pre-project planning iteration, where the business opportunity is defined and the project/program/campaign is deemed viable and/or feasible. This should be no longer than a couple of weeks. The following iteration is the planning iteration, which we discussed previously, where you are gathering support, engaging stakeholders, fleshing out budgets, building a team, and setting up the project/program/campaign environment. Subsequent iterations should all be development iterations, where projects/programs/campaigns are being developed and deployed. You're collaborating with stakeholders, implementing new functionality in order of priority deemed by the business, analyzing that new functionality to make sure it meets requirements, regularly delivering to the business, and always testing.

Interestingly enough, iterations allow an agile marketing professional to implement the status quo, show very quickly that it does not work (or maybe that it works great), and move on from there. Then he or she can go back to the sponsor and stakeholders, show them that the status quo is failing, and propose a new way forward, an incremental way forward, an iterative way forward—agile.

An important part of iterations are daily stand-up meetings, or scrums. Every day, the team is focused on completing the highest priority features in the form of working, tested marketing program features. This also gives everyone the opportunity to get on the same page as to what is happening where. This helps keep everyone working toward the same goal. As program features are delivered within the iteration, they are reviewed and accepted, if appropriate, by the product owner/sales/customer. Each day, a short, 15-minute scrum facilitates the communication of individual detailed status and any impediments or issues that are critical information for a project/program/campaign manager.

Keep in mind that in the daily scrums, attendees are not talking unless they are pigs. Everyone can hear what is happening at the most basic levels of the organization, but only the pigs are allowed to share their daily issues. This helps the agile marketing professional to know where they might have problems in the future, and enables them to clear obstacles out of the way before they become a big issue. Remember that a problem you are aware of is one you can solve (or kill!).

In agile marketing, short iterations often work better than long, drawn-out ones. This is for several reasons. First, as we talked about previously, problems become visible quickly and that gives you the opportunity to get in front of them. Second, sometimes there are problems that are visible only *after* an iteration is complete. In this case, the shorter the time period of the iteration, the more time you'll have to get ahead of the problem. Third, short iterations give you the opportunity to accommodate new requirements, or get rid of ones that are no longer valid. Fourth, improvements to existing programs are faster, resulting in the business seeing quicker results—and that's always good for you!

Step 3: Fail

Failure is the best part of the process. Really, it is! It offers you the easiest way to learn where you can continuously improve. Agile marketing teams are constantly driving toward a state of perfection with continuous improvement, adaptive planning, collaboration, design, development, testing, and integration. This fosters a dynamic, highly productive environment in which automation is critical and the output is always high-quality, valuable, working marketing programs.

So here's where your KPIs and other means of measuring your progress become critical. When you are able to measure your progress, you are able to improve on it throughout the process. You're also able to see quickly where things are going wrong. This gives you the opportunity to nip problems in the bud. It also gives you the unique opportunity to positively communicate failures to stakeholders. Pointing out your own failures before someone else points them out for you helps you mitigate the risk to your project/program/campaign. It also helps you to focus on making the project/program/campaign work. You can learn from your failed experience and make sure that, moving forward, things are done differently, and in a way that will best achieve the project/program/campaign goals.

Failures are also important to the objectives overall. It's important to weed out the projects/programs/campaigns that are either not meeting the market need, or failing in their implementation. Resources then can be put behind those projects/programs/campaigns that are working or that are important to keep the company at the forefront in the marketplace. Remember that with agile marketing, we're keeping the business and the market needs foremost in our thought process, not what is best for marketing for marketing's sake.

In agile marketing, failures are only short-term, and are easy to learn from. As we'll see in the next section, so are successes.

Step 4: Succeed

Success in agile marketing is just as short-lived as failure, but very important: it's why you've taken action in the first place! Success in agile is always changing, just as the project/program/campaign is always changing. It doesn't mean that you've pushed and pushed your people to get a six-month project/program/campaign up and running in a month. Success in agile is implementing the most critical pieces of that project/program/campaign that meets stakeholder and sponsor expectations, and then building on those.

Success is evolutionary and is always changing. Agile marketing professionals take the knowledge gathered from iterations and failures and use it to build a successful project/program/campaign. But success in agile doesn't mean you're done. The changing nature of the marketplace means agile marketing professionals will not just sit on their laurels.

In the first chapter, I briefly touched on the adoption of the elements found in the agile development process as a way to improve what marketing is doing and because marketing is traditionally and necessarily tied to the strategy of a company. The foregoing discussion about the need for marketing to have or adopt a new approach to plan and use a real process touches on the idea that we must not only understand the opportunity we have before us, but also look at ways that marketing can improve. Perhaps improve is not the correct word—let's say transform or pragmatically innovate. That all takes planning. To that end, we examine how to create agility in marketing through planning. What is this agility in marketing? Well, it is not just doing a lot all the time as a free-for-all, and, quite frankly, it is stringent in its own right. Let's take a look at agile development plan components.

An agile methodology has ten very specific principles that are to be followed in the up-front planning governance process:

- Active user involvement is imperative—you need to get the right people involved.
- The team must be empowered to make decisions—the right sponsors at the top need to be supportive.
- Requirements evolve, but the timeframe is fixed.
- Capture requirements at a high level; without too much solutioning but with a vision of what the end state could be.
- Develop small, incremental releases and iterate.
- Focus on frequent delivery of products.
- Complete each feature before moving on to the next.
- Apply the 80/20 rule.
- Testing is integrated throughout the product life cycle—test early and often.
- A collaborative and cooperative approach between all stakeholders is essential.

So how do we go about matching these principles to marketing or, perhaps more importantly, how do we make the transference from an engineering discipline to a creative discipline? Only if we accept the paradigm that marketing is creative and software development is engineering does such disparity come to life. I surmise, in fact, that engineering is creative in its own respect, and marketing is much like engineering and therefore not only about creativity—it is a process of getting people to take an action, go to a web site, call a phone number, and ultimately connect with a brand and buy a product. Product developers/engineers are looking to fill a need consumers have and develop to those requirements—real or imagined. Marketing teams need to understand the requirements of their business as well as what will motivate their buyers to create the emotional connection that will help make a campaign successful, which takes a lot of time in planning and analyzing (see—you are more like an engineer than you thought). Let's look at the aspects of this through an examination of the classical marketing model a bit more. When marketing acts within a very traditional set of processes, a lot of times it has trouble keeping up with the marketplace and the needs of the business, and oftentimes loses sight of what the customer wants.

Any marketing organization and, in essence, any type of organization that is in any type of business have some fundamental questions they must answer

1. Do you understand your customers today?

2. Are you able to articulate in a valid and relevant way to them why your products and services meet their needs best in today's marketplace?

3. Do you understand what the business needs, or requirements, are?

4. Do you understand what the market demands are?

5. Can you change and adapt your programs and campaigns in order to meet their changing needs/requirements?

Selecting the correct people to set up the product, price, place, and promotion marketing mix shows it requires a lot of skill, effort, and careful and thoughtful selection of the marketplace, especially in today's changing markets. It is often the case that it is an easy thing to conceptualize, but very difficult to implement. Having a plan is critical to this. As markets become more fragmented and more specialized, traditional marketing processes simply cannot keep up. In the discussion of the disconnect of marketing from the business, by the time marketing programs and campaigns are developed and ready for deployment, they are already out of date. Marketing therefore needs a new method in order to reach these newly segmented groups of the market and customers in order to ensure the business succeeds.

Now that we have reviewed some of the precepts of marketing and examined marketing as a discipline, and I have shared so many of my personal beliefs, we are going to examine some of the current processes of marketing and develop ideas as to how we can evolve these processes to be in line with the always changing marketplace today.

Why Do We Care About Writing Great Plans?

Knowing where to get started is one of the most difficult ideas in agile. I'd recommend starting at the beginning: plan. Planning will be different from the traditional method, and we'll explore that a little later in this chapter.

Once you've adequately planned, iterations, failures, and successes will follow. Let's jump in and get started!

Projects and product development efforts ideally start with a vision associated with a business need or direction. This vision is then typically framed in the context of a strategy and associated marketing and business goals and objectives during a management team planning session. Once all of this high-level stuff is laid out, plans on how to reach these objectives can be fleshed out. This doesn't sound too different from our traditional marketing method: management sends down marching orders, and everyone follows. A marketing plan is a document that lays out your recommendations for a business. It describes what you hope to accomplish and what precisely you will do: your objectives, strategies, and tactics.

People write marketing plans for two main reasons: to communicate a plan and to gain support. Virtually every marketing executive writes marketing plans. Brand managers create marketing plans for their brands and present these to category managers. Category managers create marketing plans for their categories, combining several brand plans, and present the plans to general managers. General managers develop plans for their divisions and present the plans to the CEO. CEOs create marketing plans for their companies, and review the plan with the board of directors and key investors and analysts. It is important to remember that even though the marketing executive or general manager is ultimately responsible for the plan, it is best created together with the cross-functional team. Sales, operations, finance, and R&D all provide critical input. Creating a marketing plan without the involvement of cross-functional groups is a bad idea because the resulting plan will almost certainly overlook critical factors. Marketing plans come in a variety of shapes and sizes. My experience with other organizations and interactions with colleagues in many parts of not only the technology industry but also manufacturing, non-profit, and consumer, to name a few, has shown me that some organizations rely heavily on written plans, while other organizations rely on presentations. I know one of the world's leading consumer products retail organizations has a reputation for using detailed memos, while another uses presentations. Some organizations use both. Written or presented, however, the basics are the same.

Complete marketing plans are typically written once a year. However, in some cases, a manager will write a series of different plans in a single year, responding to changing conditions. If a business is performing poorly, for example, a manager may well take a fresh look at it and create a new plan. Some struggling business managers do "re-plans" every month in a desperate bid to improve results. The most important thing to remember about a marketing plan is that it is a recommendation, not a review of facts. It is not the venue for brainstorming or idea generation, nor is it meant to be a reference document containing all that is known about a business. A good marketing plan clearly communicates a plan and gains support for it. There are few things that cause more work-related stress than writing marketing plans. Let's take a look at a traditional marketing plan section by section. I am using some elements from the model that I followed before applying agile for my organization, as well as a review of plans from my research. Again, marketing planning has brought about consternation, and when you take a look at the average marketing plan, it is easy to understand why.

The typical "Section 1" is the situation analysis. It is generally somewhere between 50 and 100 pages long, full of charts and information. One page might show pricing trends for the past five years. Another page has information on competitive promotion plans. Another page might show regional volume and share trends. Still another page shows historical advertising strategy. Densely packed with information, this section can go on and on.

Section 2 is often the plan itself, which is often a large collection of different ideas. There are sometimes dozens of ideas, inspired by the (mistaken) belief that more ideas are always better. There are promotion ideas and advertising ideas and new product ideas and cost-saving ideas.

Section 3 is the long and detailed financial section, which is full of financial trends and information. There is a page on variable margin trends and another page on product cost trends. There are several pages highlighting marketing spending by type: promotions, advertising, public relations, and events. Often the financial pages include projections stretching out five or ten years.

Section 4 contains an assortment of miscellaneous information. There might be a few pages on ethnic marketing programs, a page or two on risks, and some information on the timing of key decisions. The total document is at least 150 pages long. It is professionally bound with a color cover page (especially for the senior managers). Teams often commandeer conference rooms simply to have enough space to assemble the document. Finding an available copy machine on the day that plans are due is almost impossible. Brand teams sometimes take pride in having the largest marketing plan. One might overhear in the company cafeteria, "Well, our plan is so big that we had to use two three-inch binders to hold it all!"

The team then has perhaps 90 minutes to present the plan to the senior managers. Everyone who worked on the document squeezes into the conference room. There are five or more different people presenting, in an effort to give many people visibility in front of senior management. Each person is well-rehearsed and talks quickly, in a valiant but often unsuccessful bid to present all the material by moving at lightning speed. The result is a disappointment for all involved. The senior managers can't make sense of the plan; there is so much data flying around that the big ideas are submerged by the overwhelming clutter. As a result, the senior executives can't fully support the recommendations. The business team in turn gets very little feedback. Most importantly, the team fails in its core task: gaining support and buy-in for the recommendations. By the end of the typical planning process, everyone involved is exhausted and very happy to simply put the plan on the shelf, next to the plans written in prior years, all of which look strikingly alike.

Marketing plans are not going away anytime soon, and few things can do more for your career than becoming great at writing them. Explaining and gaining support for recommendations is a key step in the marketing strategy process, and marketing plans are an integral part of that process. Marketing plan presentations, in particular, will remain important because the meetings can be key venues for gaining support for a plan.

Being able to write good marketing plans will help you in three ways.

First, you can gain support for your recommendations. A good plan is simple, clear, and convincing. The recommendations seem obvious. People tend to support these plans. A weak plan is complicated, confusing, and hard to follow. People naturally ask many questions of these plans, raise concerns, and volunteer ideas. More often than not, they do not support the plan.

Second, the better you become at writing plans, the easier it will be. Make no mistake—it is never effortless, even for the best marketing professionals, but it can be significantly less painful. Some people have to struggle with the plan, wrestling it to the ground in a heroic battle. They spend hours and hours on the process, asking for additional analyses, confusing the team and themselves in the process. Others are able to efficiently produce a document. Because you may well spend two weeks a month writing marketing plans and updates, you will be much better off if you can do it efficiently.

Third, writing strong plans will actually help you deliver better results. The process of writing a plan can help you refine your ideas and tighten your focus. A strong presentation that spells out and supports your key strategies will lead to productive discussions that can improve your plan and, in turn, your business results. It is important to remember, however, that writing plans is only one part of the marketing process. You also need to spend time understanding your brand and your consumer; developing the insights, strategies, and ideas that will build the business; and executing the programs flawlessly. Writing plans is a key step in the process, but great plans alone will not build a business. Programs have to actually get into market.

Okay, so how do I do all this, you may ask—let's look at a four-step process to planning.

1. The first step is understanding the situation. Sound familiar? This is the same as knowing your constituents in the organization as well as outlining the starting point for the adaptability of this book. So again, understanding your brand, the market, and your competition.

2. The second step is developing your plan: the objectives, strategies, and tactics.

3. The third step is communicating and gaining support for the plan, using the ADAM and EVE principles not only as they relate to an adaptive approach for marketing transformation, but also within the confines of the planning process related to any marketing activity, initiatives, or even campaigns, events, and advertising integration.

4. The fourth step is one of the important parts: execution has to be iterative and so must be part of a cycle of constant planning and execution. Again, you are not re-planning but understanding that it has to be flexible, and this takes us back to the first step.

Let's return to the third step: communication and gaining support. It is perhaps one of the most important aspects of marketing planning and plan development. Agile works because the world is always changing. To paraphrase Robert Burns, "the best laid plans of mice and men," which generally refers to the fact that we cannot predict the future no matter how foolproof we think a plan is—exemplifies why the application of the agile approach after the plan is established is critically important. Writing the plan should not be part of the analysis process, nor should it be part of the strategy development process. You should write the plan when you have completed the analysis and when you have a plan in mind. The most common mistake people make when working on marketing plans is confusing understanding the situation with Step 3, writing and presenting the plan.

This mistake becomes apparent during the situation analysis section of the marketing plan. The classic situation analysis section is full of information on the business, the market, and the competition. It is almost always a vast waste of time. Large situation analyses usually just create problems by introducing information that is irrelevant or simply invites more questions. The key thing to remember is that marketing plans are not reference pieces or research reports; they are recommendations. Many people seem to think that the marketing plan should include virtually all the analysis that led to the recommendation. This is simply not the case. The process of analysis is one of exploring options, testing hypotheses, and investigating different avenues, many of which should be dead ends. The process of communicating a marketing plan, on the other hand, is one of providing a strong recommendation with compelling support. Every marketing plan should focus on three things: objectives, strategies, and tactics. These elements form the heart of the marketing plan, and this is where a manager should concentrate. The objectives are the goals for the business—in other words, what the plan is trying to achieve.

Getting the objectives right is essential; if the objectives are off, the rest of the plan will be off. Often, a manager will start the process knowing the objectives, because senior management has already clarified expectations; this is generally a good thing. There should always be a financial objective in a marketing plan, and this should almost always be profit. The core challenge for any business is delivering profits, so this goal should be incorporated into the marketing plan. In addition to a financial objective, a marketing plan may also have a secondary objective that explains how the business will achieve the financial goal. For example, a business may seek to grow profits by +15% per year while also building market share. It is critical that a marketing plan not have too long a list of objectives; limit your list to one or two items. Having too many objectives creates a lack of focus; a plan cannot do 12 different things.

Strategies are the key initiatives—in other words, the most important things the team needs to do in order to deliver the objectives. Strategies are always action-oriented; they are initiatives. Strategies are not theories, values, or principles. For example, entering a new market is a strategy. Launching a new premium product is a strategy. Increasing price is a strategy. Quality and innovation and teamwork are all good things, but they are not strategies; there is no action implied in them. Marketing plans should have only three or four strategies because focus is a key to success; managers have to identify and concentrate on the most important levers to drive the business. A long list of strategies will result in a lack of focus. In addition, it is impossible to remember a long list of strategies; people can remember three or four things, but not nine or twelve things.

Tactics are the detailed programs that will bring the strategies to life. Within any particular strategy, there may be three or four tactics; these are the specific actions that will make the strategies happen. Remember that the objectives, strategies, and tactics should all be linked; objectives should lead to strategies, and strategies should lead to tactics. Each strategy should have associated tactics; if there are no tactics linked to a strategy, it is very likely that the strategy will not happen. Similarly, each tactic should be linked to a strategy; if it isn't, the manager should question why the tactic is important. A marketing plan can be summarized by laying out the objectives, strategies, and tactics on one page. Writing a marketing plan is an important step; a manager has to take a recommendation and present it in a compelling manner. The best approach for writing a marketing plan is to start by constructing the framework; this serves as the skeleton around which the plan will be built. The challenge here is finding the story, or the flow of the document. Once you have the story, you can fill in the details. The most crucial step is adding your support and explaining why each recommendation makes sense. When you have a full draft, you revise, stripping out all the unneeded information and adding data that will bolster your case. Revise again, reworking the plan until it flows logically from page to page, taking the reader or viewer on a journey that leads smoothly to your recommendation.

Seeing the Big Picture So You Can Iterate the Details

Let's take a look at one conceptualization of the marketing process as a whole—it includes the following six items:

- *Implementation*: The actual task of getting the job done
- *Programming allocating and budgeting*: The development of short-term programs that generally focus on integrated approaches for a given product, and on the allocation of scarce resources such as sales efforts or product development time across various products and functions
- *Analysis and research*: The deliberate and careful acquisition and examination of qualitative and quantitative data to improve decision-making
- *Marketing planning*: The development of longer-term plans, which generally have stronger impact than the short-term plans from the second point
- *Strategy formation*: The development of the broadest marketing/business strategies with the longest-term impact
- *Monitoring and auditing*: The review and analysis of programs, plans, and strategies to assess their success and to determine what changes must be made

Although these are sequentially listed, each of these steps of the process is critically connected. Distinctions between a marketing plan and a program vary from organization to organization, but what is important is noting they are two distinct components of the process even if their boundaries and definition as represented here are a bit "fuzzy." One should also understand that each of the steps outlined can be subdivided into smaller elements—for example, marketing planning has subelements, which include market assessment (which is the evaluation and selection of specific product and customer markets) and "product line planning," which, in the context of the software industry, can be illustrated by "product roadmaps." Let's take a look at each of the steps of the marketing process and bring forth the key concepts.

Marketing implementation: Implementation in the context of marketing is different than implementation in other areas of the organization because the focus of marketing is generally outside the organization. Thus, marketing implementation focuses on prospects, customers, distributors, retailers, advertising agencies, etc. Additionally marketing implementation includes dealing with other functional areas to garner support and develop coordination. Most importantly, implementation is people-oriented.

Programming, allocating, and budgeting: Programs are generally related to elements of the marketing mix across all products and markets with the exception that organizations that are focused on singular products or markets develop separate programs for them individually. Allocating is a critical function for distribution of scarce resources that support programs and in some ways determine exclusion vs. inclusion. Because of the scarcity of the resources, budgeting reflects the program's allocations in a set of quantitative forecasts or estimates, which are necessarily transparent beyond the marketing function, typically including sales forecasts, which are a basis for production and product development cycles.

Marketing planning: This typically involves objectives and plans with two- to five-year time horizons and is separate from the day-to-day activity of implementation. It should be noted that implementation is reflective of the combined short- and longer-term objectives outlined in previously developed planning.

Strategy formulation: This is long-term marketing activity tied to the overall business strategy of an organization. Because marketing deals with customers and the competitive environment, it is a critical part of the total strategy process. When done well, it is impossible to separate the marketing strategy from the corporate strategy.

Monitoring and auditing: Because marketing is a mixture of art and science, quantitative and qualitative, and because it involves such a wide variety of interactive variables, it is hard to audit. Standards are few and comparisons are difficult, but a marketing audit is essential because it forces careful review of the past before new plans are developed.

Analysis and research: All marketing decisions should be based on analysis and research; it may not have to be quantitative, but it should be deliberate and match the magnitude of the decision being made. Although a lot has been written about formal analysis and research to support marketing decisions, none of this replaces common sense and good judgment.

These are guidelines showing us how to plan, iterate, fail, and, ultimately, succeed. Since we have at some level determined that we cannot easily define marketing, what may be easier to understand rather than the definition of marketing is what a market is and how we explain our offering to that market. Classically, there are many influences on the market, but at their core, they are the four Ps: product, price, place, and promotion. These four Ps define classic marketing. Each component has a very strong and complex construction in and of itself. Deciding what product to make, defining that product, pulling together the cooperation of departments to produce that product, the facilitation of what that product is and how it is perceived in the marketplace, deciding how to be competitive with respect to the product, taking into account product cost, price, and the competition, and considering the promotion of the product all require marketing. We tend to think of all of these in a classical marketing sense. All steps are followed in a linear order to create one big product, with a big launch and a lot of hullabaloo.

So a market is where we deliver and decide the result of the four Ps. With this classic marketing or traditional marketing method, we find ourselves as marketing professionals asking questions similar to the questions we have about marketing planning and writing marketing plans: how do I get knowledge about what my customers want? How do I target my customers? How do I get my product to market? What outlets are available to me or my company? What combination of direct and indirect outlets do I need to work? How do I gain the outlets I need and manage conflicting outlets? How do I manage the customer's perception of the product in the marketplace? And many more...

Based on the six-step conceptualization just outlined, it is also important to understand the lateral connection to the activities supported and influenced by the marketing process as it relates to the functional operational connections in an enterprise. This discussion of the marketing process emphasizes the importance of marketing to the ongoing success of an organization. The differentiating factor of what makes marketing both integral and necessary is that marketing has concerns in and outside the organization and in the foundational glue that drives company success. If the marketing process is not rigorously taken through each of the steps, a given company may fail in meeting its goals. This process must be supported as an integral part of business planning and part of a holistic mechanism for driving a company's objectives.

The best way to enable that holistic approach is to ensure the proper integration of leadership across the various organizations, all marching to the same goal of success. That success must be defined the same way for everybody—revenue. I had the recent privilege of talking with some of the world's business transformation leaders, and one of the ideas that kept coming forward was simply "Cash is king." I believe the more you can get people to agree to real, tangible, quantifiable goals, the more successful you will be.

After all, as I mentioned before, the measure of success is based on a continued sustainable growing influence in the market through branding as well as increasing revenue and market share. Sales and marketing have always been tied together, as they are integral to mutual objectives and success; yet there tends to be a disconnect when the organization goals are not aligned around common long and short term incentives. Getting back to the complexities of the marketing process and the necessary integration of each of the factors, organizations across an enterprise must be working in synch, otherwise there will be a lot of fingerpointing and blame when objectives are not met. Each of the steps in the marketing process and therefore the business strategy has a high dependency on a critical component for each step, and that is people. Earlier I suggested that the most important criterion for a successful marketing organization and certainly any organization is people—so adding to the classic four Ps, I am going to suggest a fifth P, people. This is one of the most important Ps and a critical factor when relating to all the elements of product, promotion, price, and placement.

Okay, so what does this have to do with agile? First and foremost, as you try to transform a process organization, or anything for that matter, you have to understand what you are starting with. The steps and procedures outlined in this chapter will bring us to a conclusion of taking the elements of traditional methodology and understanding, disciplines from "external" organizations, such as application development in this case, and aligning them with the things I feel are instinctive on some level, obvious at another level, pragmatic and innovative at a third level. Whatever the reasons, if the program is stalled because of tradition, road-blocked because of organizational constraints, or simply a lack of vision, we have to know where we start. I would venture to say one of the most important aspects of agile marketing management is being comfortable changing things yet understanding the past enough to be able to not make the same mistakes twice. It's okay to fail, but not to fail doing the same things over and over again. That, in fact, is the definition of insanity, and while some have accused me of that for some of the tactics I've tried, they've never accused me of it for trying tactics that didn't work twice in the same framework as it simply has not happened.

The role of marketing in any organization is to improve the performance of the organization by establishing and nurturing profitable relationships with customers. Marketing professionals have many different ways to accomplish this result. The practice of marketing is much more complicated than the unfortunate stereotypes of fast-talking salespeople and manipulative advertisers. On this note, I will explain the major choices that professional marketing professionals face and the ways in which marketing decisions are made. A marketing professional is the person who must decide which market opportunities to pursue, which customers to target, what products and services to offer when and at what price, how to communicate with prospects and customers, what distribution systems to use, and more. These interrelated decisions, when brought together into an integrated whole, are called a company's marketing program.

Executing the marketing program is how the organization attracts, retains, and grows its customers. The word market is a noun, not a verb, and it refers to where buyers and sellers come together to do business. When one hears the word market used as a verb, the speaker is typically using the word as a synonym for "sell," which is but a part of what professional marketing professionals actually do. Marketing professionals are at the intersection of the firm and the market. This means they have the dual responsibility of representing the market (customers, competitors, and trade) to the other members of the company and of representing the company to the market. For example, a marketing professional helps other managers in an organization understand what customers want and how this affects managerial decisions. For example, at a meeting, the marketing professional may say, "I understand how that idea would help our production efficiency, but here is what it would mean for our customers..."

A marketing professional also makes promises to customers about what the company has to offer. In fact, a lot of what marketing professionals do for customers is make promises that other members of the organization then have to fulfill. There are many aspects of marketing that have become highly quantifiable and scientific, but there still remain many mysteries about how markets operate. Some of the most basic questions are still beyond our ability to answer because they involve human behavior—the fifth P, people. Typical mysteries of marketing include the following:

- Why do people choose one brand instead of another?
- Why do people fall out of love with a product like Beanie babies? (I have storage boxes full of those lovable stuffed animals.)
- Why do people fall in love with a new product like the iPhone? (Well, I am a huge iPhone fan because of the innovation and practical applications for use—oh, wait, look at that pragmatic innovation!)
- Why does "as advertised on TV" really work? (Okay, so maybe I understand that one in general—the less than optimal commercials are a promise of a silver bullet solution or perhaps a pragmatic innovation, and the price point is a key.)

Marketing is truly more about understanding people than it is about products or techniques, and that's what makes marketing particularly interesting and challenging. The marketing professional's job is to understand people and markets, to help create product and service offerings, and to influence and serve customers. Key to this, as I have repeatedly said, including the incorporation of the Web 2.0 premise, is a marketing plan. A marketing plan is a document that specifies what marketing program an organization intends to undertake, why that program makes sense, what the program will require to be implemented, and what results are expected. It is the disciplined preparation of a marketing strategy and, as such, is pivotal to the entire organization's strategy. Preparing a marketing plan is not a simple, repetitive exercise of filling in the blanks of a checklist in a linear fashion. Rather, each circumstance requires you to decide which analysis and decisions are appropriate. You will find that you must move back and forth between the various parts of the marketing plan to ensure the parts all fit together in an integrated way. I have organized this discussion of marketing management in eight sections and categories to help you better understand where the areas you can iterate are:

- Understand the marketing challenge
    - Is this a new business startup or an existing business?
    - What are the performance objectives?
    - What decisions need to be made?
- Identify market opportunities
    - What are customer needs, wants, habits?
    - What are the competitors doing?
    - How do opportunities fit with company capabilities?
- Identify a primary target market
    - Which customers are particularly attractive?
    - Which customers are available?

- Decide how to entice customers
    - What message should be sent?
    - What mix of communication methods should be used?
- Decide on pricing
    - What should be the price at each level of distribution?
    - How should price changes be handled?
- Decide how to keep/grow the customer base
    - What customer service program should be offered?
    - What retention/development program should be used?
- Ensure the financials make sense
    - What will the marketing program cost?
    - What results are expected?
- Understand what we need to know for feedback into the loop
    - What results and experiences should be monitored?
    - What market research should be done for next time?

Understand the Marketing Challenge

The first distinction to make in preparing a marketing plan is whether this is a startup situation or an existing, ongoing situation. For example, if I have an idea for a new product that I think is new to the market and certainly new to me, then I will start in a different place preparing a marketing plan than if I have joined an organization that has been selling comforters for years, where my job may be to fine-tune the marketing program for next year. The distinction with them is that we have a startup marketing professional who is looking for market opportunities, is wondering how to get started into a market, and thus has many decisions to make for the first time (such as what price I should start with). And we have the existing or ongoing marketing professional, who is wondering what is working and what needs to be changed—but, of course, should be alert for new opportunities too.

If you are in the startup situation, I suggest reading the rest of this section as it is primarily applicable to you, but your real work starts as it relates to the marketing plan, which is about identifying market opportunities. If your role is steadier, I suggest the best place to start is with a clear understanding of what performance you have achieved and are trying to improve. This will help you decide what marketing challenges you should focus upon. For example, suppose you are a large retailer. The challenges of marketing for that company may resolve similarly to challenges of an individual store, so you may seek ways to improve store-specific approaches that are also applicable for the overall organization because, at some level, a large retailer like Macy's is defined in a lot of ways by each individual store.

Before examining all the marketing activity options, you need to know what exactly you are trying to achieve. Do you need more people to come through the door? Do you need to convert more of the current browsing traffic into paying customers? Do you need to find a way to get each customer, on average, to spend more? These questions matter greatly in terms of what marketing plan you would develop. For example, if the marketing challenge were to get more people to come into the store, you might focus attention on media advertising to ensure people know about your store. On the other hand, if the marketing challenge were to convert more browsers into customers, you might focus attention on your sales associates: do they need more training, a different compensation scheme, or what? Or perhaps the store isn't carrying the right kinds of products, and thus browsers can't find what they want to buy. Alternatively, if the marketing challenge were to increase the transaction size of customers, you might re-arrange displays to encourage more related item purchases (a technique I see used in some of my favorite clothing stores and even my husband's cigar store) or consider changes in the selection of products carried.

You also need to know where you should apply most of the improvements. It may be that a more holistic approach to making adjustments or a focus on improving the marketing strategy is primarily the direction you need to take. This means you would need to determine first whether the current marketing strategy is appropriate and change it if it needs improvement, and second, whether the current marketing strategy is being properly executed and work on that, if it needs improvement. Sometimes, it becomes obvious that the majority of the marketing approach is fine, but there is a need to make changes to part of it. For example, sometimes competitors drop their prices, thus requiring you to reconsider your price. This may or may not necessitate a review of the entire marketing approach you are following. In other words, there are so many possible marketing activities for an ongoing marketing professional that it is critical that you define the marketing challenges of most importance to you at the outset of preparing a marketing plan. Not only does this help decide what to do, but it also avoids unnecessary work on other topics and makes it easier to gauge results later.

Whether you are an ongoing marketing professional or a startup marketing professional, the question will arise as to what metrics of success to use for marketing.

Some commonly accepted measures of performance that concern all marketing professionals are as follows:

- *Total sales*: This might be expressed in dollar or unit volume.
- *Sales per customer*: This might be expressed in dollars or units per customer share of a customer's total purchases in a category (e.g., books) over time, or frequency of purchase.
- *Market share*: This is usually expressed as a percentage of the company's (or brand's) total sales relative to sales by all competitors in this category in a specified market area.
- *Sales growth*: This indicates the trend, usually expressed in percentage terms, from one period to another.
- *Total profitability*: This is expressed either as the dollar gross profit (margin) or dollar net profit.
- *Customer profitability*: This is expressed as the average dollar profit per customer or by customer group.
- *Awareness*: This is expressed as the percentage of the target market that is aware of the firm or specific things about the firm.
- *Satisfaction*: This may be measured by "happiness" or willingness to refer to a friend or colleague.
- *Loyalty*: There are a variety of measures used, but the idea is to express what percentage of customers are repeat customers vs. new customers.

There are many other measures of performance that marketing professionals use, both to set objectives and track progress. The point here is the value of establishing up front what the marketing effort is supposed to accomplish and then use those metrics as a guide for what to do and how to measure results. The only measures that really matter, though, are ultimately ones that can show what your customers will buy or have bought and most importantly what your stakeholders care about. I have seen many a great analytic marketer have reams of data that no one cares about or trusts, and if they'd only listened up front to what their stakeholders wanted reporting on, they could have been seen as wildly successful. Don't fall on your sword trying to deliver everything; figure out what's important to your top stakeholders and focus there.

Identify Market Opportunities

Identifying and assessing market opportunities are vital tasks for marketing professionals—that is, finding out what the marketing professional's organization *could* do, not necessarily what it is currently doing. Of course, identifying opportunities must be followed by selecting which opportunities to pursue. In this respect, the function of marketing is much more than simply selling what the company already makes or advertising what the company already has.

Marketing is, at its core, strategic; that is, it is about deciding what to do and for whom. In other words, marketing should lead the firm's strategy by helping the firm produce what can be sold, not just sell what can be produced. This distinction is critical in planning but also as a whole to the future of an organization. Classic discussions of buggy whips come to mind, where obsolescence drives out a market for a product unless we understand the market and the opportunities. Even in today's world, you can look at the transformation of Apple into consumer electronic vs. personal computers—taking features from one market segment, identifying what will be the next segment, and making it part of a company strategy, supported by a key marketing approach made them successful. They had a common objective all along of transforming the perception of the computer as being something complicated into a tool for use for every person and was the foundation of the marketing strategy. Marketing starts before products are made; marketing is much more than just selling existing products. Identifying market opportunities can start in one of several places: one has an idea for a new product or service and then begins to see whether there really is a market for it; one has observed problems and frustrations among customers and looks for a better "solution" than those offered by competitors; one is tracking broad trends, seeking new ideas.

Wherever you start, identifying and assessing opportunities has four major components:

- Environmental scanning
- Competitive analysis
- Customer/consumer analysis
- Self-analysis

Environmental scanning refers to close observation of trends in the marketplace. This could include tracking political developments, economic issues, social trends, and technology developments (these are sometimes collectively called PEST analysis). The challenge, of course, is not going crazy by trying to track everything in a market. The best way to do this is to have a frame of reference first. The difficulty is information overload; one of the great things and one of the worst things about the technology aspect of PEST is the amount of information available. As an example, if I am in the pizza business, I do care a lot about food preparation and consumption in general; I care about what people believe about issues like real cheese vs.

artificial, about energy efficiency, about carbohydrates in the diet; I care about extending the pizza line into other related foods and warming or packaging possibilities, etc. And, of course, I care about all kinds of other issues that affect my business. But I will have to draw the line somewhere, or I will spend all my time reading about issues and trends and have no time to do anything about my business.

The best way to do this is to start any of my business reading with a question: does this information have any bearing on my current or future business? Is it about an opportunity (something that might improve my business performance) or about a threat (something that might diminish my business performance)? If it is neither an opportunity nor a threat, then it may be interesting reading, but it is not part of my relevant environmental scan. An environmental scan is about what is happening or might happen external to my organization. As a marketing professional, I can add the most value to my organization by picking up "weak signals" in the environment and helping my team do something about those before our competitors do. If, on the other hand, all I do as a marketing professional is draw attention to the obvious, I have added little value to my team.

Timing matters in marketing: one does not want to be too early or too late in a market. It is relatively easy to prepare a list of PEST trends in any industry. It is much more difficult to develop a corresponding list of implications for a company in that industry. An implication is an answer to this question: "So what does it mean specifically for us?" For example, we have all heard about rising energy costs and the need for alternative sources of energy. So what does that mean for a particular company? What should that company start doing or stop doing in its marketing program?

Competitive analysis refers to a broad range of efforts to identify, understand, and anticipate those who would take one's customers away. Who else is offering something similar to what you are offering or planning to offer—and how successful are they? Competitive analysis includes comparison of marketing programs and marketing performance. If the competition has a much greater share of market, much greater financial resources, and so on, then they will have significant advantages that a marketing professional must overcome to compete directly. Perhaps the business should find another market to focus on. Finally, what changes are expected in the competitive environment (new competitors, new ways of competing) that will affect a business's performance? Understanding, anticipating, and dealing with competition is a core part of every marketing professional's job, so thinking about competition actually comes in at every step in the marketing process.

Competitive differentiation refers to seeking meaningful (to the customer) ways of being different (usually this means "superior") than competitors. Are there any exploitable deficiencies in competitive products or services, in their service, in their prices, in anything that matters to the customer? For example, if the competition is slow to respond to service calls, perhaps a company can differentiate itself by providing rapid response. It is important, however, to focus on factors that matter to customers, not simply to your company. The key is to look at everything from the customer's perspective and ask frankly: how will a customer decide to choose one offering over another?

"Customer analysis" refers to efforts to understand end users, buyers, and intermediate buyers/sellers. Marketing professionals are always looking for customers. Prospects are individuals, households, or organizations that a marketing professional thinks might be converted into customers— customers and clients are those people who actually buy. Consumer is another term often used to describe members of a market, but more accurately, these are the people who actually use a product or service. Customers buy products and services to satisfy their needs and wants, so it only makes sense that marketing professionals must work hard to understand what these needs and wants are.

Marketing professionals want to know what customers are looking for and how they go about making their own choices of which marketing professionals to patronize and which products and services to buy from them. For this reason, many marketing professionals start their thinking by considering individual potential customers or groups of customers (also known as segments, discussed later). These customers or segments may be in the consumer market (meaning individuals, households, etc.) or the business/institutional market (meaning organizations). Some usual questions marketing professionals pose about potential and current customers are as follows:

- What wants and needs are people trying to satisfy?
- What is particularly important to them? For example, is convenience more important than price when purchasing dinner?
- Are these needs and wants strong or weak?
- Can customers be influenced to want something a little different?
- What motivation lies behind the choice of a product or service? For example, what is the reason that they are interested in buying a new vehicle when the car they have is working just fine?
- Is the business buyer more interested in low initial price or low operating costs?

- Where do they get information about products, services, stores, and so on, as they proceed through a process of considering a purchase?
- Where do they shop, and why there? For example, why are some shoppers purchasing books on the Internet rather than from book stores?
- When do they go through this shopping/purchasing process? For example, do shoppers make their weekly grocery trip on Thursday or Saturday?

All of these questions are designed to discover insights into how the marketing professional can influence this shopping/purchasing process so that the marketing professional gets the business. In other words, research and analysis about prospects and customers are conducted not to uncover interesting facts, but rather to find actionable ideas. In your analysis of any marketing situation, I suggest you consider these questions, but as you do, focus on whether there are any meaningful implications of your analysis. For example, you may conclude that there is a group of customers who really prefer to shop for your product in the middle of the night not only because they might be night shift workers but also because they are part of a global potential that you must take into consideration. That would mean in consequence that you should next explore whether there are enough of these potential customers to constitute a viable market. Good answers to these questions require more than guesswork. Marketing professionals rely not only on close scrutiny of their experience with prospects and customers, but also on market research.

Market segmentation is a concept with great power for marketing professionals. It is very helpful in the process of target market selection and in making other marketing decisions. The basic idea of market segmentation is very simple: people differ, so we can't assume everyone is equally a market opportunity for us; therefore, divide them into different groups where each group is comprised of similar people. Some segments will be far more attractive to the marketing professional than others.

Let's consider the difference between "tweens" (7–12 years old) and "the mature market" (over 50 years old) for a marketing professional of cosmetics. Preferences for colors and fragrances, how much they are willing to pay, and much more will vary tremendously between these two segments. Based on some of my research and sessions with folks at other organizations, let's consider a large, well-known cosmetic company that has a product that is a skin moisturizer brand that has been around for a long time. They transform the brand by shortening the name and presenting the core and related products to stand for "anti-aging" (vs. moisturizing) to appeal to market segmentation products for the aging baby boomers (those born between 1946 and 1964).

Another example is a powdered beverage company that has a strong brand positioned for 5–12-year-old kids who are looking for a fun, hip, tasty drink with lots of flavor variety that moms find inexpensive. This product has been a long-term marketing success, with a dominant share in its category. Its competitors include other powdered drinks of all kinds, as well as soft drinks and juices.

There are two key consequences of market segmentation. First, the general customer-analysis questions posed previously will be answered differently for each segment. This means that without segmentation, a marketing professional may have the wrong ideas about a market opportunity. Second, when there are segments, a marketing professional must decide which segments to choose; this will be discussed in the next section.

The practice of segmentation can be complicated. For example, if the challenge were to segment the bicycle market, the marketing professional might begin by bicycle types. This would be a product-based segmentation approach and would separate children's bicycles, touring road bikes, off-road mountain bikes, and so on. The marketing professional may begin segmenting by considering different users, which is a customer-based segmentation approach and would separate weekend users, enthusiasts, racers, and so on. Similarly, the marketing professional may consider segmenting by differences in sensitivity to price (high, medium, low sensitivity), or place of distribution—specialty store, mass merchant, and so on. The choices of dimensions are endless because of the many ways people differ from one another—there is that fifth P again.

The point of segmentation is to find groups that make marketing sense. If the marketing professional chooses to focus on children's bicycles, the rest of the marketing program should be consistent with everything he or she knows or suspects about this segment of the market. For example, if the marketing professional knows that children's bikes are usually purchased by their parents and that parents are especially concerned about safety, he or she might emphasize safety in product selections, advertising, in-store merchandising, and so on. In other words, a marketing professional's understanding of segmentation leads to target market selection, which in turn leads to the rest of the marketing decisions.

Identifying and assessing market opportunities involve matching company capabilities with what will win in the marketplace. It is important you do self analysis for your own company, An attractive opportunity may exist, but not all firms can win at pursuing it. The aspect of market opportunity assessment involves understanding one's own strengths and weaknesses. Strengths are those characteristics and capabilities that are superior to competition and can be drawn on to exploit opportunities and deal with threats. Weaknesses are deficiencies. As a marketing professional, I may be particularly strong at understanding the needs of a certain segment (such as recreational power boaters) or particularly weak at finding new prospects (such as I don't accept enough media calls for interviews). Strengths and weaknesses are relative to specific opportunities and threats, not generalized statements. The combination of an analysis of strengths and weaknesses, opportunities and threats is often referred to as SWOT analysis and is common in overall business strategy formulation, not just marketing strategy creation.

Select a Target Market

Whereas the previous section was about identifying what opportunities look interesting, this section will involve deciding *what* to do. Early on in the process of making marketing decisions, the marketing professional must deal with the question, "Who are we really trying to serve?" In other words, a major marketing decision is the selection of a primary target market, which refers to those customers a marketing professional is most interested in appealing to. Having a primary target market does not necessarily mean that a business won't sell to people who don't fit the target characteristics, but rather that the marketing offer is being designed with a particular audience in mind.

A target market enables a marketing professional to focus the offer and the delivery of that offer. There can be more than one target market group; for example, a well-known fast food company targets children and adults, but targets each separately and specifically. Similarly, a discount insurance provider utilizes simultaneous ad campaigns targeting specific segments of the consuming public. Most marketing professionals find the selection of a primary target market a useful way to focus their efforts, and I suggest this approach to you in most situations. The idea is to select the part of the market that represents an attractive opportunity for the marketing professional because he or she may be able to serve it better than competitors and hence build a profitable business. The alternative, not specifying a target (which is trying to be all things to all people), is rarely successful in today's competitive, crowded marketplace. For example, many full-line department stores were once the one-stop shopping places for the majority of the population. However, they have been outmaneuvered and outperformed by specialist retailers, who target segments of the public with more compelling, more narrowly defined offers.

Again, there are as many ways to specify target markets as there are to describe people. For example, one might select the following:

- A certain age group (such as teenagers)
- An income group (such as $50,000–$100,000 in household income)
- An attitudinal or behavioral group (such as those who ride motorcycles)
- A geographic group (such as those who live in a particular city)
- A psychographic group (such as those whose lifestyle involves travel experiences rather than accumulation of household possessions)

With such a broad range of options for describing a target market, the marketing professional should avoid simplistic target market specifications such as "women between the ages of 25 to 34." The key is to meet the following criteria in selecting a target market:

- Does this definition include a large enough market to be worth serving? This is the important issue of substantial market size (and its potential growth).
- Is the target accessible to the marketing professional? For example, specifying "all Canadians" as the target market makes little sense if one is able to distribute only to those who live in Halifax.
- Does the target specification provide us with a different way of thinking about customers than our competition? Does it identify a group we can serve in a differentiated, better way than competitors?
- Does the target specification provide guidance for the rest of the organization in terms of obtaining the performance outcomes desired? For example, specifying a target customer who has "blue eyes and feels young at heart" may not help the marketing professional find, reach, or affect such customers. This criterion of actionability is very important.

Decide How to Attract Customers

As we have covered throughout this book, a lot of people underestimate what marketing is or does. They think it simply means advertising or promotion, and while promotion is one of the five Ps (certainly advertising and promotion are very visible aspects of a marketing program), these activities are but a part of the whole marketing program and only a part of the whole effort to attract customers. Marketing professionals need to communicate incentives to buy, and they do this through a variety of communication methods, including the following:

- *Advertising*: The use of mass media such as broadcast (e.g., radio, TV), print (e.g., newspapers, magazines), and electronic (e.g., web sites)
- *Promotion*: The use of coupons, samples, sales, contests, and other sales incentives
- *Point-of-purchase displays*: The use of in-store techniques such as shelf signs
- *Direct mail*: The use of materials sent through the regular postal system
- *Web marketing*: The use of the Internet and e-mail
- *Telemarketing*: The use of the telephone to contact customers via voice or fax
- *Packaging*: The use of graphics and other packaging elements
- *Personal selling*: The use of people to speak for the product or service
- *Publicity*: The use of the media to provide free coverage in their stories related to the product or service

The overall trend in marketing communications is toward dialogue with customers as opposed to monologue. Two-way communication between companies and their customers is becoming increasingly common. Not only that, but, as noted at the beginning of this chapter, customers are now using technology to talk to each other about the businesses they buy goods and services from. As a consequence, there are many other techniques being used to reach out and speak with customers and prospects. The growing use of social networking in marketing (including blogs, buzz marketing, online communities, etc.) has dramatically changed the ways marketing professionals interact with customers. In each instance of communication, typical decisions include who will be targeted, what the purpose is (the objectives), what to say (the message), how to say it (the execution, including whether the target market is involved in spreading the message or in interacting with the marketing professional), who will convey the message (media), when it will be done (the schedule), how much will be spent (the budget), and how it will be assessed (the evaluation). When developing a marketing program, all of these questions need to be addressed.

Communication Objectives

The first step is to establish objectives that are consistent with the overall marketing challenge being faced. Here are some possible examples:

- Communicate attributes, benefits, product/service improvements
- Make service tangible, more understood
- Introduce extensions, incentives, special deals
- Increase amount or frequency of use
- Decrease frequency of use
- Increase uses
- Attract new users
- Motivate/educate staff service providers

Message Design, Budget, and Media

The next step is to design the message, which some call the creative strategy. To design the message, the marketing professional considers the target market, the desired response from that target, the basic selling proposition, the desired image and tone of the message, and the attention-getting techniques that might be used (e.g., a product demonstration or testimonial from a well-known athlete). Deciding how much to spend is difficult. Typically, there are several aspects to a communications campaign, and a marketing professional must decide how much to spend on each part of the campaign.

To set the budget, some marketing professionals use approaches such as an "advertising to sales ratio," while others use an "all we can afford" approach. Some set a total amount and then divide it into pieces, while others establish what each piece might cost and then sum the amounts to create a total budget. In short, there is no common agreement on how to decide on a communications budget. Media choices include deciding which media to use (e.g., TV or radio), the placement within each medium (e.g., the section of the newspaper), and scheduling (e.g., when an outdoor ad should appear). Each choice involves many considerations, such as the ability of the medium to deliver color, the costs to reach the target, the medium's audience characteristics, when the medium is available, and what media competitors use. Each medium usually provides some statistics to help marketing professionals decide whether the prices charged are worthwhile. Here are some common audience measurement terms:

- *Circulation*: In print media, circulation measures the one-time physical distribution of the publication to any individual or household. In broadcast media, anyone tuned in once or more often to a station in a week is in that station's weekly circulation.

- *Reach*: This measures the cumulative, unduplicated target audience exposed to the advertiser's message, by media, expressed as a percentage of the target group population in a defined geographic area (also known as penetration).
- *Frequency*: This means the average number of occasions that the persons reached have been exposed to an ad during a given period of time.
- *Impressions*: The number of impressions equals the total number of ads scheduled times the total target audience exposed to each occasion.

Making marketing communication decisions is a complex business.

Evaluating Communication Effectiveness

Evaluating communications can be tricky because so much else is occurring at the same time in marketing. With the exception of carefully controlled direct marketing campaigns like direct mail and possibly e-mail, most communications are difficult to relate directly to sales results. Typically, marketing professionals begin their evaluation of a communications idea qualitatively, asking questions such as the following:

- Does it focus on benefits important to customers?
- Is it believable and compelling?
- Is it clear and memorable?
- Is it true and in good taste?
- Does it stand out from competitive campaigns?
- Does it represent the company appropriately?

Then, the marketing professionals typically move to more quantitative evaluation of communications to answer the basic question, "Does it pay off?" Measures used include the following:

- Non-behavioral measures
  - Awareness of company, product or message
  - Aided and unaided recall of the advertising
  - Opinions, attitudes, and intentions
- Behavioral measures
  - Inquiries and complaints
  - Traffic (e.g., number of people coming into a store)

- Sales (e.g., trial and repeat rates, dollars spent, frequency of purchase)

Don't Be Afraid to Try New, Untested Mediums like Web 2.0

Web 2.0, according to Wikipedia, "refers to a perceived second generation of web development and design that aims to facilitate communication, secure information sharing, interoperability, and collaboration on the World Wide Web." So it would stand to reason and be obvious that the innovation of technology must in some ways produce an innovation in marketing to address the technology advancements, mainly because Web 2.0 is about all the new ways we are using the Web. So consequently we have "Marketing 2.0," which is the label being given in tandem to the new ways marketing is being practiced with Web 2.0 concepts and tools. These advancements are prevalent in the area of the dynamics of marcom or marketing communications—the way that messaging flows between buyers and sellers to enable the exchange of goods—and the advancements are directly impacting marketing and marketing professionals as a whole. This impact revolves around the cornerstone of the Marketing 2.0 paradigm, tapping into the explosion of the idea behind "social networking." While some may not yet totally understand the interworkings of what the "social media" impact is, was, and will be on marketing and business as a whole, we need to examine the foundation of the technical advancement of personalized social enablement.

Social media will impact communication in ways that are yet to be fully realized or thought of. This is not a work of science fiction or generic personalization advertising sent to a smartphone. The social impact will be similar to online dating, with advanced sophistication so that you will not have to fill out endless questionnaires to match you to the consumables you "must have," but also what you truly need for day-to-day living. There are glimpses of this already with recommendation engines pioneered in the online space with Amazon.com. Getting from where we are to where we will be will happen sooner than we think, and the transition reflects the greatest dynamic in media communication and therefore marketing communication—more than any other impact there has been in the past.

Let's take a moment to reflect on this. It is because Web 2.0 enables data access about consumers, competition, market segments, and most importantly behavioral analysis that this will be so different. The challenge will be in putting together the correct formula to tap into how the personalization will work—or will it? What does mass media do differently than what we expect personalized behavior media to do? Mass media influences opinion. So while there is increased segmentation in the markets because consumer are wanting something slightly unique to and for them, there is the significant influence of the reasons they want what they want. So on the other side of the coin, the question is, do the technology-enabled social networks really have an impact? Let's take a look at a couple of studies I've come across in my research.

A study conducted by the US Conference Board[2] shows us that about 25% of Internet users spend time on social networking sites, with 50% of those returning to these sites multiple times a day.

As a side note, this has led to stringent policies on web access and site restrictions in 87% of the Fortune 500. This type of policy demonstrates a determined effort to prevent integrations of employees with these types of things for a variety of reasons, most of which are categorized in three manners:

- Secure infrastructure issue and violation of security policy
- Confidential information and intellectual property protection
- Privacy laws
- Productivity deterrent

There are countless others, but if we look behind these types of policies, then this social media is not just "kid stuff," and certainly it is not just young people. Recent trend in consumption of social media show that millions of Facebook users, reported that the top 50% of high-activity users were 32 years old or older. Now it is important to realize that maybe this just shows that social media is a communications vehicle for folks to "network" with their own peers in purely a social fashion and that, in the case of the leading social media site, it relates to the professional or older crowd, in that it is similar to an ongoing class reunion where friends across the miles can keep in touch about what is happening in their lives and the lives of folks they are friends with and their friends and then their friends. It also can loosely provide a means for business colleagues to keep in touch, husbands and wives to communicate if they are apart or travel for their work, etc. But most importantly it creates communities of folks with common interests and is a very impactful way to monitor or provide a vehicle for word-of-mouth (WOM). So then the arrival of Web 2.0 and therefore Marketing 2.0 represents, in some ways, a "paradigm shift" for marketing professionals and marketing as a whole.

---

[2] Conference Board, "What Others Think of You Matters: Manage and Boost Your Corporate Reputation Using Social Media," 2008.

This impact revolves around some key ideas that "Marketing 2.0" brings to the table, including the following:

- Higher confidence in the Internet and use of the Internet for commerce
- A platform for many differing thoughts and voices that increase doubt or skepticism related to marketing communications, including press releases, blogs, advertising, etc.
- Explosion of smart communication devices for unlimited access (for a fee) and availability of Internet connections
- Widespread availability of wireless networks for the home with broadband capability
- Advances in search technology and much easier searchability of the Internet
- Increased isolation of individuals and increased physical separation due to organizational "telecommuting," travel requirements, etc., resulting in desires for "virtual socialization"—social media

Now to say there is a complete paradigm shift may be overstating the influence. There are consumers that will take advantage of the ease of use related to the promises and delivery of the Web 2.0 age, but it is never a complete replacement, even though folks always make the claim as such. Radio never replaced print, and television never replaced radio. It became the means of communication, and the elements of that communication are what is important to understand. Marketing has to understand and ensure that social media is part of any marketing plan as a predecessor to any other marketing objective. Within the constraints of any marketing approach, including agile, planning is the single most important aspect.

With so many routes to market, the market segmentation plan is the key to success. So what may have been termed or characterized as traditional interruption marketing, exactly like an advertisement in a publication or a commercial interrupting your favorite program, is now a way of life. By the way, we must also take this shift in culture into account as we are understanding marketing and marketing planning. It is about not only social media and Web 2.0, but also getting customers what they want when they want— much like a DVR. Traditional marketing stems from the idea that sellers controlled what was said about what they sold, whether it was consumer goods, insurance policies, or services like banking or financial planning. The sellers also very much controlled who got to hear their messages and when they heard them. What we now must accommodate is that Marketing 2.0 shifts much greater control of information flow to the potential customer.

As I mentioned previously, the customer or consumer chooses what information to consume, when to access it, and, perhaps most importantly, has the opportunity to add to the information flow that others potential customers may see, their peers may see, and importantly the group of virtual social contacts may see. To quantify what marketing has to do has been labeled " permission or conversational marketing" or put simply, the seller has to be invited into the customer's attention. When the seller gains that attention, customers enter a conversation to express or dialogue with companies and with one another about what they want, what they like and don't like, what their experiences have been, etc. Web 2.0 tools enable uncontrollable and exponential dissemination of these conversations. In many ways, perhaps the ideas of Marketing 2.0 are a fulfillment of what I mentioned previously, and that is potential customers frequently trust and value the opinions of one another more than they do the commercial messages of corporations trying to sell them something—that is, word-of-mouth (WOM).

WOM has never been controllable by marketing professionals, but today WOM is active in ways unimaginable to traditional marketing as it existed. Truly WOM as it is enabled emulates classical best types of communication—conversational. There are two primary approaches as it relates to WOM online:

- Marketers can listen, observe, and learn (of course, they must respect privacy rights and the rules of online communities as they do this).
- Marketers can actively enter into the conversation, attempting to steer it or encourage greater dissemination of it (some refer to such interventions around WOM as "buzz marketing" or "viral marketing").

The techniques for social networking are changing constantly, but here is a list of the major ones today:

- Blog (personal; easily updated web sites plus blogging aggregators, e.g., Twitter)
- Online communities (e.g., Facebook, MySpace, LinkedIn)
- Podcasting and videocasting (e.g., YouTube)
- Virtual worlds (e.g., Second Life)
- Widgets and wikis (e.g., Wikipedia)
- Online games and contests
- RSS feeds (means "really simple syndication" to track other sites)

Depending on your point of view, all of the foregoing can be regarded as Web 2.0 features or as potential marketing tools. Sophisticated marketing professionals are experimenting with and learning about Marketing 2.0: new methods of marketing research to get more authentic views of customers; new ways to design and promulgate marketing communication campaigns; and new ways to complement distribution systems. As a consequence, new markets are being opened and new measures of marketing performance are being created. However, Marketing 2.0 does *not* mean that all of the rest of marketing and the elemental components of marketing are obsolete. On the contrary, successful use of Marketing 2.0 techniques requires effective application of the fundamental principles of marketing, whether it is marketing process, which is one of the most often overlooked aspects of marketing, especially as it relates to marketing transformation, or marketing strategy.

The advancement in capability for communication is certainly an additional paradigm, but it is not a panacea. What we must understand is that the opportunity that Marketing/Web 2.0 offers is an almost multidimensional means of market targeting, segmentation, personalization, and, potentially, influence. What it doesn't offer is the way to best take advantage of the opportunity. We will not replace traditional marketing methods, nor will we be able to incorporate all the possible permutations and combinations of very specific, targeted markets. What we can do is take into account the many opportunities provided and apply them in marketing practice.

Personal Selling

Unlike mass media or direct communications, personal selling requires people to interact with prospects and customers. Personal selling can range from simple transaction processing at a cashier's desk in a grocery store to complex team selling in a business-to-business situation. For some companies, personal selling is their prime marketing communications approach.

There are many ideas about how to effectively sell. Conventional wisdom about personal selling dictates that the marketing professional must follow these steps:

- Do your homework first (know the product, know the customer).
- Approach the customer (the opening).
- Present to the customer (focus on the benefits).
- Ask for the order (the close).

Sales training helps a salesperson learn what to say about a product or service and the company (e.g., what can be promised about delivery and installation) and helps a salesperson learn selling techniques. Selling techniques include learning how to deal with customer resistance and objections. For example, selling techniques suggest providing evidence for one's claim when a prospect expresses doubt or objection, offering endorsement when a prospect expresses agreement, and probing when a prospect expresses indifference. Highly effective salespeople typically say that they ask and listen well before they talk and show, that they focus on the customer as an individual rather than doing a canned presentation, and that they focus on product/service benefits, not features. The sales management task is to establish and support the sales force. The sales manager often has little time for selling. Much of the sales manager's job involves recruiting, selecting, training, organizing, deploying (e.g., allocating territory), motivating, and compensating salespeople, and working on the sales strategy.

Decide on Pricing

Pricing decisions are rarely made at the outset when putting together a marketing program because setting an appropriate price depends so much on what other decisions have been made. Price decisions involve much more than costs. The two major types of pricing decisions are establishing initial prices and margins and making changes to prices and margins. Pricing is a powerful marketing tool that is often highly visible to customers and competitors alike. Prices can be changed very quickly relative to other marketing decisions (such as distribution method), and the impact of pricing changes can be seen directly on financial performance.

When establishing price, think of price as a representation of what the total product/service "package of benefits" is worth to the customer. For example, a customer may be willing to pay more for diapers at midnight at a convenience store than during a regular grocery shopping trip. If so, the convenience store is justified in charging more, which in turn helps pay for the cost of being open for longer hours than the grocery store. In general terms, the marketing professional should think about establishing price within a range: the ceiling is what customers are willing to pay, and the floor is what the marketing professional is willing to accept, given costs and other constraints.

Prices may be fixed or negotiable. In many countries, negotiated pricing is more common than in North America. In North America, negotiation tends to occur only with high-priced consumer products (cars, houses, etc.) and in business-to-business marketing. Another variation in establishing prices is the distinction between bundling all options into a package vs. unbundling them. For example, some car manufacturers offer a series of options that the customer may add, with prices for each option, while other car manu-facturers bundle options together into an "all included price."

Deciding on what price to charge depends, in part, on one's objectives. For example, pricing objectives may include the following:

- Obtaining quick market penetration (a high-volume, low-margin ap-proach called penetration pricing)
- Obtaining slower penetration (called skimming the market, with low volume and high margins)
- Discouraging new competitors from entering the market or en-couraging existing competitors to quit
- Discouraging competitive price cutting
- Matching demand to capacity

Identify How to Grow and Keep Customers

A marketing professional can focus attention on acquiring new customers (called prospecting) or on developing existing customers (called development and retention). Customer acquisition costs money; studies have consistently shown that it costs more to acquire a new customer than to keep an existing customer. Retained customers often can be developed into even more valu-able customers than new customers. For these reasons, it is not surprising that savvy marketing professionals try to balance their attention between customer acquisition and customer retention and development. In these ways, marketing performance can be dramatically improved. While examining alternative ways to grow, a marketing professional may consider different combinations of customer development and new customer acquisition.

There are four major approaches:

- *Market penetration*: Focus on current customers—can we sell them more of what they are already buying from us? Can we increase their usage of our product or service, such as by convincing them to use our product at new times of the day (e.g., drinking a cola with breakfast instead of coffee or tea)?
- *New product/service offerings*: Seek to sell something new to current customers, such as a related product or service. In this instance, the marketing professional might build on the current relationship as a supplier (e.g., a retailer might add new products to her store).
- *New segments/market areas*: Seek new customers for the current product or service (e.g., enter a new geographic area).

- *Diversification*: Seek new customers and offer them new (new to the marketing professional, anyway) products and services.

One way to think about customer retention (the opposite is customer defection or churn) is in terms of the value of a customer over time. A single visit to the grocery store may mean a transaction value of only $100, or a profit of $1.50 (a net profit of 1.5% is considered average for grocery stores). However, that customer is worth a great deal to the store over several visits, over several years. No wonder grocery stores and other marketing professionals have devised so many different schemes to reward their loyal, repeat customers. These loyalty programs are intended both to retain/grow customers and to provide information about customers so that the marketing professionals can do an even better job of attracting and serving them.

The concept of customer development means increasing the value of a customer. For example, if a customer purchases a computer printer at a computer store, that store wants to develop the customer further by selling computer software, printer cartridges, paper, and other supplies. Loyalty programs differ greatly. For example, a "buy ten, get the next one free" paper punch card does not provide much marketing information for the company. On the other hand, a sophisticated loyalty program that identifies a customer and tracks what is purchased when by that customer can help develop a valuable customer database that may be used to improve marketing effectiveness.

The key to customer retention and development is not simply a clever loyalty program. Customers stay and buy more from a particular marketing professional if they believe this gives them more value than switching their patronage to someone else. Smart marketing professionals constantly look for ways to understand what customers expect of them (e.g., "What does the customer think is good service?") and what customers want more of (e.g., "Is it possible to speed up the checkout process?"). With these insights, marketing professionals can continually refine their marketing programs and maintain competitive advantage.

Ensure the Financials of the Marketing Program Make Sense

As discussed previously, a marketing plan formally expresses the strategy and implementation of the company's marketing effort. Fully developed, a marketing plan says what the company intends to do over a specified period of time, how it will do it, and why it is worth doing. It is important to realize that there is no single "right" format for a marketing program or plan; however, there are three key criteria for assessing a good program.

Does it make market sense? The first test of a proposed marketing program is whether it makes sense for the market. Is there reason to believe that the target market will respond favorably and in sufficient numbers? Is there reason to believe that consumers will regard the offer as better than competitive offers? Is there reason to believe that the trade (all members of the distribution system) will respond favorably? In other words, a marketing professional conducts a market analysis not simply for interest's sake, but rather to determine whether there is an adequate market opportunity and then to determine how to obtain it. Market information should be studied in order to derive implications for marketing decisions and performance. For example, if one learns that a competitor has just lowered prices 10%, the questions are, "What does that mean for us?" and "What are we going to do?"

Do the parts fit together well? The second test of a proposed marketing program is its completeness and internal consistency. For example, if the intent is to excel in customer service, is there adequate provision in the program for recruiting, training, and managing customer service personnel? Or if the intention is to seek customers who value high performance, does the product measure up? Is it "complete and consistent"?

Does it make financial sense? The third test of a proposed marketing program is its financial feasibility. Marketing decisions always have financial implications, and it is important for the marketing professional to figure these out. Marketing activities (such as sending direct mail or deploying salespeople) cost money and are intended to bring in revenues. A marketing program should be translated into the costs expected, the investments needed and the returns expected. Calculating the costs involved requires a careful estimation of all the costs and then a classification of those costs into different categories. Some costs are directly related to unit volume and are called variable costs.

For example, if each item sold required $30 of raw materials to make, then that $30 is a variable cost. Or if each time an item is sold, a commission of $10 is paid to the sales force, then that commission is a variable cost. On the other hand, some costs do not vary (at least within a broad range) by unit volume sold; these are called fixed costs. A marketing manager's salary may be $100,000 and not vary with changes in volume sold. The test for variable vs. fixed is whether, within a reasonable range, the costs vary with each unit of volume. The categorization of costs helps in doing some simple calculations of economic feasibility, which we'll get to in a moment. Sometimes the financial implication of a marketing decision is a change in costs;

other times, it is a change in investments. If the proposed marketing program requires that additional inventory be carried, that means an additional working capital investment. If additional delivery trucks or facilities must be purchased, these are fixed, depreciating investments. The test is whether the additional expenditure will appear on the income statement (a cost) or on the balance sheet (an investment). Advertising and other communication expenditures are regarded as costs, not investments. A marketing professional should be able to respond to the question, "What will the marketing program require financially to undertake it?"

The marketing professional is constantly being asked to forecast sales revenue because that particular estimate is so crucial to every other forecast for a company. Yet sales forecasting can be difficult to do with any accuracy, particularly in new situations.

Sales forecasts can be prepared based on several approaches:

- Previous experience (last year's results plus a change factor)
- What experts say will happen (e.g., pooling of individual salespeople's forecasts)
- What has happened in test markets (extending results to a bigger area)
- Judgment (what the manager thinks might happen, all things considered)

There is seldom a perfect method to forecast sales, but it is usually required of the marketing professional when asking approval to undertake a marketing program.

Contribution Analysis

A key question asked about a proposed marketing program is, how will this affect profitability? One way to answer this question is to prepare detailed projected statements (such as income statements and balance sheets). A faster way to do this is through "marketing contribution analysis." Both techniques should give you the same results, provided you use the same numbers and assumptions. The value of the contribution approach is that it provides a quick and straightforward way to examine relationships between price, costs, volume, and, thus, profit. The financial impact of a marketing program will boil down to what happens to these items.

A Never-Ending Process

The marketing strategy development process never ends. As soon as you start executing, you begin analyzing the situation and developing new plans. If things are going well, you start immediately thinking how you can do more and push it to the next level. If things are not going well, you start thinking about how you can fix them. Writing marketing plans never ends, either. Marketing managers are almost always writing a plan or update. That is why becoming skilled at writing plans is so important.

So I have briefly touched on the adoption of the elements related to the cyclical approach to marketing plan development and writing. This, like all things, has a foundation in agile development, and my comparison of it to a traditional method of development is discussed throughout the book. Of particular importance is the third column, which is a time qualifier found in the agile development process as a way to improve what marketing is doing. Because marketing is traditionally and necessarily tied to the strategy of a company, it is important that marketing improve.

Understand What We Need to Know for Feedback into the Loop

Failing fast is good; dying a slow death because you refuse to change course is bad for you and bad for business. Marketing is not a science, but it's not all art either. While it is impossible to anticipate all the things that happen in the marketplace and to sort out all the factors that affect marketing performance, it is possible to listen for the cues and change course. For these reasons, a savvy marketing professional constantly endeavors to learn from experience and from market research. What happened last time and, most important, why? Even partial answers help the marketing professional make better decisions in the future. Marketing professionals can get valuable insights from past experience. For example, one might track repeat purchase rates through a customer database driven by point-of-sale systems to assess a loyalty program. Or one might ask sales representatives to report on their sales call experiences, seeking insights about customer reactions to new offers. The key is to decide at the outset what measures of marketing performance to monitor and how quickly they can be monitored.

Another major set of tools for decision-making is market research techniques. Marketing research may be used to explore, to explain, to predict, or to monitor marketing. In each instance, the marketing professional is asking focused questions about the market or the marketing program and is seeking answers in a systematic way. Common marketing research techniques used both online and offline include the following:

- *Asking/listening*: Surveys, focus groups, personal interviews, complaint analysis
- *Testing/observing*: Experiments, panels, shopping diaries, video tracking

Marketing professionals might use focus groups (small groups of about eight people at a time) to explore how customers think and talk about a product or a store and thus gain some insights into how to improve. As a technique, a focus group is exploratory and is not statistically meaningful, but it is used frequently to give marketing professionals directional insights, which can then be examined with more expensive and quantitative approaches. Each of the possible market research techniques has advantages and disadvantages (such as cost, speed, accuracy, etc.), so typically marketing professionals use a mix of research methods over time. There are a host of research and tracking methods, but the essence of each is to provide good answers to questions that help marketing professionals make better decisions. This ongoing detective work is a critical part of the marketing professional's job as markets constantly change.

So marketing is all about connecting an organization to customers. It requires the following:

- Discipline to remember that customers are not all alike (and often quite unlike the marketing professional) and to go through the necessary analysis for good decisions
- Creativity to discover new ways of attracting and developing customers
- Courage to take action in an uncertain, competitive environment

If you are unable to write a great marketing plan, it is highly unlikely that you will execute great marketing programs, and even more unlikely that you will deliver great results despite the methods you may employ. Please understand that while the implication of agile means shortcuts or circumvention, it is far from that in all ways, and the most important aspect, once you've established your Garden of Eden with the application of the ADAM and EVE principles, is that you have to make sure the process begins with planning. Marketing plans are where ideas come to life. The marketing professional's world is full of ideas: new product ideas, promotion ideas, cost-saving ideas, public relations ideas, and more. Until the ideas actually find a place in a plan, however, they are simply idle thoughts. The ability to write great marketing plans is a critical skill for any marketing leader. Acquiring that skill takes practice, but it also requires approaching marketing plans with a strategic framework. I am going to outline a recommendation for how to write a great marketing plan for the agile approach to marketing. Like all skills, writing great plans requires practice and refinement. Few things will be more important in a marketing or general management career, however, so the time spent developing this skill will be a good long-term investment.

Keys to Success: Selling Is Part of Marketing!

Always remember you are selling a recommendation.. The primary goal for a marketing plan is to gain support for your ideas. You want input, certainly; but more importantly, you want support. So your focus is always on achieving this goal. You never simply communicate a plan. You communicate a plan and explain why it is the best plan possible. This approach has a huge impact on how you construct your marketing plan. It means you will look for compelling pieces of support. You will anticipate the questions, identify the reasons someone would not support the plan, and then proactively address them. You will take out information that might confuse your audience or lead to questions that will take you off track. Providing compelling support and explaining why you want to take a certain course are critical to the success of a marketing plan.

Several things can help you make a strong argument. First, always provide solid, factual information to back up your key support points. It is easy to debate and challenge opinions, but hard to challenge facts. When you are providing facts, note the source, the time period, and the specific measure. The easier it is to verify the factual information you supply, the more likely it is that your audience will accept the information as valuable support. Second, make the data compelling. The best data is simple to understand and hard to challenge. In general, the simpler you can make your information, the better.

If you must use a complex analysis, explain it fully, including your assumptions and approach. It will take time to explain, but without a clear explanation, the analysis will likely do more harm than good. Finally, always deal with the conflicting data. Nothing hurts a recommendation more than when an audience member catches a presenter off-guard by bringing up a piece of data that conflicts with the recommendation. And nothing strengthens a recommendation more than proactively identifying the conflicting information and explaining why it does not change the recommendation. If you know there are holes in the recommendation, introduce them and explain why they do not change the recommendation.

Tell a Story

People remember stories, so good marketing plans should tell a story. In a well-written plan, one point leads logically to the next and the pages flow seamlessly. In the best-case scenario, your next page answers the questions that the previous page introduced. Good stories have beginnings, middles, and ends. Good marketing plans do, too. The hard part is finding the story and sticking with it. On occasion you may find that the story simply does not hold together. The evidence might not strongly support the recommendation, and the conclusions might not follow. In this case, go back to the analysis phase and do some additional work. It may be that you have not finished with previous assumptions in the strategy development process. Remember, however, that the first story you develop is often not quite right, so you need to keep working at it. Writing marketing plans is an iterative process. Leave time to make sure your story holds together.

Keep It Simple

Simple plans are both incredibly powerful and incredibly hard to write. It is much harder to make something look simple than to make something look complex. The challenge, therefore, in writing a marketing plan is making things seem simple and obvious. A good way to keep a plan simple is to focus on what matters most: your objective and your key strategies. If you find your marketing plan getting complicated, stop writing; step back; identify the core story; and then start again, slowly adding information in such a way that things remain simple.

One of the most powerful ways you can simplify things is by using the "power of three." This idea is common practice for presentations to groups because we typically remember only three things from things we see presented, read (although I hope you remember more than three things from this book), or hear. Similar to the idea that the number seven tends to be the accepted limit for short-term memory, this "power of three" corresponds to a similar precept. Three is always the best number of strategies, the best number of tactics supporting a strategy, the best number of risks, and so on. Why three? Well, two seems light. There are only two support points? You have only two big ideas? This will not seem like enough; you can do better than that. Five or six ideas, however, will prove difficult for your audience to remember; trying to remember more than six will be almost impossible.

You can use the power of three to construct your entire document. You have three key strategies, each supported by three reasons. Against each strategy, you have three key tactics, each supported by three reasons. Occasionally a company's central planning group will issue required pages for a marketing plan, or a template for managers to follow. This certainly makes life more complex if you are attempting to tell a story. My advice is try to use the required pages to tell your story, but if it does not work, put the required pages in the appendix and use the main part of the presentation to tell your story. It is far better to tell a simple story that strongly supports your plan than to deliver the requested pages in a complex and hard-to-follow recommendation.

The other way to keep things simple is to avoid complex charts and graphics. Nothing is more frustrating than charts that are hard to understand. Some visuals resemble obscure psychological tests, open for creative interpretation. If you have a complex chart, look for a simpler way to show it. The key question is, what am I trying to show with this chart? What is the simplest way to make the point? Finally, keep the plan simple. Use an introduction and a conclusion, and emphasize the same points in each. The basic formula you learned in grade school still works: tell people what you are going to say, say it, and then tell them what you just told them. Use an agenda or table of contents. Use a simple, clear font consistently throughout the presentation. If writing a presentation, make sure headlines do not exceed two lines, and never have more than five bullet points on a page.

It might sound hard, but it really is only four steps: get the right people in place and agree to a process, iterate on what doesn't work, don't be afraid to fail fast, and keep iterating until you get to success that you can tell a story about. These four steps, when followed, are sure to lead you to success personally and professionally.

How to Get Moving in Agile

On our journey thus far, we have covered a lot of ground as it relates to the application of agile to the marketing role within or for an enterprise. I have outlined some of my thoughts and ideology about marketing as a practice, the role of marketing in an organization, examples of successful marketing outcomes, the importance of process, the importance of marketing planning, the path to driving collaboration, a case study on my personal experience and the components of that experience, and my concept of the marketing Garden of Eden with true and pragmatic components of ADAM and EVE. As I mentioned in the beginning of this book, the fundamental principle throughout this book is my steadfast belief of obvious pragmatic innovation fully supported by process and practice, with people collaborating every step of the way. Agile marketing encompasses the application of both process and procedures associated with a non-traditional marketing methodological approach. It borrows from the agile engineering discipline of application development and the application of what I am coining the "obvious principle."

You may recall from Chapter 1 there were references to obviousness.

Jack Trout's *In Search of the Obvious: The Antidote for Today's Marketing Mess* espouses an application of the ideals that form part of the baseline of my philosophy.[1] All these things come to me as part of who I am not from this

---

[1] © 2008 by Jack Trout

book; it is in my DNA; but this adds credibility and acts as the "wind beneath my wings" in everything I Let's review the five guidelines presented in *Obvious Adams: The Story of a Successful Businessman*, by Robert R. Updegraff. Here are the five guidelines from Updegraff's book:

- This problem when solved will be simple.
- Does it check with human nature?
- Put it on paper.
- Does it explode in people's minds?
- Is the time ripe?

So what I think and Trout asserts from the idea of obvious is that the pursuit of a marketing strategy is the search for the obvious. If we look at the dictionary definition of the word obvious, we find that the word means "easy to see or understand, plain, or evident." This is why obvious is so important. It is the simplicity of that message, specifically a marketing message, that drives consumerism. When a marketing message is simple, easy to understand, and evident, it works really well. Trout says that the first response to this idea is hesitation, because of the misconception that the obvious is too simple and does not appeal to the imagination. Likewise, we often think a marketing message has to be very clever and intellectually stimulating to be successful. You may recall we reviewed this concept in Chapter 1, as Trout's book warns of roadblocks that get in the way of the obvious.

A big part of avoiding roadblocks is to ensure you have good personal business investment in your marketing program. I am going to take a moment to talk about what I mean by personal investment. The bottom line is that investment in the future of the organization as a whole aligns with personal investments. Personal investments of what I call "continuous transformation" are investments for the common good, for yourself, and for the leadership qualities that you have to demonstrate for any type of change. Some key aspects of continuous transformation on a personal level include the following:

- Continually invest in yourself—knowledge can never be taken from you.
- Move beyond skills you have.
- Get uncomfortable.
- Set up scaffolding to help you build your knowledge.
- Look to outside groups to help give you objective feedback.
- Talk to customers.
- Talk to people you find difficult, and ask for criticism.
- Resolve to continually evolve.

- Help your friends (and even some enemies).
- Take the time to evangelize the agile process and the application of tools and procedures to align all the siloed organizations toward a common goal.

So now we look at the idea of truly driving a change in marketing. This is what I have done numerous times, both professionally and personally. For our purposes here, we must first establish just exactly what is meant by marketing transformation. We'll to get to the core of what it is. Let's summarize, like we would a mission statement for any transformation project.

Marketing transformation is creating, implementing, and sustaining changes in behavior, processes, and tools required to build long-term, sustainable relationships with customers, manage costs, stay ahead of competition, and maintain profitable growth.

With that said, how do we know we have to transform a marketing organization? Well, as Trout states[2] and each of us live every day, things are a mess. Some common symptoms of a marketing organization in need of transforming its processes are as follows:

- Inconsistent marketing execution
- Ineffective approaches to monitoring
- Insufficient customer intelligence
- Poor alignment of marketing resources to the best revenue opportunities
- Low sales force engagement and alignment
- Inadequate/rigid operating processes, innovative marketing techniques and tools needed to improve performance

All lead to higher sales costs, reduced revenue realization, poor customer experience, and high customer churn.

Process Alignment

It is important to not only know your organization, but also have a solid vision of your future state and an intelligent process that helps to bring together the right parts of the organization at the right time. So let's take a look at the organization and functional inputs that must exist to drive success of the agile process as it relates to marketing. Figure 5-1 shows typical inputs to

---

[2] © 2008 by Jack Trout

the agile process as it relates to the functional customers of the marketing organization. Each of these customers must be part of the transformation of marketing, as they are key to the outcome of the application of the process and its principles.

Figure 5-1. Wheel diagram © CA, Inc.

So let's take a look at the functional responsibilities of the beneficiaries of the agile process.

- Field marketing
  - Making product launches actionable for salespeople with your clients
  - Executing on strategic sales initiatives
  - Facilitating account-based marketing

- Feeding or creating the reference program where your customers refer your products or services
- Corporate marketing
  - Branding guidelines
  - Messaging guidelines
  - Facilitation of marketing process
- Channel marketing
  - Facilitation of marketing functions and process for your partners
  - Extension of branding to your partners
  - Extension of messaging to your partners
  - Implementation of marketing process
- Sales
  - Facilitation of sales process
  - Delivery of marketing messaging and guidelines
  - Delivery of sales tools for revenue attainment
  - Ensuring corporate objectives
- Internet marketing
  - Execution of brand to your customers and partners
  - Execution of your messaging to your customers and partners
  - Execution of corporate initiatives
  - Execution of marketing process
  - Driving innovation in marketing interaction
- Marketing systems
  - Driving infrastructure for all marketing activity
  - Execution of campaigns and of brand to your customers and partners
  - Technical support for marketing functions

Functional Alignment

We also have to examine the roles that functionally support the agile process in a marketing organization. The exact names in your organization may not be exactly the same, but they are called out here to ensure their alignment in the move toward functional components necessary in the agile marketing organization:

- Global program management role
  - Responsible for interfacing the business units, sales specialists, and field marketing org to create an integrated marketing

> plan to drive new revenue and sustain value from an existing portfolio

- Project manage the integrated marketing plan, working in tandem with the sourcing and product marketing teams to ensure all deliverables are met

- Operations, services, and sourcing
    - Responsible for servicing the global program, field marketing, business units and corporate teams
    - Responsible for acting as a service center for the business to provide the following:
        - Sourcing management to find the highest quality and most cost efficient way to execute the tactics
        - Deliver actionable metrics to business
        - Work with internal information services and external vendors to provide systems to enable the marketing and sales infrastructure
        - Competitive intelligence
- Product marketing role
    - Create go-to-market
    - Creation of all sales enablement tools and collateral, i.e., whitepaper, whiteboards, playbooks
    - Messaging platform docs
    - Roadmaps
- Field marketing
    - Interface with sales to create local field requirements to give to the program team to support building an integrated marketing plan
    - Execute local events/sales campaigns
    - Act as sales enablement for one-to-one marketing activities for sales
        - Presentation help
        - Sales training coordination
        - Interface with other marketing orgs to provide a feedback loop
- Teleprospecting
    - Focused on creating meetings with the enterprise accounts for your focus solution areas
    - A mechanism to help drive attendance to field events
- Event/tradeshow/sponsorship

- Responsible for event management of all tradeshows, c-level events, and sport sponsorship events not managed by local field teams, in national and international events
- Execute executive exchange programs through industry and trade magazines and events
- Branding
  - Responsible for ensuring that the corporate image is upheld while responding to changing market pressures
- Marcom
  - Responsible for the organization's voice internally and externally
  - All public relations and PR outreach, e.g., press releases
  - Employee communication
- Industry analysts relations
  - Responsible for creating/maintaining a positive image with the analysts, e.g., work to create positive industry analyst reports and for the technology industry, e.g., Gartner's "Magic Quadrant"®[3] and Forester Wave Reports®
  - Support sales and BU with relevant analyst information to drive new revenue growth
- Internet
  - Maintain and create a web presence for your organization in the global market, if applicable
  - Ensure search engine optimization for all organizational offerings and/or solutions and the overall brand
  - Provide a web platform for registration, webcasts, etc.
- Segmentation and CI
  - Responsible for acting as a service center to the business to provide information concerning the following:
    - Market share
    - Market penetration
    - Target markets
    - Competitive intelligence at strategic and tactical solution levels

---

[3] Gartner, Inc., *Gartner Magic Quadrant Research Methodology*, http://www.gartner.com/technology/research/methodologies/research_mq.jsp, 2011.

Continual Improvement

The steps to transformation in Figure 5-2 represent how marketing as an entity is the catalyst for the creation, implementation, and sustainability to deliver the transformation of a company's business. This is something I was able to facilitate and formalize for the entire company, I called it the "CIS" Create, Implement, Sustain. Specifcally, marketing drives full organizational transformation by creating a brand and platform for products and services, implementing programs and sustaining them to deliver value for employees and customers.

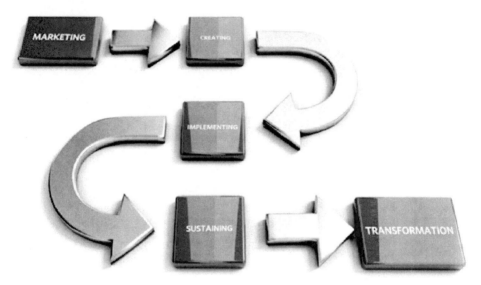

Figure 5-2. Marketing Facilitating Transformation ;Create Implement Sustain (CIS). © 2010 by CA, Inc.

Aligned with the idea of transformation are the ideas outlined in Figure 5-3, which facilitate leadership in the organization and in the marketplace. We must understand first the "symptoms" of a dysfunctional organization, and, most importantly, know that things are part of a continual improvement process. We establish the goals and focus then on iterative change for short-term successes and failures. The organization learns from both and moves forward. A colleague of mine used to scream at his team on a weekly basis "focus, focus, focus"—this is key to transformation of an organization, individuals, and teams with which you have direct and indirect influence.

Laggards		Leaders
Focus on brand identity		Focus on customer perception
Feature/Function mentality		Understand customer value
Plan Driven-Procedurally motivated		Market driven-nimble and growth focus
Lack of processes/tools drive customer relationships/leads		Consistent, repeatable, efficient processes and tools
Poor coaching, training and execution		Align incentives and performance objectives
Performance metrics misaligned with sales and BUs		Organization built on effective training and execution
Performance metrics misaligned with sales and BUs		Understand, embrace and consistently implement the strategy

Figure 5-3. Laggards and leaders transformation ideals © 2010 by CA, Inc.

Transformation Framework

Here are the essential components for the leader of marketing for driving pragmatic innovation to deliver agile marketing:

- Remove "roadblocks" and disruptions that may distract the project team from the day-to-day work effort (e.g., resolve issues, communicate those issues to the PMO so that they can be documented and brought up in PLT to clear those issues when the release manager alone is unable).
- Articulate and review key project deliverables.
- Monitor and manage the delivery of business results assigned to the release.
- Manage the release design, development, and deployment effort within schedule and budget.
- Review and intervene based on continuous monitoring of status/progress for projects within a release.
- Utilize the latest methodology and customize documents (tasks, deliverables) for application to each project included in the release. Educate project managers on the methodology and ensure

continuous compliance with methodology requirements (e.g., code review templates, unit test documentation, etc.).

- As a member of the Project Leadership Team (PLT), communicate program objectives policies, standards, procedures, and processes to project managers. Verify compliance.
- Reinforce the communications the workstream lead has given on roles and responsibilities to the project manager.
- Communicate the release/cross-project view to project managers at weekly WSL/PLT meeting.
- Provide deployment leads with applicable standards, tools, policies/procedures, and time frames; escalate as necessary to the PLT.
- Work with third-party vendors to ensure integration of projects within and across releases.
- Monitor, at a detailed level, work plans, timelines, and milestones for projects within the release.
- Identify and track cross-project dependencies as a function of the overall integrated requirements management plan.
- Identify scope changes (e.g., changes that may affect the release budget, timeline, or performance outcomes), and resolve/escalate them per change control process and procedures.
- Balance the need to minimize risk to release schedule, cost, and benefit with the need to accommodate changing customer needs.
- Facilitate the resolution of project team and cross-project team issues.
- Identify issues and risks that may affect the release budget, timeline, or performance outcomes or other releases that cannot be resolved by teams. Report issues to the Program Management Office, and escalate them as specified in the issue management process.
- Identify risks, develop mitigation plans (i.e., potential future issues), and report them to Program Management Office.

As you review these ideas or steps to complete transformation, it is also important to keep in mind the ideas I talked about before as they relate to the "iron triangle" for agile, specifically as marketing is the driving factor . (see Figure 5-4).

You should recall that the agile marketing triangle shows that any one parameter that you change affects the central goal. Ultimately, without successful marketing, revenue suffers. While sales may be tasked with bringing in the revenue, the road to that revenue is directly and indirectly related to successful marketing in the form of everything from branding to campaigns.

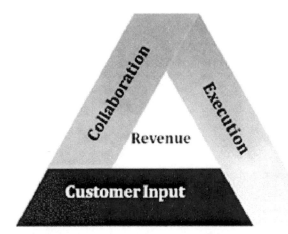

Figure 5-4. Marketing Driving Transformation iron triangle © 2010 by CA, Inc.

Similarly, as a complement to the iron triangle as an outcome-based construct, the transformation construct can be represented as the intersection of resources, budget, and "must-haves" (see Figure 5-5). All have to come together to enable and deliver the transformation of your organization integrated with the processes outlined for agile.

Figure 5-5. Agile Must-Haves © 2010 by CA, Inc.

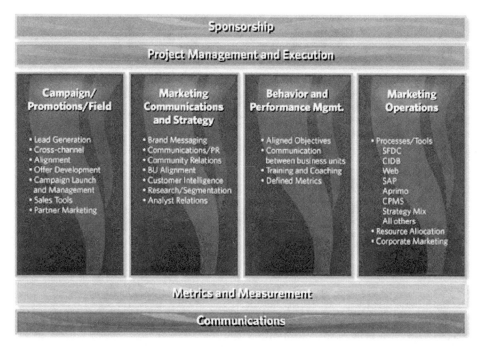

Figure 5-6. Success framework © 2010 by CA, Inc.

Ultimately the functions of the organization must try to live up to the ideals of the "to be" framework in order to facilitate the transformation and deliver. As we are in an agile transformation, our approach to this framework is to establish defined roles, knowing there will be turbulence as we fly along the path to agile marketing. This turbulence is a product of the iterative success and failure that feed into the continual improvements. Figure 5-6 above illustrates the agile state of functional alignments that have been successful for me in all of my transformational endeavors. Please note that the diagram illustrates functional alignment overlapped with the responsibilities of organizational roles.

Organizational Alignment

Part of the "to be" framework requires organizational alignment. This alignment is facilitated with strong leadership and management within the "to be" state. Managers need to create clear rules of engagement, including handoff points for important tasks. Four key ideas around alignment for delivery of the transformed agile marketing organization are as follows:

- People working together for a common goal over processes and tools
- Measurable initiatives that deliver on marketing plans
- Customer collaboration through crowd sourcing, not through guesswork
- Taking action over talking

To move from a defined relationship to an aligned one, encourage disciplined communication. When it comes to improving relations between any two functions, the first step inevitably involves improving communication. But it's not as simple as just increasing communication between groups. More communication is expensive. It eats up time, and it prolongs decision-making. I suggest that we must have precise and more disciplined communication. That means the establishment of what I define as "CallBS."

I cannot tell you how many meetings happen between siloed organizations that do not call each other on what is obviously separate from the truth. Now I certainly understand as a person who exists in the real world that we constantly have to deal with "spin" from every interaction we have. But if you are to truly try to get to a place where you can transform your organization, there has to be the capability and facilitation of accountability and transparency. I know that there are real politics, and we all have to understand there are organizational objectives and company objectives. While they may not always be aligned, this agile approach should facilitate breaking down the barriers. I suggest that holding onto misaligned objectives ultimately will deliver failure and that failure could cost more than company resources—possibly even your livelihood. The top of Figure 5-6 points out the most important thing, and that is *sponsorship*. You can be an agent for change and transformation, but most importantly that transformation must have the correct sponsorship at the executive level across multiple lines of business and organizations.

As I mentioned before, one of the keys, especially for marketing, is to align to sales. Sales delivers the revenue that keeps the company running. I am again going to discuss the importance of the sales and marketing alignment, as this is a key to transformation and the number one thing that can drive the best outcomes. If you can do nothing else, ensure you adopt an agile approach to the marketing organization through the implementation of process in everything the marketing organization does *and* align with sales. A little later on in this discussion, I will show you the marketing Garden of Eden I proposed in a previous chapter. This is very important to remember as you align your organization with the transformation model.

Sales Alignment

For any type of alignment, you must communicate—and communicate effectively and precisely. Incorporate transparency and open communication in every meeting, and ensure there are not any repercussions for doing so. People should feel safe to speak freely. To accomplish this, you should hold regular meetings between constituents and, in our case, specifically between sales and marketing (at least quarterly, perhaps bimonthly or monthly).

If we look at why marketing and sales always seem to be at odds, it is not because salespeople are egomaniacal jerks who think they know everything or because marketing are a bunch of lazy good-for-nothing ivory-tower stuffed suits, though I have seen some organizations where those generalizations could stick. It's because their missions are not aligned; sales is tasked with bringing home the bacon on a month-to-month, quarter-by-quarter basis, and marketing has a longer tail with awareness, thought leadership, and demand generation, with lead nurturing metrics being measured over a much longer time period. After all, brands are not built overnight. So how can a sales organization that loves its marketing department when it is doing well and hates them when times are slow ever really get out of being accused of being corporate backstabbers to the marketing team that wants to help, but may be a quarter behind them in delivering the leads they need today?

Remember ADAM and EVE and the snake in the Garden of Eden? No matter what we try to do, at times we will be at odds but if we are committed to the same end objectives we can overcome them. If you don't we still have the potential that when sales are disappointing, for fingerpointing from both sides unless the culture has truly changed. But change is often rapid in its execution and slow in its transformation. There will still be a blame game happening. The marketing team will blame the sales force for its poor execution of an otherwise brilliant rollout plan. The sales team, in turn, will claim that marketing sets prices too high and uses too much of the budget, which instead should go toward hiring more salespeople or paying the sales reps higher commissions.

More broadly, sales departments tend to believe that marketers are out of touch with what's really going on with customers. Marketing believes the sales force is myopic—too focused on individual customer experiences, insufficiently aware of the larger market, and blind to the future. In short, each group often undervalues the other's contributions. This lack of alignment ends up hurting corporate performance. Time and again, during research and consulting assignments, I've seen both groups stumble (and the organization suffer) because they were out of sync. Conversely, there is no question that, when sales and marketing work well together, companies see substantial improvement on important performance metrics: sales cycles are shorter, market-entry costs go down, and the cost of sales goes down.

The ongoing caution is that if sales and marketing operate independently of one another, they cannot be agile or get the multiplier effect of working together. With salespeople worried only about fulfilling product demand, not creating it, and marketers failing to link advertising dollars spent to actual sales made, it becomes obvious the two groups can't easily see the value of marketing efforts. And, because the groups are poorly coordinated, marketing's new product announcements often come at a time when sales is not prepared to capitalize on them. This disconnect happens continuously between sales and marketing, and I have to tell you I have been through countless re-orgs, alignments, new models, and department integrations to know that to succeed you have to fix. You have to investigate and identify best practices that could help enhance the joint performance and overall contributions of these two functions.

As part of the ADAM process, we must make sure we understand the constituents; this may be in the form of surveying or interviewing the chief marketing officer and sales executive leadership to capture their perspectives. Also important in the ADAM approach is to examine in depth the relationship between sales and marketing. The EVE component is the execution side of the house, and the ADAM portion is more aligned with the process side of the house. Both are iterative, both need to be flexible, and, most importantly, both are part of the agile approach as we transform marketing from a siloed business operation to a revenue-contributing integrated sales and marketing team. Figure 5-7 shows geographical as well as functional roles, and alignments applied to an agile marketing organization. Previously I discussed the importance of organizational alignment as it relates to external organizations to the marketing department, most specifically sales; this diagram shows the overlaps within the geographies and functional components within marketing for supporting agile and the business.

Figure 5-7. Functional Global Integration Model © 2010 by CA, Inc.

It is important to note that this structure is based on my conversations with several colleagues of mine throughout the technology industry and other industries globally, and the structure has proven successful with only slight tweaks for each implementation.

Key Changes Necessary to Effect Marketing Transformation

- Rightsizing of marketing goals, budget, and resources to business and sales strategy
    - Nimble and focused on a core set of solutions
    - Focused on sales enablement as well as external-facing marketing
    - Focused on fewer metrics that are actionable
    - Verticals (financial services/public sector) and partner services within the global program management office to take advantage of all resources and message appropriately to those audiences
- One CRM tool for sales and marketing
    - Provides a 360-degree view of the customer
    - Creates the same lexicon across departments

- Change the mindset of marketing to become an enabler of the business
- Expert team in operations/sourcing that can be leveraged across marketing and the business
    - Knows when to bring it in-house or source it for the best quality and cost
- Technical marketing responsibilities clearly defined with accountability from start to finish
    - Create a SVP marketing role over all BU product marketing teams responsible for the quality of product marketing
    - Ownership from start to finish of messaging, collateral, and defined sales enablement tools. (The current state is that this is broken between product marketing, corporate marketing, and field marketing.)
    - Budget and resource empowerment to get the job done— collaboration across former boundries including external sourcing available thru Global Program management which the technical marketing team can leverage when needed

So there you have it: a structure and approach to enabling agile for your marketing organization. Of course, there will always be some degree of tweaking as it relates to your specific environment, but I have to emphasize that the most import aspect is the ADAM and EVE approach to collaborative facilitation of synergies across organizational boundaries. This approach and framework, coupled with the awareness that the solution is usually always obvious, should be pragmatic and, most importantly, innovative. As throughout most of the book, you have seen how I have illustrated that there is a significant amount of evidence from marketing gurus, colleagues, and implementations that my approach to this transformation does work. I also am in a continual improvement process for myself and continue to evaluate applicability of different approaches to problems from many sources of, dare I say, inspiration. The next chapter of this book will address how to utilize crowdsourcing in an agile environment and how that applies to the concept of agile marketing and your own transformation as you take the leap into an agile world.

Crowdsourcing or Once Again Formalizing My Practice

So not to put too fine a point on it, but once again there is a validation, by adoption and trends in the marketplace, of my principles and manner of operation as a marketing professional. Crowdsourcing is once again an application of the principle of *obvious pragmatic innovation*. You may recall that, as I've discussed previously, there is a formalization of "this manner of doing business" coined obvious pragmatic innovation, which is a foundational premise of this book. It is my sincere hope that the adoption of engineering principles, specifically the agile methodology, to other areas of operational concerns in your organization—for this book, it is marketing—has become obvious. So what I am saying about crowdsourcing is that there are many leading companies adopting this concept as one of the feeds into their product enhancement sourcing, and this mechanism is a natural fit into agile and therefore adaptable for agile marketing. Before we begin that discussion, I would like to include a recent interview I conducted as part of my continuing research on agile adoption in the marketplace. I was asked to be a speaker at this organization's online "innovation forum" because I was able to assist in facilitating the utilization of their technology as a supporting element for my company's internal and external virtual webcasting and event initiatives, in a pragmatic and innovative way. As part of this process, I was fortunate enough to have a discussion with their president and CEO, Mr. Sharat Sharan, about my forthcoming book, and he informed me they were utilizing agile for their product development. I asked to talk with ON24's CTO and vice president of engineering, Jayesh Sahasi, about agile, and he graciously agreed.

Michelle: *Please tell me a little history of ON24.*

Jayesh: *Sure. ON24 was founded in 1998. Originally it was a financial information network. It was focused on creating and syndicating video and audio content for the financial industry. And then, in the years following the bursting of the whole dot com bubble, ON24 had to move from that business model, which wasn't really, as you know, gaining any more traction at that point.*

We leveraged our expertise in streaming—moved toward providing live video and audio streams wrapped with interactivity and webcasting, and ON24 was born out of that. We came to another fork in the road around 2007, 2008, when we saw an opportunity to incorporate and build out an industry-leading virtual show offering. So the combination of all three areas has gained a lot of traction in the last couple of years, and we're seeing a lot of interest in that.

So, that basically is what got us to today and to the very interesting and exciting things we're working on now.

Michelle: *Fundamentally what is your business and how has it evolved over time, Jayesh?*

Jayesh: *Basically, we're in the business of providing webcasting and virtual events. And the areas we focus on the most are demand generation and corporate communication. ON24 provides absolutely the most reliable and trusted solutions that enable companies to plan, produce, and deliver, in a very cost-effective way, their online events—including, as you know, things like internal communication. So, for instance, a CEO addressing the troops. Or, it could be a global sales meeting or something like that. We also do a lot of lead generation type of webinars, which directly impact and improve how our customers are perceived in the marketplace. We do continuing education webinars, which include the ability for the educational participants to be certified or receive a certificate at the end with continuing education* *credits. A significant number of people in the accounting business do that with us.*

We, of course, also have the virtual events side of the business; we do virtual conferences, virtual career fairs, and we've started recently adding this whole capability into a new product line called Event Portals. It basically takes real-world conferences, trade shows, or other events and brings them online with fully indexed searchable content, audio, video, interactivity, and mobile access—this, of course, includes interoperability with elements like social media and real-time capability.

So, that's really, you know, the areas of business that we are in, and it's really been instrumental to growth. We've started with webcasting, we added in virtual shows, and now we're taking real-world shows and bringing them online using event portals.

Michelle: What's your standing in the marketplace?

Jayesh: ON24 really is the 800-pound gorilla in this space and truly defines the space for the industry. Specifically we are the premier webcasting and virtual events solution. In this category, there are very few pure play companies similar to us; where there are, it has been consolidation of vendors entering into the market. For example, other organizations offer some elements of this space, like a phone conferencing provider including webcasting and virtual events, but their main business remains phone conferencing. Another example may be an organization that offers virtual events, and they have some bits and pieces of webcasting as well—so they're in the space, offering some solutions, but that's not their core business.

Michelle: When did you join the company?

Jayesh: I joined ON24 back in 2000, September 2000. Pretty close to the deflation of the dot com bubble.

Michelle: I understand that there is a recent (organizational) shift to bring marketing under your responsibility. Would you please tell me what factors influenced that change?

Jayesh: Let me correct that. ON24 has a separate marketing department so, that's not reporting to me, (they) work closely with sales. They are responsible for lead gen, PR, and various functions and are very critical to ON24 and our success in the marketplace. What I run on the marketing side is more what is typically thought of as product marketing and product management. That is the part under me, in addition to engineering, which is basically software development and quality assurance. So, I run that.

And in terms of your question, we made that recent change in the alignment bringing product marketing and management together for a couple of reasons. One was that we wanted to reduce the silos that we were seeing in the organization. We wanted to have one department responsible for communicating. We used to have one department responsible for communicating with sales, and another department responsible for driving products and features, and yet another responsible for implementing the changes. So, having all of these under a common umbrella, it's really focused us so we had this new role of product owner that was introduced.

It drove down all of the barriers, and it turned out to be much more efficient. We also wanted to be in a position where we had a lot more accountability. So, the product owners—as they've been defined as of now—are responsible for the success or failure of the product. And we can align the incentives appropriately as a management team. This person has control of the product priorities and what gets built and is the same person that is responsible for sales enablement and customer enablement. So, closing that loop was very important for us. And that's really been the main reason driving that decision.

Michelle: I heard the term "product owners" that have responsibilities encompassing traditional product marketing and product management functions. Product owner is an example of agile terminology. Will you discuss what impact agile has on your development time, time-to-market, and how that's implemented at ON24?

Jayesh: Sure, in more traditional models where, as you know, people develop their requirements up front, they toss them over the wall for execution, and then developers are supposed to go build something. What those requirements actually do is pose a lot of challenges. What I mean by that is when we encountered real-world situations, people actually started developing with all sorts of edge cases or exceptions. There were many conditions that the product manager never even dreamed of that started coming to light and required endless amounts of rework, mismatched expectations between the product manager, and developer, and QA team.

When you move that model to agile, the focus becomes more one of communication. Collaboration and communication are fundamental to the agile approach. At the inception of the project, it's not so much a focus on sitting down with volumes of documentation being necessary up front. In fact, experience has taught us that at the beginning of a project, it turns out to be when we really know the least about what the final product will be. Therefore trying to determine this all the way up front is not necessarily the best time to be developing extensive documentation.

Agile says, if you need documentation, first of all do as little as possible. And do it at the end when you know what is actually going to be delivered. So you know what actually is going to be going out.

By focusing on that communication, what happens is everyone in that scrum team comes along for the ride. They are aware of the requirements, they are aware of things as they change, what is driving each of those decisions, they are aware of the trade-offs that are being made. So, everyone is in lock step, and there is no disconnect requiring rework or mismatched assumptions and things like that, which tend to hamper the success of a project.

So, the result of all of this is that development becomes much faster because we don't waste so much time on requirements that aren't understood, or rework because we are not going down the wrong path until someone notices a problem with their requirements. But more than just the speed of development, which obviously is faster, for us at least in agile, working on the items that are prioritized by the product owner, one by one in sequence, ensures that we get the absolute best return on our investment.

We're not spending all our time on issues of marginal use, utility, or impact to the business just because they were written down in some document and we're rigidly following that requirement document.

So, agile kind of forces you to re-evaluate the cost of developing every little feature or tweak in the context of the big picture. And then it allows everyone the luxury of adapting that requirement based on new information.

So, you'll be surprised how much time that actually ends up saving and how much closer that end result is in alignment with the real needs of our customers and our business.

Michelle: How does agile impact a product owner in the traditional role of product marketing?

Jayesh: Okay. So in our case, we have a product owner who's responsible for product management as well. So, this person is defining what gets built. He's also the marketing person who is then communicating with the internal and external stakeholders about what's getting delivered. So, agile allows this product owner to know as far ahead of time as anyone what is actually going to be in a release.

If they're intimately familiar with every single feature, every trade-off that was made during development, they're able to communicate that very effectively rather than having that responsibility being split between different roles.

This person is also the one who defines and tracks the items in the product backlog. So these are the items that get worked on based on business priorities, based on technical concerns and on efficiency and scalability considerations.

Feedback from someone who is in a product marketing role is also directly fed into this prioritization process. So, again, having the same person *wearing both hats means that nothing is lost in the translation. They are the ones who are talking to the customers, and they're the ones who are prioritizing what gets done. So, it really streamlines the process and works very well.*

Michelle: *How has agile adoption of the product owner role as you've implemented it impacted the business of ON24 as a whole?*

Jayesh: *It's really allowed us to have a very razor-sharp focus on what is important for the business. It allows us to pivot quickly to address the changing market conditions, e.g., if something new comes in and a sales guy's talking about a particular problem, issue, or request that they're getting from a customer. That feedback goes directly to the product owner, and it could go into the next sprint right away if it is important enough. You don't have to wait for the next release; you don't have to wait for anything except just communicating it to the product owner. And it gets prioritized and added in and executed very quickly. So it allows us to work much smarter, allows us to deliver the maximum ROI.*

Michelle: *Do you think adoption of agile is revolutionary or an evolution in the way you are able to do things to possibly impact your business?*

Jayesh: *Absolutely, it's positively impacting our business. But in many ways, it is an incremental change to our prior development methodologies. What I mean is there was this whole rational unified process or, as you are aware, different spiral-development methods that were non-waterfall, which were the precursors to agile in some ways. So it's incremental over that, and some of these things I had seen and started to implement as the CTO for my development organization. What agile delivers along with the change is that it is a collection of best practices and is very practical in its approach to software development.*

Change is inevitable. So in other methods or previous development methods, you can stand there like a wall and try to block change. But no one can really block that change. Saying things like: I'm not going to take new requirements. Or saying that there is a code freeze right here, and there's a requirement freeze right here. It basically means you'll end up delivering things that are not the best for the needs of your business. So in that sense, agile is more realistic, but it has been for me an incremental change over the previous development model. But on the other side, there are definitely some parts of agile that are very revolutionary. Like having the whole concept of these empowered self-organizing teams with constant communication with the team members. The blurring of those boundaries between developer and product owner and QA. Everybody is a scrum team member; everybody can potentially do a lot of tasks that are outside of their natural role. For example, a QA person can do other things than just doing testing in the whole scrum model.

So it certainly makes enough people uncomfortable to be called revolutionary, I think. So really, it depends on how you look at it.

Michelle: *Do you think you're 100 percent agile or are you a hybrid?*

Jayesh: *In the real world, I'm not sure if anything as messy as a development process can be 100 percent anything. But we do aim to be 100 percent agile. We're still a work in progress, and we constantly strive to improve our implementation of these agile methodologies. But we're getting there. We don't have hybrid as a goal, but if you had to pin me down, we're probably a hybrid aiming toward 100 percent agile.*

Michelle: *It seems as though application development seems to borrow from engineering disciplines—in this case, agile. Do you think this a good way for us to learn?*

Jayesh: *Absolutely. I mean it's a scientific approach to developing a process. I mean, developers, engineers in general, spend a lot of time thinking about how to make things efficient. And a lot of time thinking about what is the real-world impact of some things.*

So having an abstract process that looks beautiful is not good enough. I mean, actually when the rubber hits the road, it has to work. What the industry has learned for the last two or three decades has evolved into this agile methodology.

It is certainly something that should be looked into, primarily to see if agile is suitable in an organization outside of development. My company as a whole is more general in approach when compared to my organization. Our methodology is all about communication, about respect, respect toward people and their time and their capabilities. And just a concept of trust and communication.

These are core to successful agile and are generally applicable everywhere.

Michelle: *Would you highlight a couple of tools you use to support your agile process-related development?*

Jayesh: *Specifically for agile, we just use GreenHopper, which is a plug-in for JIRA, which is a change management system, and it provides us all the tools to be able to measure our performance, have the planning charts and the task boards and the burn-down charts and all the agile elements.*

Michelle: *So, what do you worry about?*

Jayesh: *Well, in our industry, we know that the only thing that is not going to change is things that are going to change and at ever increasing rates. All this change doesn't bother me. I don't spend a lot of time worrying about our product. I think we have great leadership. We have a fantastic team— really talented engineers and product people.*

So that innovation we've shown already. To help us get to this position, I think it's our sustainable competitive advantage. So I don't worry about that stuff. But if I did have something to worry about, it would be about getting disconnected from our customers.

ON24 is a really customer-focused company. Our best product ideas, like you said before—crowdsourcing—they come from a lot of our customer requests, from strategic clients as well as just the general population of our clients. And also we have this annual customer advisory board meeting where we have a lot of our strategic customers come in and talk to us.

So, I think getting disconnected from our customers, that's the one thing that I worry about. And we are taking steps to mitigate that and to involve them even more, whether they're online communities where they can interact with each other and with us and give us ideas. So, that probably answers your question, I think.

Michelle: You've mentioned that you use customer input to help make decisions. Is crowdsourcing something you utilize as an active method?

Jayesh: It's not directly or formally used in the sense of making all of our product decisions based on external people or a bunch of stakeholders driving the decision. But in another sense, we have this large professional services organization that is executing events every day and in touch with all of our customers pretty much on a daily basis.

We poll them very frequently. So in a sense, they aggregate the customer-client input, and they are the source of a lot of our innovation, a lot of the new features that we build. But all of those come in, and crowdsourcing is just one piece of the puzzle.

There are also strategic priorities for the company that we need to address; things like scalability and those concerns, which may not be obvious for some but are important, even though not necessarily from someone on the outside looking in. So we have to balance all of those together, and all those inputs are important. So while crowdsourcing or the wisdom of the crowd is just one part, certainly is one piece of the puzzle, it is not the entire picture.

Michelle: Can you see the application of the agile constructs and these approaches to other areas in your company?

Jayesh: Yes, absolutely. I mean, for example, you'd have a closer working relationship between marketing and sales. That could be fostered. You'd see more communication, better metrics, doing smaller—call them "experiments" and "iterative development" of projects or things you do as initiatives within marketing. Also rather than big marketing events, smaller, focused customer engagements, and allowing for the process of the retrospective that we have in agile. I think to improve the process, to learn from *the project that you've recently done and incorporate that learning in the next cycle.*

Those features certainly are interesting; you can do that. You can translate other features almost one to one. You can have sales/marketing items. Like a project backlog, you'd have a project backlog or something like that. You can do some of the daily scrum meetings to eliminate the bottle-neck if you focus people on what they should be working on in a given day. And have shorter projects, like I've mentioned.

Very important for any department or organization but increasingly for marketing is the need for metrics. Marketing metrics are becoming increasingly important, so just having a true process, any process would probably help, and agile has some very good tools to be able to understand and track the velocity of the project. So, what your team can deliver to have those extra metrics and not just goals that you set ahead of time. No one actually revisits how well you did against the goals. Agile delivers more than just typical marketing numbers like leads generated. And that would help tremendously.

Also just being able to do course corrections, and to be agile, to be able to react as new information comes in or early results about a campaign come in. To be able to adjust your course. All of those fall neatly into to the agile world. I think there are definitely a lot of things that you can learn from agile and apply to marketing, other departments.

As this interview took place, at the latter stages of the development of this book, I was, of course, greatly pleased with the dialog, as a validation not only of the premise of this entire book, but also, most importantly, that others are instituting these types of ideas and being successful with them. I could not have said any of the things in the interview better myself. This is a great example of the impact that adoption of a formalized ideology—agile—by an organization has transformed the business to assist in improving the bottom line. We see that agile, as a transforming element to drive obvious pragmatic innovation, is being used successfully. In this example, they have integrated two traditional marketing roles into their development organization as the implementation of the agile product owner. Also, Jayesh points out the fundamental ideal of learning from engineering disciplines to apply to software/application development is not only logical but also fundamental to the constant need for business to improve through organizational transformation. Importantly, agile has impacted their time to market and therefore their bottom line. Figures 6-1 and 6-2 are an overview of ON24 and what it sells.

ON24 Corporate Backgrounder

ON24 is the global leader in webcasting and virtual events. ON24's solutions provide companies worldwide with a full range of applications and services for corporate and marketing initiatives such as lead generation, conferences and events, product launches, continuing professional education, internal communications and executive announcements.

No other provider can match ON24's size, reliability or scalability.
- In 2009, the company delivered more than 20,000 events and grew more than 30%
- Its two fully redundant data centers, unique in the industry, ensure superior reliability
- In addition, the ON24 network, with it's patented platform technology, is capable of delivering the largest webcasts in the industry

ON24 Products and Solutions

ON24 provides a broad line of innovative webcasting and virtual events solutions, supported by services such as pre-event promotion, professional event delivery and post-event reporting and analytics.

ON24 Webcasts
ON24 Webcasting
Engages with an audience with high-quality video and audio presentations. These are highly scalable, customizable events, provided live and on demand.
ON24 Webcast Center
A feature-rich web-based application for publishing interactive audio or video webcasts to audiences of thousands.

ON24 Virtual Show
A flexible communications and demand generation solution that provides a virtual venue for events such as tradeshows, conferences, partner pavilions, and training summits.

ON24 Virtual Briefing Center
An innovative new virtual environment solution, the ON24 Virtual Briefing Center serves as an interactive, persistent and dynamic online destination.

Insight24®
A Business-to-Business rich media network of webcasts, podcasts, videos and online demos for business and technology professionals. Insight24 provides timely and relevant information to facilitate decision-making.

ON24 Customers

More than 750 organizations in publishing, technology, life sciences, government and financial services, including Cisco, United Business Media, Credit Suisse, GE Healthcare, IBM, the National Science Foundation and Oracle, rely on ON24 for webcasting and virtual event solutions for a variety of applications, including demand generation, corporate communications and online training.

Executive Management

Sharat Sharan, President and CEO
Eoin O'Connor, Vice President of Finance
Jayesh Sahasi, CTO and Vice President, Engineering
Ed Van Petten, CIO and Vice President, Network Operations
Denise Persson, CMO and Vice President of Marketing
Scott Ray, Vice President, Professional Services
Michael Nelson, Vice President, Sales
Tom Masotto, Vice President of Business Development

©2010, ON24, Inc. | 201 3rd Street, San Francisco, CA 94103
More details at: www.on24.com, email: solutions@ON24.com or call 1-877-202-9599

Figure 6-1. ON24 Corporate Backgrounder © 2010 by ON24, Inc.

ON24 Fact Sheet

The Global Leader in Webcasting and Virtual Event Solutions
* Over 700 customers in technology, publishing, conferencing, life sciences and government
* Partnerships with leading B2B publishers and top conferencing providers
* The solution of choice for demand generation, corporate communications and online training
* Event delivery success rate – 99.9%
* 185 employees
* Offices in San Francisco, New York, London, and Singapore

Superior Expertise and Resources
* 10-year track record with more than 8 years of online event delivery experience
* On track to deliver more than 32, 000 webcasts and 300 virtual shows in 2009
* 4x bigger than its nearest competitor
* San Francisco-based development/support staffs that are 3x larger than any others in this space
* 32-person technology team, enabling global innovation and service delivery

World-class Product Line
* Webcast event platform superiority
    * Customizable, dynamic user experiences
    * HTML and flash-based audio and video event delivery
    * Real-time reporting and lead scoring engines
    * Mobile device application

* Leading virtual show technology
    * Best-of-breed integrated webcasting and virtual show platform
    * Ideal for virtual trade shows, user conferences, partner expos and company meetings
    * Generates more leads, more effectively and efficiently
    * Average attendee time in ON24 Virtual Show: 2.5 hours

Scalable, Redundant Network
* Two fully redundant data centers - first in the industry- for superior reliability
* Capable of delivering the largest webcasts, with over 15,000 viewers, in the industry

Global Service and Delivery
* Offices in EMEA and Asia Pacific
* Global partnerships in EMEA, Asia Pacific and Latin America
* Multi-Language support
* With more than 80 professionals, the industry's largest Client Services organization

© 2010, ON24, Inc. | 201 3rd Street, San Francisco, CA 94103
More details at: www.on24.com, email: solutions@ON24.com or call 1-877-202-9599

Figure 6-2. ON 24 Fact Sheet © 2009 by ON24, Inc.

Discussed in the interview, and mentioned at the beginning of the chapter, was the concept of crowdsourcing. In the case of ON24, it is utilized possibly not as a formal process but as inputs to the product owner. These inputs characterize the foundation of and include the ideas related to crowdsourcing. Let's take a quick look at the concept and its application in industry.

Beyond the Team: Crowdsourcing

So "crowdsourcing" was coined by *Wired* magazine's Jeff Howe in 2006, but the general idea has been around for a long time. There are those who believe that opinions matter, and while I may tend to subscribe to the old joke about opinions and other things we all possess, it is an interesting way to understand your market, customers, prospects, etc.

Crowdsourcing, at its most basic level, is about collaborative thinking toward a common goal. When you don't have the answers or resources, you find someone who does or a group of people whose collective knowledge can help you attain or reach a resolution to what you are trying to accomplish. Direct application of the formal term of crowdsourcing is an idea that we all do every day in one form or another—we seek opinions of our colleagues, peers, team members, and friends. Here is another example of and a validation of the fundamental concept of this book. That is to say, the principles I have put forth as obvious practical innovation are formalizing my approach to not only marketing but also life. What I have done through this book is crowdsource my ideas with thinkers in the industry through examples given by thought leaders like Ries, Trout, and Moore, to name a few. A slight variation on the idea, but still in line with the concept.

Getting back to the discussion historically, this concept of crowdsourcing has been challenging in the business realm on a larger scale, due to the complexities of driving all the opinions into an easily implemented form. In the past, pen had to be taken to paper and the speed of communications channels was not very conducive to collaborative brainstorming sessions. Now, though, we have the Internet. Ironically, the "power" of this platform was established really around a crowdsourcing project in and of itself. Collaboration could suddenly be broadcast around the globe with one click and responded to with the same ease.

Today, by definition, crowdsourcing is when a business takes a responsibility that is usually designated by an internal group or individual and outsources it to an undefined group of people in the form of an open call. This is different than a focus group in a variety of ways. A focus group is precisely that: focused as part of research. This accomplishes similar things in a broader spectrum. Some call it "open innovation," while others think of it simply as an extension of the open source concept.

Whatever it's called, it works. Entire research and development teams of some businesses now consist of crowdsourcing. Your organization no longer has to pay large fees to designers or creative consultants. Many businesses now use crowdsourcing to develop new products based on direct input from the target audience. All in all, businesses are building temporary teams larger than ever imagined at very little cost, launching crowdsourcing as a key component in business innovation that is pragmatic in application. Proponents of crowdsourcing are quick to tout what works. When done correctly, crowdsourcing offers the opportunity to develop something new while simultaneously creating brand awareness and building vested relationships with customers or prospects. So it is really a combined initiative of practical innovation, research, development, and marketing all in one.

Most often, benefits of crowdsourcing align with the agile approach and include the following:

- Expanding options and solutions beyond what is immediately available within your organization or company due to resource or budget constraints
- Reducing costs by following a model that drives responsiveness to ideas and or solutions that work, instead of the traditional means of research and development that require payment to all the failures of innovation (you may recall the discussion about programming only for features that are applicable from the foregoing interview)
- Providing a means to funnel and redirect attention to a business's other marketing efforts; ideal when used an extension of social media and as a marketing tool, crowdsourcing pairs effortlessly with many social media marketing efforts or traditional advertising.

There is always the other side of the coin. As I mentioned at the beginning of this discussion, the trouble with asking opinions of a crowd is that everyone has one—so when not thought through or approached strategically, crowdsourcing can do the following:

- Take a much longer time than anticipated to take an idea from development to implementation; crowdsourcing often relies on the culmination of ideas from many people; it can be time-consuming facilitating and managing the process, especially if individuals lose interest and no contract is in place to require them to finish.
- Exhaust the crowd; like everything else, where there are successes there are also failures. One of the primary approaches to the practice of crowdsourcing is to reward the "best idea" as a winner through some form of compensation. What sometimes happens is that some members of the crowd will repeatedly invest in meeting demands and end up without anything to show for their efforts.

- Produce lackluster results; if a business's crowd is not in tune with their stakeholders, crowdsourced products or solutions become moot points.
- Create missed opportunities; often products and solutions require funds to develop. If a business does not provide funds or immediate gratification to the crowd in its open call, the best or most thoughtful solutions might not ever appear.
- Produce a "false positive"; sometimes the nature of the incentive or of the target crowd who starts to endorse an idea may get others in the crowd to follow along. This can be seen in any interaction where there is public exposure of the trends for support of ideas.

So how do you combat these downfalls? Well, as with everything else, obviously, pragmatic innovation—adopt agile into the approach for implementation of the concept: plan, fail, iterate, succeed. That should sound familiar. Let's talk about how we might do that.

Agile Crowdsourcing: Plan

When developing a crowdsourcing strategy, you need to take into consideration the following:

- Goal or outcome desired
- Participants
- Logistics and resources
- Timeline for completion
- Possible incentives for reward

With this in mind, the three most common objectives and strategies of crowdsourcing are content development, product development, and marketing. These usually focus on one of two crowds: professionals or consumers. Strategies will also have varying costs to execute, ranging from little to no expenditure, to time spent weeding through submissions, to significant costs in execution through high-powered marketing campaigns.

Content Development

Some businesses use crowdsourcing to create content. This can be achieved by calling upon a crowd of professionals such as designers, web developers, or writers to produce content on an as-needed basis or, by asking target audiences to create their own content. With online sites, creators can bid on the needs of businesses and individuals, like logo design or web coding, while businesses set the price points, details, and deadlines.

Creative companies are taking it further and basing their entire existence on crowdsourced content development. There is a video media company built around a social network where viewers can make and upload their own segments, post comments on other uploads, and vote on which segments should air. Community members can also post news items to the web site that they think should be covered. Other users, along with reporters, pick up the beats. Since launching across traditional media and online platforms, the company has won Emmy awards for its peer-to-peer content and is the only 24/7 cable and satellite television network and Internet site produced and programmed in collaboration with its audience.

Probably the flagship example of crowdsourced content is Wikipedia. This online information source is a collaborative compilation of knowledge in encyclopedia form. Anyone can add or edit, although rules do apply. The entire site is free, the organization itself is a non-profit organization, and contributors are not compensated for content. Their impact on the online industry has been tremendous, terminology surrounding the idea and name has entered mainstream vocabulary, and countless folks have tried to emulate and adopt it both for and not for profit.

Product Development

Sometimes businesses seek more than just content—they use crowdsourcing to create new products or services. Much like content development, product development can call upon a crowd of professionals or tap the target audience itself. One online T-shirt retailer has built a crowdsourcing community similar to the one created by the video media company. Except instead of news, the end results are T-shirts. Anyone can become a member of the community and upload or comment on T-shirt designs. Then, users vote during a specified period, and the winning designs are produced and made available to all customers. Winning designers also receive a small cash prize. What started as a hobby for college students grew into a full-fledged online community that now includes forums, trend spotting, photo sharing, online resources, design scholarships, and more. That retailer reports annual sales in the double-digit millions.

Solutions can also be considered products in the world of crowdsourcing. I came across an example of a large toothpaste company that paid $25K to a retired engineer and crowdsourcing hobbyist who claimed to have a solution by the time he finished reading the challenge (obvious to him). After failing to solve the conundrum in-house, researchers at the toothpaste company turned to crowdsourcing (innovative) and got their result less expensively and faster (practical)—talk about obvious practical innovation.

Crowdsourcing and Ideation

The term *ideation* adapts the idea of crowdsourcing to the very specific objective of collecting ideas. These ideas are used for the crowdsourcing of product enhancement ideas from your customers and have become a game changer for product development. Historically, and as was discussed earlier in my talk with ON24's CTO, most companies have relied on one-to-one communication with customers to get feedback and set priorities around product enhancements. Issues would come up, and customers would find either a gap in the product or a need for something that had not been planned by product management. Usually these enhancement requests were either entered into the same help desk system as product defects or tracked another way from bug tracking systems to spreadsheets. The end results of systems like these were the creation of enhancement request black holes. Enhancements that were direly needed would be escalated, and that seemed to be the main way for customers to track and find the status of their requests. You had to either be a major customer or constantly nag in order to get heard. In other words, the system was closed. It was opaque.

Ideation upends that system by replacing it with one built on transparency and openness. Ideation turns enhancement requests into conversations. Ideation places context around the priority and value of an enhancement for all of the product's consumers, not just the VIPs or squeaky wheels. How does it work?

Ideation asks customers to post their ideas and allows them to see ideas that other customers have posted. Customers can then vote their colleagues' ideas up or down. They can start discussions around the ideas, improving and contributing to the initial thought. The ideas can be categorized for the customer in numerous ways. It can be based on the idea's popularity or activity like comments and votes up or down. The top ideas can display those with the highest net votes or ideas can be categorized around a single product. But the most important way that an idea can be categorized is its status, and this is where the game really does change. Customers can now see into the life cycle of the enhancement request, and they can watch it go from a new fledgling concept into something that product management is considering, all the way until it is either rejected or accepted as part of the product. It is that unprecedented view into the process that moves ideation beyond just a way to collect new features for a product and into a valuable tool for customers and product managers alike.

However, product management has reason to be apprehensive about a system like this. It seems designed for mutiny. What if a seemingly simple idea uncovers deeper issues? What if product management was holding off on certain features that the company didn't want to reveal because it gave them a competitive advantage? What if there simply weren't resources to address a popular idea? It could easily be seen as handing over the keys of the asylum to the inmates. But it can also be seen as a chance to provide explanations and insight into the product. It helps set product management's priorities in a way that extends across all customers, not just a few. Most importantly it builds trust with the customers: trust that the product managers are listening, and trust that the product managers are acting and commenting, participating in the process with the customers. This kind of trust translates into customer loyalty. It translates into new sales and increased renewals of licenses. It provides a backbone for the post-sales product life cycle.

What if there are too many ideas? Imagine 50 ideas about basically the same thing but each stated differently. This is where intelligence has been built into ideation. Whenever customers create an idea, they are asked to provide two chunks of content: a title and the summary. When they create their title, the ideation system checks for similar ideas and suggests them to the customer. If customers see basically the same idea they were about to post, they can check that idea out and vote it up instead. If they have a new twist on it, they can comment and add to the discussion around the idea. This in turn streamlines the process for product management. In the old system, when the communication was one to one, the product manager had to hunt down all of the duplicates manually.

Marketing

Looking for the best way to create a marketing message or a tactic to incorporate into an existing marketing strategy that fosters engagement and brand champions? Ask the audience.

Each of us who is a fan of football and the Super Bowl is familiar with the large amounts of money that have historically been spent on advertising. Let's take a look at an extension of ideation of a large snack manufacturer.

Since 2007 this snack company has put together what has proven to be one of the most successful crowdsourced ad campaigns ever. It involves one of their signature snacks featured as a way for fans to get to go to the Super Bowl. In the months leading up to the Super Bowl, consumers are challenged with creating their own commercial featuring their product. Submissions are narrowed down to six finalists, who each win $25,000 and a trip to the Super Bowl, and then the voting turns over to the average Joe. From there, the top four submissions are aired during the Super Bowl on national television, and—yes, there's more—if any of the ads get first place in the *USA Today* Ad Meter, the creators of that ad will get $1 million.

Initiate the Wave

The previously identified strategy options fit into one or a combination of the crowdsourcing models identified here.

1. *The online marketplace*: This model was really the pioneer for Howe's definition of crowdsourcing. The basic idea of this model fits in with content creation or product development objectives and makes it possible for many businesses to exist on crowdsourced matchmaking alone. One of the earliest modern examples of such a model is a photo provider. It has a web site where photographers— with skill sets varying from novice to professional—from all over the world upload photos, illustrations, b-roll video clips, and flash images for anyone to purchase and use, royalty free. Prices range from about $1 to $40 an image. This company now boasts the world's largest collection of royalty-free images, and since its debut in 2000, it has virtually obliterated the need for non-profits, design consultants, and individuals to budget big bucks for images obtained through professional photo shoots or stock images. The key to its success is its community of contributors—without the crowd, the marketplace simply wouldn't exist.

2. *The competition model*: Often referred to as the most common form of crowdsourcing, the competition model can be aligned with practically any crowdsourcing strategy. Unlike the marketplace model, which actively uses all crowdsourced content and leaves it up to the consumer to discern what content to pay for, the competition model usually seeks submissions to one very specific call, and then the one who initiated the call chooses the best submission and pays only for that content in the form of compensation or prizes. Essentially, in competition models, the crowd part is only really relevant

in that individual ideas are collectively compiled with one goal in mind, as opposed to collective collaboration among a crowd. Crowdsourced marketing efforts such as the Doritos campaign fall into this model, as do platforms like Behance, crowdSPRING, and 99designs. But, instead of reaching out to the consumer through competitions, they usually work like this: A client comes to the site, and posts an explanation of the project's needs and the reward offered. Clients then pay a nominal listing fee and wait for creators to submit results. The major benefit of this model is that instead of issuing a request for proposal and receiving a handful of submissions, the well of possibilities in this model is significantly larger. 99designs claims that most open calls attract more than 50 submissions. Other benefits include the opportunity for briefs and concepts to change and evolve over time, based on user submissions and feedback, and the significant opportunity that those who submit ideas become engaged and invested in the brand.

3. *The ideas bank*: Idea banks are based on true collective collaboration, and no compensation or prize for idea generation is ever offered. The point of this model is simply collective feedback. A business or individual has an idea or solution and reaches out to the crowds to gauge how on-target this idea or solution is before implementation. The closest non-crowdsourcing example is market research that usually precedes product development. While there are sites that exist to collect ideas from the masses, many businesses are simply providing ways for audiences to contribute via a company site. One can see that Starbucks has done this through the implementation of the My Starbucks Idea campaign. In a nutshell, Starbucks used its web site to create a cross between a crowdsourcing community and a suggestion box—users create an account, tell Starbucks what they want to see in its stores, and vote on others' ideas. This model has become a driving force in Starbucks products and services.

Home or Away: The Platforms

Many ways exist to help businesses implement these crowdsourcing efforts, a few of which have been mentioned briefly. How a business goes about making an open call for crowdsourcing depends on the audience and the strategy. Sometimes, it makes the most sense to pair crowdsourcing with traditional communications tactics and tools, while other times it makes sense to target the crowds most willing to help. A great way to do so is through crowdsourcing platforms. These platforms allow a business to leverage an existing system or channel to make the open call. If a business is seeking the solution to an internal issue—such as the need for design work or a way to streamline production—then it is seeking crowdsource submissions from experienced professionals. Examples of platforms that may make the most sense include the following.

Content Development Platforms

These solutions are perfect for posting design, web development, or copywriting calls.

- *Behance*: Design
- *crowdSPRING*: Design
- *99Designs*: Design
- *TopCoder*: Web development
- *Genius Rocket*: Video, design, web, and copywriting

Research and Development Platforms

These are appropriate for gleaning the crowd for solutions to problems, obstacles, or equations in order to develop a new product or streamline a process.

- *InnoCentive*: High-level problem solving across many industries and platforms, used by big names like NASA, Proctor & Gamble, and Eli Lilly
- *Hypios*: Problem solving at all levels for companies ranging in size from small to large
- *Inkling*: Platform for highly targeted prediction markets—the focus group gone digital

Social Media Platforms

If a business is seeking to crowdsource research or content directly from consumers for the consumer, consider the following platforms.

- *YouTube™ or Vimeo™*: Video content
- *Facebook*: Social network

- *Twitter*: Micro-blogging tool
- *Ning*: Create your own social network

These sites all have one thing in common: community. Users can upload, share, rate, or comment on content and connect with each other virtually. Because these sites fit so well with the concept of community that crowdsourcing is based on, they are fantastic for serving as the medium for making the call or serving as the requested medium of submission.

The-Whole-Kit-and-Caboodle Platforms

Some crowdsourcing platforms exist in unlimited form. Anyone can post requests that range from translation services to proving that ghosts are real to solving societal issues such as world hunger.

- Amazon.com's Mechanical Turk
- Big Carrot

Word for the wise: Be sure to employ traditional marketing measurement tools to assess the full impact of crowdsourcing and return on investment. When considering a crowdsourcing strategy or solution, don't forget the fine print. The standard practice seems to be the inclusion of legal disclosures that specify that any and all submissions automatically become the intellectual property of the company sponsoring the competition, hosting the conversation, or requesting the information.

Motivate and Spur Participation

Many experts say that the secret to successful crowdsourcing is in the incentives offered. Just like many other areas of business, a reason has to be given, a benefit made obvious, as to why audiences should care. The same holds true in crowdsourcing. It would be nice if bragging rights would be reward enough for crowdsourcing solutions, but the reality is that cash payment or prize incentives are what really entice crowds to participate in the first place. Build your crowdsourcing strategy in a way that makes it worth the crowd's while and compensate them accordingly.

If your company doesn't have the means to provide monetary incentive, build your business's crowdsourcing strategy around a different value—like the sense of community and brand ownership offered to users of My Starbucks Idea. Even though users aren't compensated for implemented ideas, they see proof that a brand cares what they think.

Next, focus on getting the word out. If your business is crowdsourcing for internal purposes and using a content development platform like the ones listed previously, communication will be taken care of in large part by the platform. However, if you are using crowdsourcing as a means of obtaining and providing value to external audiences, it would be best to have a defined communications strategy—it will need to be promoted via multiple channels and should be incorporated into a marketing plan. Secure the infrastructure and involve full-time staff. Don't overlook employee input or existing processes when considering a crowdsourced solution.

Consider transparency and balance: transparency in communicating with employees what the plan is and how they are expected to fit into that plan; and balance what makes the most sense to be done in-house vs. what to crowdsource. Lines may have to be drawn that exclude or welcome employees to participate in crowdsourcing as members of the crowd. For example, put the entire internal team in charge of helping to make the final decision on what crowdsourced submissions are implemented or considered through internal voting instead of designating one decision-maker. Or, consider crowdsourcing internally: Need a new logo? Ask employees to submit ideas.

Crowdsourcing and Agile Marketing

The basis of crowdsourcing comes from the idea of collective intelligence. So how do we define collective intelligence? Jeff Howe, the guy that came up with the term crowdsourcing, says it this way: "A central principle animating crowdsourcing is that the group contains more knowledge than individuals," which is a large expansion of the "two heads are better than one" concept. Just that foundational principle of collective intelligence is a demonstrative part of the cyclical nature of agile. So you can begin to see how this idea ties into agile marketing. James Suroweicki says, "Even if most of the people within a group are not especially well informed or rational, it can still reach a collectively wise decision." This is the science that explains why, when asked for a lifeline on *Who Wants to Be a Millionaire?*, the crowd guesses 91% correctly, whereas experts have a 61% likelihood of getting the right answer. The answers that come from crowdsourcing are called collective intelligence or wisdom of crowds. Yes, two terms for the same thing.

So what does it take to achieve collective intelligence? Will any group of people do? Crowdsourcing has three unique requirements to deliver collective intelligence: (1) a diverse crowd, (2) a qualified crowd, and (3) the right size of crowd.

Crowd Must Be Diverse

Crowdsourcing requires a mix of people who aren't too much alike. If you had the undivided attention of every genius on any given topic, you would get very accurate answers to questions. Contrary to popular belief, a group of the most highly accredited or accomplished brains on a topic does not produce the best answers. Crowdsourcing shows that breakthrough solutions more reliably come from a diverse enough set of minds to go at the question from different angles without the bias inherent in like-thinking people. Remember the example of the toothpaste company.

Crowd Must Be Qualified

Crowdsourcing takes people who are interested and capable. Qualifying a crowd is as easy as finding people with an interest in the subject with the technical skill to provide the answer or perform the task. For answers on how to better operate your business, the best crowd is likely your employees and partners. They know the company and are motivated to make it work better.

Crowd Must Be Right Size

The simpler the crowdsourcing question, the larger the crowd needed.

Crowdsourcing involves many models where the simple majority does not rule; instead different members vote with different weight, or perhaps expert moderators have influence. To keep it simple, though, let's talk about crowdsourcing where the majority will pick the winning solution. How many people does it take for the majority answer to be right? The answer depends on the simplicity of the question, but really the jury is still out on the minimum size of a crowd for collective intelligence. Jeff Howe mentions 5,000. Some say it could be fewer. But as with everything else, be pragmatic and innovative, and do not be surprised if the answer to each question is obvious.

Crowds Worth Considering

Selecting the right crowd is important. I would suggest that you consider your employees/stakeholders across all aspects of your business. There is a great deal of knowledge and experience that can come from your employees. The method is more important than numbers in this case. The key to success here is flattening your organization so that all employees feel they can contribute their ideas.

In addition to your employees and as indicated earlier with the implementation discussion of the ideation concept, getting direct feedback from your customers is very valuable as a target crowd. In this case, the crowd should be made up of people who are already passionate about your brand, people who are passionate about what you sell. You should also include folks that are not your fans. "Keep your friends close but your enemies closer" is a great way to possibly gain insight. Constructive criticism is good, unless it is criticism that is just complaints without insights.

Of course, you should always consider the broad public, including expert outsiders, especially when thinking about innovation—bringing qualified diverse thinkers together to assess and discover solutions has proven to lead to breakthroughs. To achieve this, you will need a large group of all types—hobbyists, hecklers, and experts. The crowd size in this type of application will have to be large—think thousands or tens of thousands. Recall the physics solution and the toothpaste company example from earlier in this chapter. To make this work, you'll need people with a variety of backgrounds, as everyone will approach situations differently.

For the application of public policy, the crowd would be the citizens or constituents to bring democratic practices down to a grassroots level. Crowd size is dependent on the number of citizens in the jurisdiction (city, country, voting ward). You'll want to structure things so there is a good cross section of those directly affected by the policy, not just those with a keen interest in being politically active.

Difference Between Crowdsourcing, Open Innovation, Mass Collaboration, and Co-creation

So we have covered some ideas about crowdsourcing as a term and a concept. There are other similar innovations or rather ideas that are similar in their conception. One of these is something called *co-creation*. Co-creation is creating a work or product by standing together with those for whom the project is intended. Scholars C. K. Prahalad and Venkat Ramaswamy introduced the idea of co-creation in their 2000 *Harvard Business Review* article, "Co-opting Customer Competence." They developed their arguments further in their book *The Future of Competition*. Still another source has produced studies where there is an attempt to uniquely distinguish the idea of co-creation from related concepts such as crowdsourcing, ideation, mass customization, and mass collaboration. They did this by saying that the foundational aspect of psychoanalytical decision-making as well as innovation are the roots of the co-creation concept in its intellectual evolution.

So is there really a difference? Probably not. Apply obvious pragmatic innovation. Some people are more comfortable with one term over another. It is not so much the terminology that is important but rather the application. I think it really boils down to whose book you buy, and it should be my next book on individual aspects and studies on application of obvious pragmatic innovation. Since you already have this one in hand, the terminology is not quite as important as the adoptability and application for whatever areas of the marketing department it may fit.

Crowdsourcing Beyond Ideation

Typically company web sites have visitors for very specific reasons: to find facts, get answers, and get support. As professional networking and collaboration tools become more prevalent on a company's product community site, the reason for visits is beginning to change. Customers can now find answers and receive support from other customers, and they often turn to peers for help before they open issues through the official support channels. With the proper encouragement, this experience will be passed on, and the customers that were helped by their peers will contribute back and answer questions themselves, leading to a virtuous circle.

With that in mind, product communities have many avenues for participation: message boards, blogs, comments, and content ratings. Each is a way to communicate. It allows communication between company and customer as well as between customer and customer. Message boards provide space for discussions as well as a place for questions to be answered. Blogs allow experts to explain new ideas and viewpoints. For both message boards and blogs, comments enhance the posts and ratings convey value.

As more and more adaptations of the ideas of crowdsourcing become "main stream," measurement also has to be adjusted beyond the success or failure of the "open call." These measures should be in line with the typical measures associated with any type of route to market; especially when businesses crowdsource their customers and prospects, there is the opportunity for much greater impact. This impact includes brand awareness, overall impressions, or traffic incurred to a site. Crowdsourcing can be a great way for businesses to harness the power of collective and collaborative thinking to innovate and work with audiences toward a common goal, while providing brand awareness and incentive for engagement. What's more, the opportunities to use crowdsourcing and the potential outcomes of crowdsourced efforts are practically limitless. So use this in an iterative fashion. Plan, fail, iterate, succeed, and, most importantly, listen to the obvious answer. By now I am hoping you see the promise of the ideas fundamental to agile, and that is collaboration with measurable fail points to success.

One of the key aspects that I have not discussed throughout this book is the fundamental application of technology to support your marketing projects. I actually did have a chapter dedicated to the use of project management software, specifically my company's (CA Technologies) Agile Vision™ product as a way to manage marketing programs and initiatives. So as not to be deter from the vision of this book and the lessons learned in my career so far, I concluded that the section may have seemed a bit more of a plug for the product so it was excluded. That said, I have used this technology both because it is a market leader in the Project and Portfolio Management (PPM) software space but also because in my continual strive for marketing transformation and application of the feedback loop of agile marketing I believe that in your own organizations you should always "drink your own champagne." This means use your own products wherever and whenever possible this provides the feedback loop into product marketing and development (as long as we have broken down the silos we discussed earlier) and as a tool for marketing success stories to your customers.

Because marketing programs are projects similar to technology projects and they are so closely linked these days I see no reason agile methodology adopted within a project management technology can't be utilized for marketing.

So let's take a look at a couple of roles in marketing and how the agile method roles we have talked about throughout this book can be applied to the roles in the agile methodology.

Project management software that supports agile will have the agile roles so for a marketing match up you can use; Scrum Master can be seen as your Campaign Manager, Product Owner can be your Product Marketing Manager for the solution you are marketing as he or she is your internal customer who hopefully can help get your external customer feedback. The team consists of all the creative "developers" writers, graphic artists, promotions, events people you may need to move your project along. The key is that you now can apply all roles to roles that are accounted for in a project management technology that has the agile roles built in or any way you may want to manage your project along its agile lifecycle.

We have now traveled down a seemingly lengthy road in this agile marketing journey, I have discussed the fundamental idea of the application of my Obvious Pragmatic Innovation to everything I do and the precepts of marketing in the Garden Eden with ADAM and EVE. Agile is very real and can make you successful. If you don't quite get it right the first time you will know quickly and you can iterate that is what agile is all about. I think you will find that agile as a whole and can support any transformation and adoption to your organization. You can go out to major vendors like Accenture and SFDC see they too apply agile methodologies to their marketing practices, especially where technology and marketing meet with interactive marketing.

Accenture's own marketing interactive website can be found at

http://www.accenture.com/us-en/Pages/service-agile-intelligent-marketing-video-summary.aspx

They invite their customers to learn about their journey towards agile.

So you see when organization as large as Accenture buy into agile for marketing I would think that is at least compelling enough for you to consider it for your organization.

Hopefully this book has taught you a lot about agile and how it can be applied to marketing. If you still need to know more please feel to contact me as I am tied into an extensive array of social media networks (sounds like a topic for one of my next books), at the very least you can certainly expect another iteration of this one . . . welcome to the agile world!

References

There are so many thought leaders, books, articles, blogs, and tweets that I have read and followed that have contributed to the writing of this book. I would like to reference just a few of the influences that have validated the ideas I have put into practice.

- Ambler, Scott W. "Agile Project Initiation Survey." 2009.
- Gartner, Inc. *Gartner Magic Quadrant Research Methodology.* http://www.gartner.com/technology/research/methodologies/research_mq.jsp. 2011.
- Gladwell, Malcolm. *Blink: The Power of Thinking Without Thinking.* New York: Little, Brown, 2005.
- Harvard Business Publishing, *Harvard Business Review.* http://hbr.org/.
- Michelli, Joseph A. *The New Gold Standard: 5 Leadership Principles for Creating a Legendary Customer Experience Courtesy of the Ritz-Carlton Hotel Company.* New York: McGraw Hill, 2008.
- Moore, Geoffrey A. *Crossing the Chasm.* New York: HarperBusiness, 1991.
- Ogilvy, David. *Ogilvy on Advertising.* New York: Vintage, 1995.
- Ries, Al and Laura Ries. *The 22 Immutable Laws of Branding.* Harper Paperbacks, 2002.
- Ries, Al and Jack Trout. *The 22 Immutable Laws of Marketing.* New York: HarperBusiness, 1994.

- Smith, Craig and Alexander Hiam. *Marketing for Dummies*. Chichester, UK: Wiley, 2006.
- Trout, Jack. *In Search of the Obvious: The Antidote for Today's Marketing Mess*. Hoboken, NJ: Wiley, 2008.
- Trout, Jack. "The Law of Perception," in *Branding Strategy*. 2007.
- Vizdos, Mike. *Implementing Scrum*. http://www.implementingscrum.com/section/blog/cartoons/.
- Vogel, Craig M., Jonathan Cagan and Peter Boatwright, *The Design of Things to Come* (Upper Saddle River, NJ: Prentice Hall, 2005).

Index

22 immutable laws of branding, 17–21

22 immutable laws of marketing, 13–17

99Designs platform, 208

A

acceleration, law of, 15

active stakeholder participation
technique, 115

ADAM (admitting, defining, assigning,
measuring) process, 80–86, 185

adaptability, 33

admitting, defining, assigning,
measuring (ADAM) process,
80–86, 185

advertising
law of, 19
overview, 153
Super Bowl, 205

advertising channels, 89–90

agile crowdsourcing, plan for, 202

agile development planning
principles, 130

agile marketing
crowdsourcing and, 210–212
four Ps and marketplace, 37–38
instituting flexible methodology,
30–31

making priority, 88–91
processes, 39–41
changing market and new
demands on marketing,
40–41
implementation, 39
marketing planning, 39–40
quality
enabling, 32–33
using technology to augment,
33–35
as solution, 41–44
streamlining perception, 31
teamwork resolution, 31–32
whom message serves, 35–37

Agile Model-Driven Development
(AMDD), 115

agile software development
active stakeholder participation
technique, 115
agile marketing based on, 113–114
Agile Model-Driven
Development, 115
Big Design Up Front, 116

aligned relationships
moving from defined relationship
to, 104–106
moving to integrated relationship
from, 106–112
overview, 102

alignment
    in collaborative leadership, 79–80,
        85, 105
    functional, 175–177
    organizational, 182–183
    process, 173–175
    sales, 184–186
allocating in marketing process,
    137–138
alternative channels, 89–90
AMA (The American Marketing
    Association), 12
AMDD (Agile Model-Driven
    Development), 115
analysis and research in marketing
    process, 137, 139
analytics, and customer retention, 92
analytics strategy, of case study, 73
Apple, 17, 146
application development, agile
    active stakeholder participation
        technique, 115
    agile marketing based on, 113–114
    Big Design Up Front, 116
appropriateness, 33
attributes, law of, 15
attributes of quality, 33
audience measurement terms, 154
auditing in marketing process, 137–138
awareness, as metric of success, 145

B

B2B companies, 92, 98
B2C companies, 98
balance, in crowdsourcing, 210
Behance platform, 208
behaviors in marketing organizations, 29
best marketing plans, focus on, 78
blogs, in crowdsourcing, 213

borders, law of, 21
BR Detail Count, RTVM, 54
BR Priority, RTVM, 54
BR Summary Count, RTVM, 54
BR Summary, RTVM, 54
brand equity, 100
branding, 17–21, 177
budgets, 154–155
    in marketing process, 137–138
    planning within, 124
    selling projects to sponsors,
        124–125
    as source of friction between
        sales and marketing, 97
    in transformation framework,
        181–186
Business Assertion, RTVM, 54
business impact, 33
Business Requirement, RTVM, 54
business strategy
    long-term objectives of, 122–123
    short-term analysis of, 121
    short-term objectives of, 121–123
buy-ins, 78
buyers, decision process of, 114
buying funnels, 108–110
buying process, over-generalization
    of, 18

C

CallBS, 183
campaign development, in
    collaborative leadership, 79
case study, 45–75
    analytics strategy of, 73
    functional delivery of, 74
    personas in
        overview, 68–69
        types of, 69–72
category, law of the, 14–20

CCOs (chief customer officers), 94
change
  in agile process, 194
  law of, 21
Channel Enablement, 85
channel marketing, 175
charts, 170
chief customer officers (CCOs), 94
chief revenue officers (CROs), 108
circulation, 154
CIS (Create, Implement, Sustain), 178
classical marketing model,
  shortcomings of, 131
client managers, 97–98
co-creation, difference between
  crowdsourcing and, 212–213
co-locating marketers and
  salespeople, 105
collaboration, 48, 212–213
collaborative leadership
  ADAM process and EVE principle,
    80–81
  customers
    cultivating, 91–93
    facing, 98–99
    metrics, 100–101
    service and support, 99
  eliminating silos, 86–87
  four-step process, 82–86
  making agile priority, 88–91
  marketing
    conflict between sales and,
      96–98
    different roles for, 95–96
    reinventing, 93–94
  relationships, 101–103
    aligned, 102
    creating stronger, 103–112
    defined, 102
    integrated, 102–103
    undefined, 102
collaborative thinking, in
  crowdsourcing, 200–201

collective intelligence, 210–212
color, law of, 21
comments, in crowdsourcing, 213
communicating marketing plan,
  135–137
communication
  in agile process, 192
  in crowdsourcing, 210
  disciplined, 183
  disciplined, in collaborative
    leadership, 104
  evaluating effectiveness of, 155
  objectives of, 154
  regarding problems, in
    collaborative leadership, 82
  in sales alignment, 184
  significance of simplified, 66–67
  in transformation framework, 180
communication methods, 153
company, law of the, 20
competition crowdsourcing model,
  206–207
competitive analysis, 147–148
competitive differentiation, 148
compromises, in collaborative
  leadership, 87
conflicts, between sales and
  marketing, 96–98
conservatives, 24
consistency, law of, 21
constructs of marketing, 48
consumer marketing, 22
content development, 202–203, 208
continuous transformation, on
  personal level, 172–173
contraction, law of, 19
contribution analysis, 165
conversational marketing, 159
corporate marketing, 175

costs
    fixed, 164
    time, and scope relationship,
        47–48
    variable, 164

Create, Implement, Sustain (CIS), 178

credentials, law of, 19

credit card companies, cultivating
    customers by, 92–93

CRM (customer relationship
    management), 98, 186

CROs (chief revenue officers), 108

cross-functional team, creating
    marketing plans with, 132

Crossing the Chasm (Moore), 23–25

crowds
    diversity of, 211
    qualifications of, 211
    size of, 211
    worth considering, 211–212

crowdsourcing, 189–214
    and agile marketing, 210–212
    benefits of, 201
    definition of, 200–202
    development
        of content, 202–203
        of products, 203–204
    difference between open
        innovation, mass
        collaboration, co-creation
        and, 212–213
    disadvantages of, 201–202
    and ideation
        crowdsourcing beyond,
            213–214
        overview, 204–205
    marketing, 205–206
    models for, 206–207
    motivating participation in,
        209–210
    plan for agile, 202
    platforms, 207–209
        content development, 208

    research and development,
        208
    social media, 208–209
    whole-kit-and-caboodle, 209

crowdSPRING platform, 208

cultural friction between sales and
    marketing, 97–98

customer analysis, 148–150

customer-cultivating organizations
    client managers in, 97–98
    customer-facing functions, 98–99
    customer service and support, 99
    metrics, 100–101
    reinventing marketing in, 93–94

customer development, 163

customer equity, 100

customer-focused marketing, 84

customer input, 48

customer interactions, 50–51

customer lifetime value metric, 100

customer profitability
    focusing on, 100
    as metric of success, 145

customer relationship management
    (CRM), 98, 186

customer support team, in
    collaborative leadership, 79–80

customers
    attracting, 152–153
    in crowdsourcing, 212
    cultivating, 91–93
    facing, 98–99
    growing and keeping, 162–163
    in ideation process, 204–205
    metrics, 100–101
    ON24 focus on, 196
    perceptions of reality, 13
    promises to, 141
    relationships, focusing on, 91
    service and support, 99

cyclical analytics, 73

D

D-Day strategy, 24

daily stand-up meetings (scrums), 128

defined relationships
  moving from undefined
    relationship to, 103
  moving to aligned relationship
    from, 104–106
  overview, 102

Delta Airlines, 99

designing, message, 154–155

development
  agile process in, 195
  of content, 202–203, 208
  of products, 203–204

development framework, agile
  marketing, 123

differentiation, competitive, 148

digital advertising, 89–90

direct mail, 153

disciplined communication, 104, 183

displays, point-of-purchase, 153

disproportionately aligned marketing
  organizations, 47

diversification, 163

diversity, of crowds, 211

division, law of, 15

documentation, 126, 192

downstream marketers, 110

duality, law of, 14

dysfunctional agile application, 80

E

early adopters, 24

early majority, 24

economic friction between sales and
  marketing, 96–97

employees, in crowdsourcing, 211

engineering, similarities to
  marketing, 130

enhancements, product, in ideation
  process, 204–205

environmental scanning, 146–147

EVE (evaluate, validate, execute)
  principle, 80–81, 83, 185

Event Portals, ON24, 191

events, 176

evolving, overview, 114

exclusivity, law of, 14

execution, 48

expansion, law of, 19

extensions, law of, 20

F

Facebook, 208

failures
  law of, 15
  learning from, 166
  as step in planning, 128–129

fast food industry, 87

feedback, 166–168

fellowship, law of, 20

field marketing, 174–176

financial objectives in marketing
  plans, 136

financial section of marketing plan, 133

financials, ensuring sense of, 163–165

fixed costs, 164

fixed pricing, 161

focus groups, 167, 200

focus, law of, 14

forecasting, sales, 165

four Ps (product, price, promotion,
  place), 37–38, 139

four-step process, 82–86, 135–136

frequency, 155

functional alignment, 175–177, 182

functional delivery, of case study, 74

functional global integration model, 186

funnels, buying, 108–110

G

gaming industry, 89

Genius Rocket platform, 208

Geo/Country, RTVM, 55

global integration model,
    functional, 186

global program management role, 175

goals, marketing, 186

graphics, 170

Green Eggs and Ham (Dr. Seuss), 2

GreenHopper plug-in, 195

H

"house diagram," 66–67

hype, law of, 15

Hypios platform, 208

I

ideas banks, 207

ideation, and crowdsourcing, 204–205,
    213–214

implementation, marketing, 137–138

impressions, 155

improvement, continual, 178

In Search of the Obvious, 3, 171–172

incentives, in crowdsourcing, 209

incubation plans, 84

industry analysts relations, 177

inflexible marketing, 3

Inkling platform, 208

InnoCentive platform, 208

innovation, 6–11, 21, 212–213

innovators, 24

integrated relationships
    moving from aligned relationship
        to, 106–112
    overview, 102–103

intelligence, collective, 210–212

internal resources for projects, 124

Internet advertising, 89–90, 175–177

investments, 165

"iron triangle" model, 47–48, 180

issue management, 180

Item Type, RTVM, 54

iterations, as step in planning, 127–128

J

JIRA change management system, 195

K

Kapur, Dee, 6–10

key performance indicators. *See* KPIs

kick-off meeting, 126

KPIs (key performance indicators)
    importance for project
        failures, 129
    setting, 126

L

ladder, law of the, 14

laggards, 24, 179

late majority, 24

law of acceleration, 15

law of advertising, 19

law of attributes, 15

law of borders, 21

law of candor, 15

law of change, 21

law of color, 21

law of consistency, 21

law of contraction, 19

law of credentials, 19

law of division, 15

law of duality, 14

law of exclusivity, 14

law of expansion, 19

law of extensions, 20

law of failure, 15

law of fellowship, 20

law of focus, 14

law of hype, 15

law of leadership, 14

law of line extension, 15

law of mortality, 21

law of perception, 14

law of perspective, 15

law of publicity, 19

law of quality, 20

law of resources, 16

law of sacrifice, 15

law of shape, 21

law of siblings, 21

law of singularity, 15, 21

law of sub-brands, 20

law of success, 15

law of the category, 14, 20

law of the company, 20

law of the generic, 20

law of the ladder, 14

law of the mind, 14

law of the name, 20

law of the opposite, 15

law of the word, 19

law of unpredictability, 15

leaders of marketing, 179–182

leadership, collaborative. *See* collaborative leadership

leadership, law of, 14

leadership team
importance of in agressive timeline, 59
planning, 113

legal disclosures, in crowdsourcing, 209

liaisons, 105

life cycle, technology adoption, 23–25

life events, tailoring products to, 93

lifetime value, customer, 100

line extension, law of, 15

long-term objectives, in business strategy, 122–123

loss leaders, 100

loyalty, as metric of success, 145

loyalty programs, 163

M

marcom, 177

market areas, expanding into new, 162

market penetration, 162

market research, in customer-cultivating organizations, 98–99

market research techniques, 166

market segmentation, 149–150, 158

market share, 100, 145

marketing
22 immutable laws of, 13–17
agile, crowdsourcing and, 210–212
challenge of, 47, 143–145
conflict between sales and, 96–98
consumers, 22
crowdsourcing, 205–206
defined, 12
different roles for, 95–96
ensuring financials make sense, 163–165

identifying opportunities, 145–151
implementation, 137–138
management, overview, 142–143
outdated methods for, 28
plans. *See also* planning
    importance of, 142
    writing, 132–137
reinventing, 93–94
seeing process as whole, 137–143
selecting target, 151–152
selling as part of, 168–169
as service department, 27

Marketing 2.0, 156–160

marketing process, 137–139

marketing professionals, 141–142

marketing program, 141

marketing systems, 175

marketplace model, 206
    changing, and new demands on
        marketing, 40–41
    and four Ps (product, price,
        promotion, place), 37–38

markets, defined, 24

mass collaboration, difference
    between crowdsourcing and,
    212–213

mature market, 149

measurement, in crowdsourcing, 213

measures of success, 144

media, 154–155

meetings
    daily stand-up, 128
    kick-off, 126
    schedule for agressive timeline, 58

message boards, in crowdsourcing, 213

message design, 154–155

message, marketing, 172

methodology, 10, 30–31, 179

metrics, 110–111
    customer, 100–101
    increasing importance of, 197

of success, 144

mind, law of the, 14

mission statement for
    transformation, 46

models, for crowdsourcing, 206–207

monitoring in marketing process,
    137–138

Moore, Geoffrey A., 23–25

mortality, law of, 21

must-haves, in transformation
    framework, 181

My Starbucks Idea campaign, 207

mysteries of marketing, 141–142

N

name, law of the, 20

negotiated pricing, 161

network advertising, 89–90

Ning, 209

Nokia, 99

O

objectives, 48
    asking sponsors and stakeholders
        for intended, 125
    importance of failure to, 129
    long and short-term business
        strategy, 122–123
    in marketing plans, 136
    pricing, 162

Obvious Adams, The Story of a
    Successful Businessman, 3, 172

obvious pragmatic innovation, 189

obvious principle, 3–6, 171–172

offline market research techniques, 167

ON24, 190–199

online market research techniques, 167

online marketplace model, 206

open calls, in crowdsourcing, 200

open innovation, difference between crowdsourcing and, 212–213

operations, 176, 187

opinions, in crowdsourcing, 200

opposite, law of the, 15

organization types, and collaborative leadership, 86

organizational alignment, 182–183

outsourced customer service, 99

ownership of problems, in collaborative leadership, 82–83

P

package delivery industry, 88–89

packaging, 153

participation of stakeholders, active, 115

penetration, 155, 162

people, marketing mysteries of, 141–142

perceptions
    law of, 14
    of reality, 13
    streamlining, 31

permission or conversational marketing, 159

personal investment in marketing programs, 172–173

personal selling, 153, 160–161

personas, in case study
    overview, 68–69
    types of, 69–72

perspective, law of, 15

PEST (political developments, economic issues, social trends, and technology developments) analysis, 146

planning, 113–170
    communication
        evaluating effectiveness of, 155
        objectives of, 154
    contribution analysis, 165
    customers
        attracting, 152–153
        growing and keeping, 162–163
    getting feedback, 166–168
    iteration, 127
    keeping simple, 169–170
    marketing, 39–40
        challenge of, 143–145
        ensuring financials make sense, 163–165
        identifying opportunities, 145–151
        seeing process as whole, 137–143
        selecting target, 151–152
        selling as part of, 168–169
    message design, budget, and media, 154–155
    never-ending process, 166
    personal selling, 160–161
    pricing, 161–162
    principles, agile development, 130
    steps involved in
        fail, 128–129
        iterate, 127–128
        plan, 123–126
        succeed, 129–131
    storytelling, 169
    trying untested mediums, Web 2.0, 156–160
    writing, 131–137

platforms, for crowdsourcing, 207–209
    content development platform, 208
    research and development platform, 208
    social media platform, 208–209
    whole-kit-and-caboodle platform, 209

PLT (Project Leadership Team), 180

PNCV (Product New Contract Value), 48

point-of-purchase displays, 153

policies on web access, 157

political developments, economic issues, social trends, and technology developments (PEST analysis), 146

Postal Service, US, 88–89

power of three, 169–170

pragmatic innovation, 6–11, 21

pragmatists, 24

pre-project planning iteration, 127

predictability, 33

presentations, marketing plans as, 132

presenting marketing plans, 133–134

pricing
overview, 161–162
as source of friction between sales and marketing, 96

pride, product, 41

principles of agile development planning, 130

Priority Mail, 88–89

problems, dealing with in ADAM process, 82–86

process alignment, 173–175

process, buying, 114

process improvement programs, 83

Produce or Perish behavior, 29

product development, 203–204

product-driven management, 93

product enhancements, in ideation process, 204–205

product marketing role, 176

Product New Contract Value (PNCV), 48

product offerings, 162

product owners, 192–194

product, price, promotion, place (four Ps), 37–38, 139

product pride, 41

professionals, marketing, 141–142

profitability, focusing on customer, 100

program leadership team, planning, 113

program management role, global, 175

program, marketing, 141

Project Leadership Team (PLT), 180

project management governance model, planning stage of, 113

project manager assignments, 62

project (program, campaign)
budget planning for, 124
documentation of, 126
failure of, 128–129
internal resources for, 124
iterations, 127–128
picking teams for, 125–126
selling to sponsors, 124–125
sprint planning, 126
success of, 129

promises to customers, 141

promotion costs, as source of friction between sales and marketing, 96

promotion, overview, 153

prospecting, 162

publicity, 19, 153

Q

quality
attributes of, 33
enabling, 32–33
law of, 20
using technology to augment, 33–35

R

reality, perceptions of, 13

relationships, 101–103
 aligned, 102
 creating stronger, 103–112
  moving from aligned to
   integrated relationship,
   106–112
  moving from defined to aligned
   relationship, 104–106
  moving from undefined to
   defined relationship, 103
 defined, 102
 integrated, 102–103
 undefined, 102

Release Delivery Manager role, 63–66

reliability, 33

Requirement SME, RTVM, 55

requirements gathering, 127

Requirements Traceability Verification
 Matrix (RTVM), 52–55

research
 development platform, for
  crowdsourcing, 208
 marketing process, 98–99, 137,
  139, 166

resources
 law of, 16
 in transformation framework,
  181–186

responsibility, in collaborative
 leadership, 79–80

retail, customer retention in, 92

retention, customer, 162–163

revenue
 in agile triangle, 180
 "iron triangle" model and, 48–49
 objective of agile marketing
  triangle, 74

rewards, shared, 110–111

risk management, 180

Room Without a View behavior, 30

RTVM (Requirements Traceability
 Verification Matrix), 52–55

S

sacrifice, law of, 15

Sahasi, Jayesh, 190–197

sales
 ADAM process, 82–86
 alignment, 184–186
 forecasting, 165
 functional responsibilities of, 175
 growth as metric of success, 145
 involving in agile marketing, 79–80
 versus marketing, 13
 and marketing, conflict between,
  96–98
 per customer, as metric of
  success, 145
 relationship to marketing, 77
 roles for marketing, 95–96
 sources of friction with marketing,
  96–98
 types of relationships with
  marketing, 101–112

satisfaction, as metric of success, 145

scanning, environmental, 146–147

scope changes, 180

scope, time, and cost relationship,
 47–48

scoring model for analytics
 adoption, 74

scrum teams
 in collaborative leadership, 79–80
 overview, 12

scrums, 128

Section 1 of marketing plan, 133–136

Section 2 of marketing plan, 133

Section 3 of marketing plan, 133

Section 4 of marketing plan, 133

segmentation, 149–150, 158, 177

segments, expanding into new, 162

self analysis, 150–151

selling
over-generalization of role of, 18
as part of marketing, 168–169
personal, 153, 160–161

service department, marketing as, 27

service offerings, 162

services
cultivating customers in, 92–93
overview, 176

Shampoo Super Genius Marketer, 29

shape, law of, 21

shared rewards, 110–111

short-term analysis of business
strategy, 121

short-term objectives, in business
strategy, 121–123

siblings, law of, 21

silos
eliminating, 86–87
overview, 80

simplified communication, 66–67

singularity, law of, 15, 21

situation analysis of marketing plan,
133–136

social media
for crowdsourcing, 208–209
impact on communications,
156–160

social networking
in marketing, 153
platforms, 50

solution delivery methodology, 56

solutions, as products in
crowdsourcing, 203

sourcing, 176, 187

sponsors, selling projects to, 124–125

sponsorship, 176, 183

sprint planning, 126

SR Count, RTVM, 54

stakeholders
active participation
technique, 115
asking for intended
objectives, 125
in crowdsourcing, 211
planning buy-in for, 113

Starbucks, 207

startup marketing situations, market
challenges, 143–145

storytelling, 169

strategies
adjusting according to market
challenges, 144
formation in marketing process,
137–138
in marketing plans, 136

streamline processes, 46

strengths of company, 151

sub-brands, law of, 20

success
law of, 15
metrics of, 144
overview, 24
as step in planning, 129–131

summaries, in ideation process, 205

Super Bowl advertising, 205

support for marketing plan
recommendations, 134–137

System/Process Requirement,
RTVM, 54

systems architect, for marketing
campaigns, 87

systems engineering concepts,
86–87, 89

systems, marketing, 175

T

tactics in marketing plans, 136
"tailored interaction," 50
target markets, selecting, 151–152
teams. *See also* collaborative
    leadership
    cross-functional, creating
        marketing plans with, 132
    picking for projects, 125–126
    presentation of marketing plans,
        133–134
teamwork resolution, 31–32
technical marketing
    responsibilities, 187
technology
    adoption life cycle, 23–25
    using to augment quality, 33–35
telecom industry, 81
telemarketing, 153
teleprospecting, 176
Tesco, 92–94
three, power of, 169–170
time, cost, and scope relationship,
    47–48
time-to-market, 192–193
timing, importance in
    marketing, 147
titles, in ideation process, 205
TopCoder platform, 208
total profitability, as metric of
    success, 145
total sales, as metric of success, 145
Touch Point Contact, RTVM, 54–55
tradeshows, 176
traditional marketing model,
    shortcomings of, 131
transformation
    continuous, on personal level,
        172–173

    framework of, 179–182
    key changes necessary to effect,
        186–187
    mission statement for, 46
transparency, in crowdsourcing, 210
Trout, Jack, 3–6, 13–17, 171–172
tweens, 149
Twitter, 209
two-way communication, 153

U

undefined relationships, 102–103
unpredictability, law of, 15
Updegraff, Robert R., 3, 172
upstream marketers, 110–111
US Postal Service, 88–89
USAA, 94

V

variable costs, 164
visionaries, 24

W, X

WALL-E, 84
weaknesses of company, 151
Web 2.0
    marketing within, 49
    overview, 156–160
web access, policies on, 157
web marketing, 153
welcome message to team, 60–61
whole-kit-and-caboodle platform, for
    crowdsourcing, 209
Wikipedia, 203
WOM (word-of-mouth), 157–159
word, law of the, 19
word-of-mouth (WOM), 157–159

workstream lead, 62

writing plans, marketing, 131–137

Y, Z

Yes Man, 27

YouTube, 208